15 TOOLS

TO TURN THE TIDE

15 TOOLS
TO TURN THE TIDE

A STEP-BY-STEP PLAYBOOK FOR EMPOWERED NEGOTIATING

SETH FREEMAN

WM

WILLIAM MORROW

An Imprint of HarperCollins*Publishers*

HarperCollins books may be purchased for educational, business, or sales promotional use. For information, please email the Special Markets Department at SPsales@harpercollins.com.

FIRST EDITION

Designed by Kyle O'Brien

Library of Congress Cataloging-in-Publication Data has been applied for.

ISBN 978-0-06-322623-4

23 24 25 26 27 LBC 5 4 3 2 1

To my wife, Cary, my children, Hannah and Rachael, my parents, John & Gina, and my students. Thank you.

Contents

15 Tools, in Brief

How it helps-
What it's called

Break through impasse-
Three Little Words

Get really ready-
I FORESAW IT

Bring a 1-pager-
**Topics, Targets,
and Tradeoffs Grid**

Manage emotions-
Roleplay

Find powerful helpers-
Who I FORESAW

Find a dream counterpart-
Targeted Negotiation

Help meetings work-
Golden Minute

Talk good-
Reframe

Do Good for Them,
Great for You-
Win Warmly Recipe Card

Deescalate-
Exactly! **Challenge**

Unify your group-
Common Interests Hack

Be a boss whisperer-
APSO

Change a mind-
If We Agree/If We Disagree

No other offers? Find wisdom-
Notional BATNA

Test an offer-
**Measures of Success
Dashboard**

15 TOOLS

TO TURN THE TIDE

Introduction

Imagine you're at work one day when you get a call that could decide your company's fate—and yours. It's Brenda, an executive from the healthcare center that's your firm's biggest client. Your team is hard at work designing a computerized welcome screen that the client's patients will use when they first arrive. Brenda asks you, "How close are you to finishing?"

"Everything's fine," you tell her. "We're on track to have it ready for you, as we promised, in sixty days."

There's a pause. "Yes," she says, "that's why I'm calling. We need it in thirty days." You almost drop the phone.

"Brenda," you tell her, "I *really* don't think that's possible."

She is not pleased. "Well," she asks, "would you please check with your team?"

"Of course," you say, and you excuse yourself to talk with your designers, who immediately laugh you out of the room. You report the bad news to Brenda. The call ends, and you return to your work, only to get a message ten minutes later from your boss, Dave: "Get in here now." You race over.

Dave is on a speaker call with Brenda's boss, Betty. Betty is very unhappy. If the firm doesn't deliver the welcome screen in thirty days, she says, it will lose them as a client. Dave looks stunned, like a rabbit in front of an oncoming truck. Wisely, you push the mute button and whisper, "Tell her you'll call her back." He does.

"OK," Betty says, "but I need to hear back from you in twenty minutes because I'm going into a meeting with my bosses." She hangs up.

"Get. Everyone. In. Here. Now," says Dave, and you quickly summon all the designers. But as soon as Dave states the challenge, all hell breaks loose. Every designer shouts it's impossible to deliver the welcome screen in thirty days. Dave pushes back, saying, "Look, these people can turn our lights off. We have *got* to deliver it in thirty days." The conversation spirals down a hole:

"Can't!" "Must!" *"Can't!"* "MUST!" What would you do at a moment like this?

Shanice, a student of mine, faced this crisis; she was the manager who received Brenda's call. And what Shanice did in the next few moments was not normal: she deployed her negotiation training. But because she did, something strange happened. By the time the boss called back, Shanice had helped him and the team discover a response—a counteroffer, really—that thrilled Betty. Hours later, Betty called back to sing the firm's praises, promising more work, and Shanice was a hero.

How do you turn around a near-death business experience like that? How do you save the day, negotiating when you feel powerless and you're pressed and distressed? And more generally, how do you advocate for yourself, your family, your team, your charity, or your company when you feel as weak as Bambi, and the other side seems as powerful and determined as Godzilla? That's what this book is about.

The Challenges You Face

It's hard to negotiate. I know; I've worked with thousands of students and clients around the globe, and when we first meet, they often tell me so. They find negotiation difficult whether they're UN diplomats or small business owners, senior executives or junior managers, lawyers or clients, graduate students or kindergarteners. In fact, the word "negotiate" comes from two Latin words, *neg ōtium*, that literally mean "not leisure." Which means that for at least two thousand years, people have struggled with negotiation. And they've struggled especially when they've faced serious adversity, like Shanice faced, even though it's at just such moments that we need to be at the peak of our powers. If there's one question negotiation instructors like me get more than any other, it's this: "Yes, but what if you're negotiating in a tough situation?"

Specifically, what if

You face a "Godzilla" counterpart—a powerful or intimidating person who makes you feel so weak on the eve of talks that it feels like you will have no ability to respond if they start by saying no, or "you must"?

You feel so stressed that you forget what you planned to say and struggle to keep your mind in the game as the talks unfold?

You're under time pressure and don't know how best to use the limited time you do have?

You face a damned if you do/damned if you don't dilemma as you try to convince a boss to change course?

You feel you have no choice but to say yes?

You feel pressure to agree, but you can't tell if yes is wise?

You face stress from anxious colleagues and counterparts because of recession, inflation, or another economic crisis, and don't know how negotiation can help you turn things around?

You want to be decent and humane *and* solve your problem, but the adversity you face seems to make it impossible to do that?

There are hundreds of books about the art of negotiating. Many are excellent, offering time-tested principles for reaching wise and satisfying outcomes. These include, for example, intentionally preparing, knowing and developing your best alternative to a negotiated agreement, setting a range, getting creative, and cushioning your first offer. As my students and I have found, and as research shows, these principles can help you (and your counterparts), often in remarkable ways. But they don't offer some important things you need to actually negotiate well under pressure.

First, they leave out some vital insights—like what to do with your emotions, or what to do when you seem to have no choices, or how to know when to say yes and when to say no. And second, most books assume that once you've encountered principles, you've learned them and you're ready. But real life is more demanding than that.

Alas, while knowing about principles helps, what matters most is being able to deploy them in real-life situations. That's especially true in times of stress, adversity, or powerlessness—the times we most need these principles, and the times they're hardest to recall and apply. Our minds go blank; we feel over-whelmed and confused.

That feeling is normal: pilots, nurses, military commanders, surgeons, ath-letes, and others who perform in high-pressure situations all struggle to cope with stress and adversity. And yet, they've all found something that helps them overcome these challenges and perform well, even when it seems impossible.

The secret is tools: acronyms, checklists, mnemonics, sayings, recipes, roleplays, cue cards, and the like, each of which by design helps them cope and succeed. For example, astronauts and pilots use checklists (as pilot Sully Sullenberger did to help pull off the miracle landing on the Hudson River). Military leaders in the heat of battle use acronyms like ADDRAC (Alert! Di-rection! Description! Range! Assignments! Control!). And Olympic athletes use visualization, a kind of roleplay, just before they perform. Like them, you as a negotiator need tools—well-customized instruments that work unusually well, even when you feel flooded, or you're the least influential person at the table—that enable you to *deploy* key insights in high-stress moments.

But tools aren't just coping devices, they're also valuable learning aids, as teachers know. That's why teachers break up learning into chunks and give scaffolds for each chunk: steps, templates, charts, rubrics, cues, maps, and so on. Each makes learning digestible, memorable, and portable. Each makes it easier to practice and master core skills.[1] Negotiators need scaffolds too.

How the Tools in This Book Can Help You

Having a strong tool kit helps you learn the great principles of negotiation and actually apply them. It can help especially when you're short on time, lacking in confidence, and under stress. For example, these tools can help you

> manage emotions that often defeat negotiators, and cope as Olympic athletes do

remember and apply key insights when stress makes your brain blur, as astronauts and football coaches do

find nonobvious, satisfying solutions to big problems under pressure, as top Silicon Valley designers do

know what to say to a boss in a crisis, as nurses and copilots have learned

quickly get everyone collaborating when they seem hostile and alienated, as seasoned mediators do

discover ways to overcome power imbalances.

As professionals in many fields have learned, good tools are like apps that equip you the moment you need them. They're a way to cope with adversity. They ease your cognitive and emotional load so you can think and act more effectively in real time. They distill a wealth of wisdom and experience into a ready-to-use packet.

15 Tools to Turn the Tide will equip you for these challenging real-life situations. It includes a host of unique, ready-to-deploy methods that, by design, help you to not only gain key principles but also to use them. They help you get ready, perform, assess, and even lead when you face difficult conversations, challenging conflicts, and tough negotiations. While many negotiation books offer you tools, what they usually mean are principles. Here, you'll find portable, memorable instruments that help you turn principles into wise action.

I've written this book to serve you whether or not you have formal negotiation training. Like thousands of my students and my junior clients, novice negotiators will find the tools are an excellent scaffold for learning. Like my senior clients, experienced negotiators will find that the tools refresh and enrich what you once knew, and add a lot. And whatever level you're at, you'll find the tools help you negotiate well when it counts.

We start the book with tools you can use to prepare, then explore ones that help you handle the talks, and then ones that help you decide whether to accept an offer. The tools here have helped thousands of people deal well with adversity and stress, whether they're novice or veteran negotiators. As we'll see, even children can use—and have used—these instruments to reach excellent results.

You can use the tools alone or in combination as your needs require. While most are easy to remember, you don't have to; simple templates I'll give you can prompt you, supporting you and reminding you as you go.

Especially written for you if you *don't* love to negotiate, *15 Tools to Turn the Tide* reassures you that you can often do remarkable things. One reason: while we often think negotiation means sharp, aggressive bargaining, experienced negotiators know you can achieve more for yourself and others with integrity and wisdom, creating agreements that make the other side happy and your side *very* happy. In the process, the tools help you shift your dealings with others from the freaked-out premise of scarcity to a reasonable premise of abundance; from knee-jerk competition to wise value creation and claiming; from a "shoot first, aim later" approach to problems to a purposeful one that moves with deliberate speed; from inhumane to humane dealings. From being ineffectively defensive to wisely being strong and kind. The key is to have the equipment for that journey.

Drawing on my decades of experience and research, I've designed most of the tools myself. Each bakes in one or more critical negotiation insight. Since many of these insights focus on being hard on the problem but soft on the person, they can help you deal with big problems with humanity in ways that often enrich the relationship—and do very well for yourself. Many capture the great negotiation principles; several add important new ones. And because each gives you power, often in surprising ways, each is particularly useful when you face adversity, which is key.

The Tools in Action

To make the tools come alive, I'll illustrate them with stories of negotiators who survived "near-death" negotiation experiences and triumphed. For example, you'll learn the story of a young executive who saved a ruined merger, preserved his and his boss's careers, and created millions of dollars in value when everyone thought it impossible. A homeless singer-songwriter who turned down a $1 million contract from a record company, avoiding traps in the offer and negotiating a far better deal that allowed her to soar—unlike so many other recording artists, who wind up bankrupt. An alternative energy company that overcame rising supply prices and negotiated unique deals suppliers loved that saved it $100 million in a single year. And a fundraiser who convinced her initially reluctant corporate donor to enthusiastically increase its donation fivefold—in a recession.

Many other stories are not about money at all but about something at least as important. You'll meet the dentist who negotiated the release of his despairing fellow passengers after their plane had been waiting on the tarmac in a hurricane for six hours. The eleven-year-old boy who finally convinced his reluctant father to get their family a cat. The young man whose fiancée's bereaved father excluded him from everything having to do with his late daughter—the circumstances of her death, her personal effects, her memorial service—until the young man used tools to help turn the father's hostility into inclusion and friendship. And the all-but-fired U.S. general in World War II who persuaded his highly resistant commanding officer to let him land on Utah Beach in the D-Day invasion, perhaps saving that part of the invasion and resulting in his being awarded the Congressional Medal of Honor. (To protect privacy, I've changed names and other identifying facts of nonpublic figures, always erring on the side of understating how well the stories went.)*

Nothing always works. As enthusiastic as I am about what I want to share with you, I will trust you to understand that even the best equipment won't always save the day. But knowing how to deploy good tools definitely can improve the odds.

So, how *did* Shanice save the day? She listened and asked pivotal questions

---

* Except when I explicitly note that I'm sharing a hypothetical narrative, each story is based on a true case and retains the essential challenge, circumstances, principles, arc, and results. The protagonist intentionally used the ideas I'm illustrating in each case. In a couple of instances, I've combined such stories into a composite to illustrate an insight more succinctly. Where numbers are involved and might help identify someone, I've typically chosen more conservative ones. I'll also share studies throughout the book to add depth and empirical breadth. One thing about studies: as you may know, the sciences (natural and social alike) have been struggling lately with a reproducibility crisis; a third to half don't bear scrutiny. Ugh. So, while I'll draw on studies, take them with a grain of salt. But be encouraged: the ones I'll share reflect insights I've seen evidence for in my own and other practitioners' work.

when everyone else was arguing, drawing out insights and information when everyone else could only use their reptile brains, and so summoned from the group an idea that no one would have otherwise imagined. That's great, but seriously, how are you supposed to do something like that? Is there anything that can make it easier, especially when you're under pressure? As we'll see, the answer is yes: you can do everything Shanice did and more by deploying the very first tool we'll explore in Chapter 1, something called Three Little Words. Those three words capture the insights she used and prompt you when you need them so you can save the day too. It's the first of many tools we'll explore to help you know what to do—and then do it.

PART I

Get Ready

There is no such thing as bad weather, only bad clothing.
—Scandinavian proverb

Break through impasse:
Three Little Words

Get really ready:
I FORESAW IT

Bring a 1-pager:
Topics, Targets, and Tradeoffs Grid

Manage emotions:
Roleplay

Find powerful helpers:
Who I FORESAW

Find a dream counterpart:
Targeted Negotiation

Heavyweight prizefighter Mike Tyson famously said, "Everyone has a plan until they get punched in the mouth."[1] But consider his title bout with Buster Douglas.

Douglas, a journeyman heavyweight, was an extreme underdog when Tyson fought him in Tokyo on February 11, 1990: oddsmakers had pegged him at 42 to 1. The press gave him no chance. To make matters worse, his wife had left him, and his mother died days before the bout. Tyson, the reigning heavyweight champion, was a lethal fighter who had routinely knocked out opponents in the early rounds. He approached the Douglas bout as another easy payday and hadn't bothered to train much for it.

But unbeknownst to Tyson, Douglas took a different approach. Studying his opponent, he noticed Tyson had so dominated adversaries that he hadn't needed stamina for later rounds, and that previous opponents had allowed Tyson to attack from the start. To capitalize on those insights, Douglas worked out a plan to use superior quickness to attack early, evade whenever Tyson attacked, clinch whenever he got in trouble, and make Tyson move. The idea was to tire him out for the first several rounds, then go on full attack. To everyone's surprise, it was apparent from the start of the fight that Douglas was not afraid. More shocking still: the bout unfolded almost exactly the way Douglas had planned. To Tyson's and the world's astonishment, Douglas knocked Tyson out in the tenth round to become the new heavyweight champion.

It was Tyson's first loss, and it made his famous line ironic. Tyson had dismissed planning and lost; Douglas harnessed it and won, against staggering odds. As Tyson himself put it later, "I learned a valuable lesson: you always need to prepare."[2]

The same holds true for negotiating. So, in Part I of the book you'll find tools that help you do the kind of preparation that can dramatically improve your odds for success.

CHAPTER 1

Use Three Little Words to Find Hope

THE TOOL: THREE LITTLE WORDS

Use this tool when . . .
- you face a painful impasse
- you face a serious conflict
- you have too much responsibility and not enough authority
- your firm or industry faces strong price pressure
- you face a resistant prospective customer
- you face a resistant donor.

Use this tool to . . .
- break through impasse
- resolve a serious conflict
- influence even when you lack authority
- turn a commodity business around
- make a sale
- raise money for charity.

My purpose in this chapter is to prove a claim that, on its face, seems outrageous: whether you are a manager faced with an existential business crisis, a head of state trying to end a war, or an eleven-year-old boy longing to get a cat, you can overcome seemingly impossible odds, and often quickly, with the help of Three Little Words: Interests, Facts, Options.

What If You Have Twenty Minutes to Save Your Firm?

Remember Shanice, the manager we met in the introduction whose firm faced an impossible deadline from their biggest client? How exactly did she save the day? As soon as she saw the design team and the boss were getting nowhere arguing about it, Shanice asked a seemingly dumb question:

"Wait," she said, "*why* can't we deliver the welcome screen in thirty days? What are we concerned about?" The team immediately overwhelmed her with a long list of software issues. "OK, OK," said Shanice. "Why do you suppose the client needs the welcome screen in thirty days? What are they concerned about?"

An odd silence filled the room. No one knew. So, Shanice asked follow-up questions to suss out the Facts. Doing that revealed a strong hypothesis: the client probably needed the welcome screen to launch its new pilot health care center in thirty days. Then Shanice asked about Options: "Well, is there any way we can help them launch in thirty days, even if the software isn't ready then?" Suddenly the team shifted from arguing to brainstorming. Moments later, Shanice called time. "That's twenty minutes. We've got to make the call now," she said.

With Shanice standing by, Dave called Betty back. "Betty," said Dave, "we think we have something for you, but before we share it, we wanted to check: *Why* do you need the welcome screen in thirty days?" They'd guessed correctly: the client needed to launch the pilot health care center then, and the welcome screen was critical.

"Well," said Dave, with Shanice prompting him, "Betty, if you need the finished welcome screen in thirty days, I must tell you that *no* reputable design firm could get it to you that quickly; some of the key features will take two months to complete. But if your goal is to launch the pilot health care center in thirty days, we can help." He then listed several ideas they'd come up with, including this: "The missing features can be done manually in a back office, and we have staff here we could lend you who can perform those tasks during the launch, and then step down when the welcome screen is fully functional. Would that help?"

"You would do that for us?" said Betty. Suddenly, Betty was thrilled. She had a potential solution to offer her own bosses. The call ended happily.

Hours later, Betty called back to say they'd try to manage without help for now but might use the support later. And then Betty added this: "Regardless, you are going to get a lot more business from us because you guys are rock stars."

How did *that* happen? When Shanice got that initial call, she had seen her job flashing in front of her eyes. But somehow, she had managed to turn the crisis around so that by the end, the client was *more* excited to work with Shanice's firm, and Shanice was a hero. How?

Three Little Words: Interests, Facts, Options

By in effect asking her team to think the way a creative negotiator does, Shanice turned a potential crisis into a triumph. The client was delighted with the solution Shanice's questions had revealed, and the relationship between the firms *improved* because of the conflict. There's a word for what Shanice offered: service. Even when she couldn't give the client what it thought it wanted, she found a way to serve its Interests.

I love Shanice's story because it illustrates that even when it seems improbable, you can discover hidden harmony and hope with negotiation principles. But there's also a reason I *don't* love Shanice's story: it's hard to remember principles like that in an emergency. We need help, a mental app, if you will, that can guide us in the moment. We need a tool.

So, let's take a closer look.

Three Little Words

Interests. One of the most powerful ideas I've found for fostering peace and prosperity is a practice called interest-based bargaining, which was pioneered in the 1920s by management scholar Mary Parker Follett and popularized decades later by the excellent book *Getting to Yes*. If you're already familiar with it, rest assured there is much more insight to gain in this chapter and throughout the book. For example, later you'll discover several nonobvious ways to apply the idea to help you lead, sell, find new business opportunities, and even raise money for charity. If you're not familiar with it, I'm delighted to introduce it to you.

The heart of the idea is simple, yet not obvious: focus on Interests, not positions.

A position is a demand: "Deliver in thirty days!" Or "higher salary!" An Interest is the *why* behind that demand. It's the deeper concern: the underlying need, the motivation. Thinking about Interests can often change the game for the better, shifting the conversation from impasse toward mutual satisfaction.

Shanice shifted her group's futile argument over positions into a conversation about Interests. That shift became the foundation for her transforming work. Similarly, while a job candidate may think the only thing that matters to them is a higher salary, asking "Why do I want it?" can reveal a valuable insight, such as this: "I need to provide more for my family."

Focusing on Interests allows you to look beyond demands and envision creative solutions. Instead of just pushing for a higher salary, the candidate might be happy to get better benefits, an accelerated raise, a guaranteed bonus, stock options, tuition reimbursement, moving expenses, day care, and so on. Knowing your own Interests can help you ask for good things that are easier for the other to give you. And knowing the *other's* Interests can help you offer Options that serve the other well. So, the first step in deploying the Three Little Words is simply to jot down what Interests you each have. Usually that means listing some deeper needs. You don't have to delve into the utterly profound; just a few material and perhaps emotional needs is fine. For example, our job candidate might list "provide more for my family, opportunities for advancement, fairness, and satisfying assignments."[1]

Facts. Before you talk to the other person—learn, learn, learn. Excellent negotiators are invariably excellent researchers. They work the Internet. They call friends. They run the numbers. They live, in short, by the four-hundred-year-old wisdom of Sir Francis Bacon: "Knowledge is power."

To the point: top sports agents like Bob Woolf and Scott Boras earned their reputations as excellent negotiators in part by becoming outstanding learners.

Woolf kept files of every NBA player's salary and benefits, including unpublished information he learned from fellow agents, which sometimes enabled him to know more about a team's payroll than they knew themselves.[2] Boras hired economists and statisticians to help him craft evidence-based $100 million offers for his baseball clients.[3] Learning Facts saves you from many negotiation traps, enables you to understand your counterparts, and reveals benchmarks you can use to set your targets. It also builds your confidence and helps you discover Interests and Options you might have missed.

Shanice, of course, didn't have time to do in-depth research. But she did the next best thing: she asked follow-up questions so that her team could at least make educated guesses about the Facts of the client's situation, the technology, the team's capabilities, and so on.

Similarly, a job candidate or an HR executive is typically more relaxed, confident, and open when she learns several things before a job negotiation. She might, for example, find the going rates for similarly qualified candidates in similar places and what demand is for the people with those qualifications. She might also learn what creative deals other firms are offering, and what the candidate's (or the firm's) budget looks like. The key is to err on the side of learning too much.

One reason you rarely see truly excellent negotiating on TV or in movies is that much of what really matters is not very exciting. Hollywood screenwriters always want to up the stakes: increasing the risk, the danger, the action, and the time pressure, which is precisely the opposite of what excellent negotiators do.[4] Skilled negotiating is boring to watch. Contrary to popular belief, the idea isn't to think quickly on your feet, talk fast, bluster, and bluff your way to glory. Negotiation can create feelings of anxiety and fear in part because we think we have to carry on like hyperaggressive talkers to be effective. While some negotiators succeed that way, for most of us, the strategy backfires and creates needless stress. So, don't worry if you don't feel nearly as tough or adept at negotiating as people on TV seem to be, or if doing research seems disconnected from what "real" negotiators do. Great negotiators do their homework.

Beyond the obvious ways to do Factual research, there are several, less common ways worth considering:

Phone for power. Calling an expert can produce a wealth of insight. A traveler can learn valuable things from a travel agent, a house hunter from a broker; just make sure you're discreet and appropriate. Likewise, reaching out to friends and contacts for guidance and referrals can give you valuable information and, as we'll explore more fully later, allies who can help in several other ways too.

Information interview. Chat with appropriate people you know and those they refer you to and ask them for information and additional referrals and so on, a method journalists and agents swear by. Learn about Facts, personalities, feelings, relationships, norms, "how we do things around here," needs, and more. Just be thoughtful and discreet.

Play with spreadsheets. Playing out how different offers could affect your budget, your cash flow, and the like can reveal crucial negotiation insights.

Research like your counterpart. One of my favorite practices is to search the Web as if I were my counterpart. For example, if I'm a supplier weighing an offer from a purchasing agent, I'd do well to check, among other things, a top purchasing agent website called Procurious.com. It includes blog posts about purchasing agents' worries, constraints, and preferred Options, along with tips, news, discussion boards, reports on the latest trends, and more.

Look at financials. Another valuable way to understand the other side is to review its financials, or have a financially skilled teammate do it. And of course, checking your own financials is vital too. To the point: any time you can review a budget, you're implicitly learning about Interests: "Hmm, we have pretty high housing expenses. Covering them is one reason I need more compensation—an Interest. I wonder if that suggests any Options. Does the employer offer a home buyer's program?"

Talk to a lawyer. Experienced attorneys can be wellsprings of knowledge about what is reasonable in the market and, of course, what the law is.

Read your counterpart's public information. Often a firm reveals a lot about itself online, such as its mission, vision, organizational structure, and competitors, and, in its SEC filings, blogs, and handbooks, surprising details about its policies and concerns.

Read journals. Industry magazines can reveal surprisingly helpful information about trends, rates, and likely Interests your counterpart has.

Find other hidden gems on the Web. Industry surveys can be revealing, and bloggers have valuable stories and data. Also, some sites aggregate critical research, saving you time. And online groups may have members who can share practical wisdom.

These research methods (and others) are catnip to a seasoned negotiator.

When we explore our next tool, ⤴ [Chapter 2], we'll look more fully at some research questions that are so valuable they deserve special attention and separate treatment. Suffice to say for now that gathering the Facts is a core component of any good negotiator's toolkit.

Options. Now that you know the Interests and Facts, you can generate possible creative deal terms to satisfy the Interests. An Option is anything you could offer or ask for that might partially serve at least one person's needs. It can be a small part of a rich, complicated package—or the one solution by itself. Each should be an idea you and the other negotiator might accept. In Shanice's case, her effort to learn the Interests and Facts led the group to develop several Options. One of them—for Shanice's group to manually operate the welcome screen—so served the client's Interests that Betty was immediately pleased. The first Option we think of doesn't work most of the time. That's precisely why experienced negotiators don't quit with one or two Options.

In a milestone study titled "The Behaviour of Successful Negotiators,"[5] Neil Rackham and John Carlisle compared forty-eight widely acknowledged excellent negotiators with forty-eight mediocre ones. What distinguished the excellent from the so-so? One striking finding: excellent negotiators, on average, developed many more Options, typically five *per topic.*[6] Well, I don't want you to be an excellent negotiator, I want you to be outstanding, so I recommend brainstorming six or more per topic. Brainstorming many Options improves the odds you'll find at least a few that work well. In fact, generating *lots* of Options is a hallmark of leading design firms like Silicon Valley's renowned IDEO, founded by David Kelley, a collaborator of Steve Jobs. IDEO designers don't develop five but dozens or even hundreds of ideas, then cherry-pick the best.

One easy way to generate Options is to simply look at your list of Interests, pick one, and ask, "What creative ideas would satisfy this Interest?" Then pick another. Or pick two, one for each negotiator, and ask, "What Options would satisfy both Interests?" Another way is to require that at least one idea must be silly, strange, or weird, simply because giving yourself license to go crazy can often reveal good, unusual ideas. For example, Shanice might have thought, What if we invite Betty to kidnap our design team? That might have led to an idea that proved brilliant: sending Betty a couple of temporary volunteers.

I've found that in five minutes, one person can readily generate a few Options, a pair can produce six or more, and a class can come up with two to three dozen. So, you can often come up with more and better Options if you can brainstorm with one or more teammate(s).

There's no need to worry about getting precisely six Options per topic when you're brainstorming; just jot down lots of ideas and then see if you can group them into logical categories. Then, when you spot one set that has only a couple of ideas, you can add more to it.

Help in the Face of Different Business Challenges

As we'll see, the Three Little Words can help you overcome many different business challenges. Here, consider one most entrepreneurs dread: dealing with landlords. That was the problem my future student Frank faced when he was operating a deli in a strip mall in northern New Jersey, hoping to make enough to earn the tuition to business school. Alas, he made little profit at first. A key reason: a terrible lease. It charged Frank a high rent and barred him from putting up a big sign or serving hot food. The saving grace was a clause promising the landlord wouldn't rent space to competing delis. Then one day, Frank noticed a new deli opening at the far end of the mall. Furious, he went to his lawyer and asked him to sue the landlord. The lawyer listened and agreed the landlord probably had breached the lease. But then the lawyer did something odd. Rather than recommending litigation, he asked Frank to tell him more about his needs and his situation. Then he asked Frank to give him a couple of weeks to see what he could do. A couple of weeks later, Frank's lawyer called saying, "How would you feel if I could get you permission to put up a big sign, permission to serve hot food, and a thirty-three percent cut in your rent if you'd agree to let the other deli into the mall?" Frank was stunned. "You could get that for me?!" The lawyer said, "Yes, the landlord's willing. And you'll probably get more business having a competitor nearby." Frank happily agreed, and found the deal helped him make so much money he got to business school a year earlier than he'd expected. What changed? In effect, the lawyer had used the Three Little Words, shifting the focus beyond winning to satisfying Frank's Interests, mastering the Facts, and developing creative Options both sides could accept.*

Strong and Kind: Why the Three Little Words Are So Powerful

One of the most compelling reasons to use the Three Little Words is that they help you be something that often seems impossible: strong *and* kind. How? By letting you be hard on the problem, soft on the person. They let you say, in effect, "I must fight for my concerns, but I'm happy to do it in a way that serves you well too." That means you can enhance the relationship, even as you care for your needs.

Years ago, one rainy Thanksgiving eve, I found myself in Queens, trying to catch a taxi to take me into Manhattan. Finally, a cab pulled over. I got in and told the driver my destination, only to hear him say, "No, I'm not going there."

I was stunned and angry. "What do you mean?" I said. "You have to!" (It's illegal for an on-duty New York taxi to refuse a fare.)

But he was adamant. So was I. So, we each sat there. He refused to move. I refused to get out. Time passed. What to do? Then I asked him, "Can you tell me please why you won't take me to Manhattan?" (Interest.) He replied, "Because I'm just about to go off duty and head home for the holiday away from Manhattan, and I don't want to spend the next two hours fighting traffic back and forth." Long silence. I started to look through the window to gauge the sit-

---

*His story was so compelling that Harvard's Program on Negotiation chair Robert Mnookin later featured it as the iconic opening narrative in his book for lawyers, *Beyond Winning: Negotiating to Create Value in Deals and Disputes.*

uation: the weather, the availability of other cabs, demand for cabs, proximity to the subway, and so on. (Facts.) Suddenly, I saw another available cab two blocks away—too far for me to run to in the rain, but waiting for a fare. That gave me an idea. (Option.)

"Look," I said, "if you'll drive me to that other cab and he says he'll take me, I'll get out." The cabdriver brightened. "You got it," he said. We reached the cab, confirmed he was willing to take me to Manhattan, and I gladly got out. "Hey, man," the first cabbie said, "thanks. Sorry I couldn't take you." I said, "No problem at all. Happy Thanksgiving." Deploying the Three Little Words changed me from being angry, ineffective, and silly to being strong and kind—and helped us both feel satisfied and grateful.

Three Little Words Lead to Nobel Peace Prizes: How the Tool Reveals "Impossible" Agreement

The Three Little Words can help resolve conflicts that might seem, on their surface, intractable.

In 1994, Israel and Jordan found themselves at an impasse over a long-sought treaty to end their hostilities. A core problem was that both sides demanded control of precious water rights to Lake Tiberias. For years the two countries had treated talks about the water as a zero-sum game, fighting over the water and often wasting it. But then negotiators began to think about the water differently. They realized Jordan needed a way to store water for periods of drought, and find more, while Israel needed to protect its long-term water security (Interests). Drawing on extensive scientific and technical knowledge (Facts), they found a novel solution (Option). The idea was to let Jordan store a substantial amount of water in the lake during the winter—that is, agree not to draw on it then but in the dry summer—and get additional water by using Israel's desalination technology. In return, Israel got year-round access to a goodly amount of lake water. That solution pleased both sides and led to the Israel-Jordan Treaty of 1994.[7]

Similarly, two of the Three Little Words helped Israel, Egypt, and the United

States resolve a critical dispute over control of the Sinai Peninsula. Early in the Camp David peace talks with U.S. president Jimmy Carter, both Israel and Egypt insisted on sole control, a seemingly unsolvable impasse that nearly ended the talks at the start. Then someone asked each nation's leader *why* they wanted the Sinai. Egypt's Anwar Sādāt explained Egypt wanted sovereignty; Israel's Menachem Begin said Israel needed security. What did they mean by this? Sādāt meant Egypt wanted the maps of the world to recognize the Sinai as belonging to Egypt, the Egyptian flag to fly there, and Egyptian civilians to settle there. Military presence wasn't essential. Begin meant Israel wanted no surprise attack and a buffer zone with no military. All of which revealed a set of Options: What if Egypt got the maps, the flag, and the civilians as it wished for the Sinai, but both sides agreed there'd be no military in most of the territory, creating a buffer zone protecting Israel (along with real-time U.S. satellite images to help Israel track any Egyptian troop movements)? Both leaders said yes. That breakthrough removed one of the key stumbling blocks that helped both countries enter the Camp David Accords in 1978.[8] The accords, though controversial, ended long-standing hostilities between the two nations, producing peace between them that's lasted for decades. For their efforts, each nation's leader—Begin, Sādāt, and Carter—won the Nobel Peace Prize.[9]

The Limits of the Three Little Words

The Three Little Words have their limits. First, you can't resolve every conflict using an Interest-based approach. For example, it often doesn't work when conflicts are mainly about tribalism, ethnic rivalry, or so-called wicked problems, which by definition have such a tangle of causes that they're all but impossible to solve.

Second, there will be times when you find your problem demands more insight, more savvy, more perspective, more power, and more care than even the Three Little Words can give you. Fortunately, the second tool, ➤ [Chapter 2] I FORESAW IT, can help.

Third, the Three Little Words don't tell you how to *divide* the pie. That's important: negotiators who naively focus on being creative, with no thought about how they'll deal with the competitive side, can get hurt. But rest easy: other tools we'll explore will give you that support—most important, much of the Topics, Targets, and Tradeoffs (TTT) grid, 📋 [Chapter 4] and the Winning Warmly Recipe Card, 🏆🏆 [Chapter 7], among others. Indeed, if, like me, you've felt uneasy negotiating for more of the pie, you'll find those tools handy and valuable since claiming wealth can often be a vital form of justice and a vital way to care for those you serve.

All that said, we can achieve remarkable harmony, even between longtime adversaries, using the Three Little Words. I've witnessed this goodness hundreds of times in my students' work. I've seen the Three Little Words help my clients thrive. And I've also seen those words work in my own service as a trained mediator, where I've used them to broker agreement between many people who at first could barely stand to be in the same room with each other.

But if the Three Little Words are as simple as they are powerful, can they work even for a child?

So Simple an Eleven-Year-Old Can Do It

Jamal, eleven, had been trying for months to get his dad to buy him a cat. Jamal had used all the bread-and-butter persuasion gambits eleven-year-old boys usually rely on: nagging, pleading, pouting, complaining. But, his efforts had only succeeded in making him and his dad frustrated with each other. Then one day, Jamal found himself with his babysitter, Yiling, who happened to be a graduate student of mine. Jamal shared his frustrations with Yiling, who offered to teach Jamal the Three Little Words.

After Yiling left, Jamal readied for a conversation with his dad by putting the Three Little Words to use. Then he went to his dad and asked him if they could have lunch together. "O-K," said his puzzled father. Over lunch, Jamal said, "Dad, I wonder if we can have a conversation about getting a cat." His father sighed. "Jamal! We've been over this! Look, *I* want a cat too. But you know we can't get one. Your sister's allergic, I can't spend time cleaning up all the cat hair, and you're eleven—how do I know you'll take good care of it? It's out of the question."

But then Jamal said something that shocked his father: "Dad, you're right: those are good things to be concerned about. So, I did some research, and I found out there's a kind of cat that most kids aren't allergic to. I think it's called a Bengal. It doesn't shed much at all—that's why they're popular. And I found this group—I think it's a charity—that can lend us a cat for a few weeks so you can see if I keep my promise to take good care of it." Stunned silence. Then his father said, *"Then, we're getting a cat!"*

In my professional life, I've seen thousands of negotiations, some for hundreds of millions of dollars, but Jamal's is one of my favorites. His story illustrates that even an eleven-year-old can overcome adversity by deploying the Three Little Words. Learning them helped develop Jamal's maturity, creativity, poise, proactivity, and respectful engagement, qualities we want in our children and ourselves. How did Jamal do it?

When Yiling asked, Jamal was quickly able to list his father's Interests: protect Jamal's sister's health, keep the apartment neat, and avoid unwisely trusting an irresponsible child to care for a cat. That insight became the foundation for Jamal's transforming work.

Jamal then took the time to research Facts online, and that's how he discovered that Bengal cats are a popular allergy-friendly breed. It's also how he found an organization I'll call Second Chance Rescue, which lets people foster a cat for a few weeks. Jamal quickly realized that discovery also happened to be a brilliant creative Option, one that served everyone's Interests well.

Mastering the Facts nurtures that feeling you get when you've done your homework on the eve of a big exam and know you're ready. One reason Jamal was so relaxed, confident, and solicitous was because he knew his stuff.

Leading Without Authority with the Three Little Words

But Jamal's and Shanice's stories, and Israel's, Egypt's, and Jordan's, only start to capture the power of the Three Little Words. One of the most widespread problems leaders face is that they have too much responsibility and too little authority. As Hedrick Smith points out in *The Power Game: How Washington*

Works, even presidents often find they have far less power than we think they have. If you're a middle-level manager, a project team leader, a committee chair, a C-suite executive, or the nominal head of the family, you probably already know this problem. You've found you can't simply tell people to do everything you need them to do to help you get tasks done. What to do?

A surprising answer: negotiate. As many studies and books have found, a good portion of what leaders do all day is negotiate with colleagues and subordinates.[10] But how?

The Three Little Words can help. By thinking them through beforehand, discussing them with the other(s) you'd like to lead, and seeking outcomes that make them *want* to cooperate. By doing that, you often can get better results and more buy-in than you would if you had unilateral authority.

Consider this story. With no authority over her work colleagues, Rachael used the Three Little Words to lead them so well she helped save their department during tough times at her auto parts company. She enabled them to agree to wise budget cuts, and do it in a way that hurt little and changed her relationship with them from rivals to friends.

As a recession loomed, Rachael's engineering design department needed to give senior management a proposed budget, so Rachael and four fellow engineers who each led small teams all submitted proposals to Wanchee, their department manager. But Wanchee rejected them, saying that the total expenses would be far too high. None of the lead engineers knew what to do. Each stuck to their demands, and discussions soon turned ugly. Worse, everyone was distressed when Wanchee threatened to cut each lead engineer's budget by 33 percent across the board. Tensions rose, and factions started to form. Rachael sensed the department was facing disaster. What to do?

Rachael first carefully reviewed the different teams' budgets, and the projects they had proposed, to discern what Interests each lead negotiator most cared about and master the Facts. She then brainstormed several Options her colleagues and she could use to lower costs. Then she met with the other lead engineers and suggested they work together to see if they could produce a budget that satisfied each of their fundamental Interests. And she further encouraged them to collaborate by reminding them that deadlock could lead to worse budget cuts that could cripple the department, hurting everyone. Sobered and encouraged, the other lead engineers shifted from anger to openness.

She then began to ask them each why they needed what they'd requested. Why, for example, did Alexander, one of the lead engineers, need four new 3D printers? After listening to each colleague carefully, Rachael drew from her own research and brainstorming, asking whether Alexander could live with three if, instead, during off hours Rachael shared with Alexander one of the four printers she was ordering? Through their discussion, Rachael helped the other lead engineers satisfy Interests with Options by identifying several creative ways they could share, helping them create complementary schedules, and spotting other low-impact/high-savings compromises. By the time the budget was due, Rachael and the other lead engineers had found ways to share five printers, eliminate requests for four others, and cut their computer hardware order without hurting their projects. As a result, the final budget they submitted came in almost $800,000 below their original proposal. Wanchee praised Rachael for her excellent work. And just as significant, the engineers had gone from seeing each other as competitors to collaborators, and each of them was happy.

Rachael's approach was not unique. As we'll see later, presidents, managers, and even generals often use a similar approach, as many studies confirm.

The idea, then: when you lack the authority and relationship you need to perform your duties, use the Three Little Words to bridge the gap, negotiating with colleagues to win the support you need.[11]

The Most Powerful Way to Sell in Three Little Words

Beyond management, the Three Little Words are also at the heart of one of the most effective, well-researched selling methods ever devised.

Neil Rackham and his team of thirty researchers studied 35,000 sales calls in over twenty countries in the 1970s and 1980s, research salespeople still widely rely on today.[12] The research spanned ten years and may be the largest study of selling ever conducted. It showed that, contrary to popular belief, conventional sales methods for small consumer goods failed miserably when applied to more complex transactions. Rather than telling the customer how great her product is, Rackham's team instead advised a salesperson to ask her customer a series of simple questions. See in this example if you can spot the photocopier salesperson using concepts baked into the Three Little Words:

Q: Tell me about your firm and its copying work? [Customer answers.]

Q: I see—you're growing, so cash is tight lately. You copy ~1,000 brochures a week. What difficulties have you experienced with your current copying? How satisfied are you with copying lately? [Customer answers.]

Q: I get it—you feel you're doing OK; you have a jam two or three times a week that stops copying for an hour or two, but you usually fix it. Which business areas are most affected when the copier breaks down two or three times a week? [Customer answers.]

Q: I see; you've often had some late deliveries and some unhappy customers, and some overtime labor charges that typically cost you ~$200/week. So that's about . . . $10,000 a year? How might a more reliable copier reduce overtime and affect repeat business? [Customer answers.]

Q: So, it sounds like your current copier occasionally breaks down, which costs you ~$10,000 a year in overtime. Sounds like better reliability would save you that money and ease your cash crunch. Also, I gather better reliability would improve your odds of not losing another $12,000 customer. Do I hear that right?

Rackham showed that simply by asking a first question about the customer's situation (Facts) and then a series of more penetrating questions about her Interests, the salesperson could make the customer eager to hear what Options the salesperson had to offer to serve those Interests. And the salesperson could do it *without saying anything about the product.* It's the opposite of the old sales saying "Always be closing." Rackham's method, called S.P.I.N. selling, instead says, "Always be listening for the Three Little Words." As Rackham notes, this approach lies at the heart of consultative selling,[13]also known as needs-based selling, which has become one of the most lucrative selling methods today.

This approach has helped my own sales work as a consultant. Early in my career, a bank asked me to pitch my training work, so I came in and gave them a stem-winding presentation they seemed to love. I never heard from them again. Later, once I'd learned from Rackham, I took a radically different approach. I'd begin each conversation with a prospective client by saying, "Let me listen so I can learn more about your needs." Then I followed up with questions similar to Rackham's and tailored what I offered them accordingly. I won more business that way.

Here, then, is a thought experiment: people often say of a great salesperson that "she could sell freezers to people living in the Arctic." How would you sell to them?

Using the Three Little Words and Rackham's approach, you'd discover a little-known Fact: if you leave food outdoors in winter in the Arctic, it often freezes so hard it becomes unusable. This fact reveals a nonobvious Interest: the need to store food more *warmly,* which freezers do. And you'd discover another little-known Fact: warming local temperatures make outdoor storage in the Arctic summer increasingly unreliable, which reveals another nonobvious Interest: steady food temperature control. Which may explain why many people living in the Arctic *do* buy freezers.[14]

Fundraising in a Recession with the Three Little Words

The Three Little Words can also help you raise money.

Bridget was volunteering for an AIDS fundraising event. When she reached Milind, her contact at one of the charity's corporate donors, Milind told her that the firm unfortunately wouldn't be able to contribute that year, even though it had given $5,000 the year before. "I'm sorry to hear that," Bridget said. "I hope you're all right. What's going on with the firm these days?" Milind told her the firm was facing a recession, sales were down, its marketing campaign targeting young urban professionals was fizzling, and the CEO had ordered a spending freeze. Bridget told him she was sorry for their troubles, which Milind appreciated. A few days later, Bridget called Milind back. "I got to thinking about your marketing problem," she said. "So, I did some learning and found out our annual fundraiser at Chicago's Field Museum next month has historically attracted about one thousand young urban professionals with salaries ranging from $75,000 to $250,000 and average earnings of about $110,000. It occurred to me that's your target demographic, and we've found that corporate donors get a lot of brand awareness and goodwill from participating. We could feature your name and logo and let you set up a booth to give out promotional material. Would that be of interest to you?" Milind was so excited by the idea that he asked Bridget to let his firm cosponsor the event for $25,000, a fivefold increase from the previous year. And all that despite the recession.

Bridget's experience illustrates an insight championed by Howard Stevenson, a Harvard professor who has helped raise over $2 billion. In his book, *Getting to Giving: Fundraising the Entrepreneurial Way,* Stevenson observes that a key to attracting charitable giving is to focus on the donor's motivations and then find meaningful ways to help the donor participate. Put another way, a key is to focus on the donor's Interests, learn Facts, then offer creative Options the donor will likely respond to well. That's just what Bridget did. Her story is particularly apt for our purposes: fundraising is always stressful, she had every reason to feel powerless, and the recession meant she faced particular adversity. Yet she turned everything around beautifully.

In fact, you can use the Three Little Words to turn things around for your entire company—or industry.

Using the Three Little Words to Reinvent Your Industry—No Such Thing as a Commodity

Back in the 1960s, chicken was a commodity—consumers couldn't distinguish one poultry producer from another. Then the head of one poultry firm noticed that consumers cared about more than just the price of chicken; they cared about color, quality, and cut. So, in the early 1970s, after careful research, he started promoting chicken with a pleasing yellow color, packaged with brand tags bearing a quality guarantee, offered whole or in select parts.[15] Those creative Options, backed by memorable advertising, helped Frank Perdue become a household name, turned his company into a top performer in the industry, and ushered in a new age of brand-name chicken. How did he do it? The Three Little Words.

As Tom Peters and Nancy Austin observe in their classic work, *Passion for Excellence,* there is no such thing as a commodity. In industry after industry, from chemicals to dairy to chicken, Peters and Austin found cases where an innovator identified undiscovered, unmet Interests commodity buyers had, learned a lot, and then rolled out a suite of improved choices that transformed the marketplace.

I've witnessed this dynamic in real time. Years ago, I asked students to take fifteen minutes to apply the Three Little Words to the bulk plastics industry, an alleged commodity business. Within minutes they'd produced over thirty creative Options a plastics producer could offer to serve buyer's hidden Interests, from just-in-time delivery to manufacturing advice, from guarantees against currency fluctuations to variations in color, quantity, delivery, storage, and billing. When we finished, an executive raised his hand and said, "I've been in the plastics industry for four years, and it's taken us that long to realize what this class has discovered in fifteen minutes—that we can't just haggle over price anymore and that we have to get more creative."

All of which means you may be able to revolutionize your firm, your industry, and your profession by asking what unmet Interests customers and clients have, what Facts you need to learn, and what creative Options might serve those Interests well.

Getting Seriously Ready for Anything

The Three Little Words—Interests, Facts, Options—can often help by themselves. But there's more. Their initials, IFO, are the first part of a larger tool students and executives prize and rely on, a tool that can help even when the Three Little Words alone can't. Regardless, it's a tool that can ready you in several ways for even the most challenging negotiations. That tool, the

I FORESAW IT, is rich enough that it deserves its own discussion first as in ⤴ [Chapter 2]; and second as in ⤴⤴ [Chapter 3].

Tool in Brief

Three Little Words: Interests, Facts, Options

Challenges

1. *The Basic Challenge.* This week, whenever you face a difficult conflict or a negotiation, see what happens if you slow down, focus on Interests, research some Facts, brainstorm creative Options, and then go talk it over with the other person. What does it take to do that? And what effect does it have on the conversation?

2. *No Such Thing as a Commodity Challenge.* This week, transform your business (or industry) by thinking deeply about hidden needs your current (or future) customers have. Do some research about it, and then develop creative products and services you could offer them that no one is currently providing.

3. *Three Little Fundraising Words Challenge.* This week, think about your donors' Interests, do Factual research about them and your charity, and see what nonobvious creative ideas you might offer your donors to make giving more meaningful for them.

4. *The Consultative Selling Challenge.* This week, instead of regaling your prospective customer with lots of reasons to buy, see what happens if you intentionally ask questions about your customer's Facts and Interests, listen closely, ask follow-up questions, and only then welcome conversation about how Options you can offer can serve those Interests.

Build a Swiss Army Knife for Adversity

Imagine you are on an airplane. You've just finished a hellish twenty-two-hour flight, but the plane can't offload because a hurricane has all but shut down the airport. So, the plane sits on the tarmac for the Next. Six. Hours. By the last hour, your fellow passengers are close to mutiny. No one knows what to do. But sitting next to you is a man named Bob Barsky, a dentist who has had enough. So, Dr. Barsky does one completely legal thing anyone could have done, and within forty-five minutes, everyone is off the plane, safely in the airport terminal, crisis over. What did Dr. Barsky do? For most of us, the crisis would have seemed unsolvable. But a single question helped Dr. Barsky save the day. It was one of several powerful questions that await you if you know how to use the I FORESAW IT mnemonic.

I FORESAW IT is a ten-letter tool negotiators use to get ready for any important negotiation or conflict. Each letter stands for a word, and each word a question that skilled negotiators answer before they enter key talks. We've already discussed three letters in the tool—Interests, Facts, and Options—but here we will cover six more letters standing for other powerful questions you can ask yourself and others. (We'll cover the last letter later in more detail. 📋 [Chapter 4].) These questions help you in many ways. They reveal hidden opportunities, allies, and traps, and help you build rapport and deal with resistance, better understand the people and the problems, discover leverage (and weaknesses), spot easily overlooked influencers, discover persuasive benchmarks, and more.

Stuck on the plane, Dr. Barsky heard a flight attendant invite passengers to write complaints to the airline's CEO, Allen Dodge, at the airline's headquarters in Chicago. That information prompted him to do something no other passenger thought to do. Guessing the CEO lived in an affluent suburb near the airport, Dr. Barsky did a bit of research and learned Dodge's phone number, then called it. Dodge wasn't there, but to Dr. Barsky's surprise, Dodge's wife answered. She felt mortified when Dr. Barsky told her the situation. Dodge's wife immediately called airport operations, and soon after, Dr. Barsky's plane got clearance to go to a gate. What was the question Dr. Barsky asked? "WHO is influential here?" the question captured by the *W* in I FORESAW IT.

And that's just one letter. What if you had the full "Swiss Army knife" full of helps for adversity? Because often problems are more complicated and seemingly intractable than Dr. Barsky's. A complex merger is collapsing. You face intense pressure to cut costs but your suppliers seem determined to raise prices. The key details of a new job are at stake. A family is in peril because a family member's death has led to seemingly unsolvable conflict over how to deal with his estate. You're stranded in a distant land, and your first solution *doesn't* work. If only you could walk around the problem in real time, see its several facets, and discover several ways to win. By design, I FORESAW IT helps you do just that. Its several parts can match the size and complexity of the challenge.

So, let's first see what it consists of, then see it in action in an existential business crisis.

I FORESAW IT in Brief ✈

Interests. Each party's underlying needs, and also any common interests. That is, separate lists of concerns we each have, and a list of concerns we share.

Factual and Financial Research. Facts. Useful information and spreadsheets. In other words, the answers to good research questions we produce through our conversations, reading, and number crunching.

Options. Creative deal terms. That is, a list of different items we might agree on: separate, potentially attractive things one of us could offer the other.

Rapport, Reactions, and Responses. Early ways to signal goodwill, likely objections you'll get during the talks, and possible replies. Put another way, brief early talking points to set the right tone, worrisome things the other might say, and, for each worrisome thing, a good comeback.

Empathy and Ethics. How things look from the other's perspective, and what ethical dilemmas you each face. In other words, what the matter might look like if you were to speak in the other's internal voice, and, separately, moral problems each of you might have with the matter you're discussing, and with possible solutions.

Setting and Scheduling. Where and when you'll negotiate. That is, in what place or medium should you negotiate with what ground rules, and at what hour, what day, and in what sequence?

Alternatives to Agreement. Things each of you might do alone if you can't agree. That is, separate lists of choices you each have that you could turn to to serve your Interests without the other's involvement.

Who. People away from the table who can influence the talks. In other words, besides you and the other negotiator(s), who else can have an important effect, perhaps because they're powerful or knowledgeable, they have a veto, they can provide something vital, and so on?

Independent Criteria. Benchmarks, objective standards. (A special form of factual research.) Put another way, knowledge from sources you both trust that can tell you what's reasonable.

Topics, Targets, and Tradeoffs. A summary of key highlights from your I FORESAW IT work. That is, a simple grid that distills your key learning into a handy glance-and-go one-pager.

(To show you what one looks like, later in this chapter I'll share a sample of an I FORESAW IT plan based on one a traveler created in just a few minutes to help solve a travel disaster.)

So, what happens when you put the tool to use in the face of a potentially job-ending and deal-ending challenge?

Saving a Merger, Millions of Dollars, and Several Careers with I FORESAW IT

Diego was sitting at his desk one day at Beta, Inc., when his boss called in a panic. Acme, the company that had just agreed to acquire their firm, had announced a new policy that threatened Beta, her career, and Diego's. What to do? Diego's story demonstrates that this mnemonic can help you save your career and create millions' worth of wealth.

Acme was an engine manufacturer based in Cleveland. It had recently acquired Beta, the firm Diego worked for, an engine parts firm based in the New York area. Now, Acme had decided to charge each side for transition fees that would cost Beta an eye-popping $20 million. The charge was so stiff that it would turn the economics of the acquisition upside down, making it a money loser for Beta. What to do?

Knowing preparation would be key, Diego immediately turned to I FORE-SAW IT and began doing intense Factual Research. He learned that Acme's primary goal was to cover the cost of making the two firms technologically compatible. (For example, Acme would need to replace Beta's Macs with PCs like Acme's.)

Separately, he scoured the financials, calling colleagues to learn how different firms charge their divisions for transition costs.

Then Diego went to see his boss. Deeply distressed about what seemed like certain disaster, she had no idea what to do. So, Diego just listened to her for a good while, then started to walk her through the first few parts of I FORESAW IT. Soon, the boss began to calm down and see glimmers of hope. She called in two other colleagues to participate. Together, they identified Interests each side had, and used these Interests and Diego's Factual *and Financial* Research to help them develop a dozen different Options. Having bad ideas, he found, made the best ideas stand out. Then they worked through the rest of the I FORESAW IT mnemonic.

While completing the mnemonic, they discovered something everyone had overlooked: under their merger agreement, Diego's firm had the right to keep its Macs and other hardware, and would, to avoid internal disruptions. That meant costs would soar if the firms didn't solve the incompatibility problem. Which meant Beta had a more powerful Alternative to Agreement than his boss had imagined. It also meant both firms had a Common Interest in wisely cutting shared costs.

The best Option they uncovered was a reorganization no one had thought of. Under it, Diego's division would only need to pay its share of the direct cost of making the two firms' hardware compatible, but it wouldn't bear other transition costs. The method would also reduce the need to replace Beta's hardware, saving Acme money, and wouldn't create any financial issues.

Diego's boss was so heartened by these insights that she told Diego he had to be Beta's ambassador to Acme. So, Diego set about fleshing out the I FORESAW IT plan on his own.

Further research confirmed the reorganization idea was workable: two other firms in the industry had used this very approach, and there were no time bombs in the idea that would explode years later. The other firms' experiences were powerful Independent Criteria that the idea was fair and workable.

Thinking about the Setting and Scheduling of meetings and Who could be most influential, Diego arranged to meet with Acme's CIO, the most amicable of its senior executives, to win support for the idea and build a coalition. Diego knew if he could get this one executive on board, she would be able to convince Acme's COO. With the support of both of them, he thought he could win over the CFO.

Empathy, intentionally looking at the problem from Acme's perspective, revealed something else: the CIO would respond best if Diego focused on the numbers and appealed to her Interest in shareholder value, and to the Common Interest of cutting costs.

At first Diego's excellent preparation helped him win a positive response from the CIO, but then Diego faced near disaster: while the CIO assured Diego she understood his proposal, she added she felt it simply wouldn't work for Acme. At that point, Diego felt like screaming. Fortunately, Diego "went to the balcony" and politely took a crucial five-minute break.

Regaining composure, he returned and asked a dumb question: What was he missing? What was the problem with the proposal? The CIO replied Acme simply had never done it before. Why not? The CIO went blank and, after a long pause, shook her head and said she had no idea. So, the CIO asked her team to spend the next three days going through Diego's model.

Then, the CIO called Diego to tell him they had almost fully embraced his proposal, with a few adjustments. Diego was delighted. The CIO added that she had already reached out to the COO and CFO, both of whom had embraced it too. The ultimate agreement: Beta would be charged $2 million to buy some new equipment, but Acme would cancel the other charges.

The net effect was that Diego's division and the firm as a whole saved over $5 million in operating costs, and his division avoided a $20 million charge and therefore was able to show a net operating profit after the acquisition. Diego was a hero, winning praise from his boss and his CEO.

Diego concluded that without I FORESAW IT, he would not have been so successful. Without it, he would not have felt confident enough to even get involved. Also, if he had, he would have tried to argue with Acme executives without preparation. The key, he realized, was systematic readiness.

He's not alone. For decades, students and clients have said in anonymous surveys that I FORESAW IT is one of their most valuable business tools; many continue to use it many years after they first learned it.

Gavin Kennedy, a negotiation expert, once wrote that "preparation is the jewel in the crown of negotiation. Get this right (and *merely doing it is not enough*) and your performance in a negotiation dramatically improves" (emphasis added). Field research supports the point: there is a right way and a wrong way to prepare; a way to waste time and spin your wheels, and a way to put the same amount of time to powerful use. But how? As Diego's story illustrates, having I FORESAW IT helps you put your time and energy to best use. One study found that five of the eight differences between excellent and mediocre negotiators came down to differences in preparation.[1] Each of the preparation practices excellent negotiators favor is baked into I FORESAW IT.

Getting the most out of your preparation time is especially important when you face a crisis and time is short. These moments tempt you to fight, flee, or freak—to just argue your case, skip town, or flounder around as time ticks away. I FORESAW IT calms you down, lets you walk around the problem and discover hidden hope and power. And when you use it with a team, you can get them calmed down too, and thinking together about the problem in a structured, systematic, revealing way.

Notice that Diego didn't feel the need to go through the mnemonic in order; he jumped first into Factual and Financial Research and moved around from there. While the mnemonic follows a basic sequence, you don't have to use it that way; you can jump around, because several parts tend to inspire ideas that go in other parts, so there's a natural self-reinforcing quality to it. However you choose to use it, I FORESAW IT can help you.

But what if you hate planning, or simply feel it will take too much time or energy? Rest easy: after I've finished introducing you to I FORESAW IT, I'll share seven ways you can use it even when time or energy is in short supply.

Planning, Not a Plan

Eighty percent of the value of I FORESAW IT comes from thinking and learning about the problem in fresh ways. While what you write down can be a valuable reference tool, don't feel you have to religiously leaf through your I FORESAW IT notes in the thick of the talks. It's the act of thinking and learning that most strengthens you. Great improvisational musicians like Jimi Hendrix and John Coltrane practiced ten or more hours a day,[2] preparation that empowered them to experiment. Similarly, once you've done your homework well, you're up for a big exam even if it's closed book.

That said, it's useful to bring your I FORESAW IT plan with you (or entrust it to a negotiation teammate) so you can summon it when needed.

As we'll see, you can also distill many of the most important insights from your I FORESAW IT plan into a simple tool we'll discover later, ⬚ [Chapter 4], that lets you use it like a coach's play card, giving you the ability to "glance and go" in the thick of the talks.

A Closer Look at Each Part

Now that you have a sense of the mnemonic, let's take a closer look at each part. While we've covered much of what you need to know about the first three letters, ⚙ [Chapter 1], there's a bit more to say about them.

Interests. List underlying needs.

Separately list yours, hers, and common. See if you can spot several of each. List several. Include intangible Interests such as face-saving. Give special attention to Common Interests—that is, specific, nonobvious shared goals— which are so important we'll discuss them in detail later, ♞♥ [Chapter 11]. For major talks with a large organization, or with multiple organizations, it pays to list the Interests of each significant player on each side.

Factual and Financial Research. Learn, learn, learn.

What do you need to learn? Many things. For example, depending on the matter: What are market prices? What do key documents say? What do experts say? Published information? What is the other person's reputation? What do the budget, cash flow, balance sheet, and other spreadsheets reveal, and how will different outcomes affect them? What is the history of the relationship? What are the cultural norms? How is the other person's organization set up?

Err on the side of learning too much. When you face a big negotiation challenge, you may feel lost at first. That's normal and healthy; stay with it. Write down your questions and the answers you uncover.

Options. Brainstorm possible deal terms.

Don't worry about crafting a complete proposal here, just list as many *qualitatively* different and partial deal terms as you can. That way you can use them later, alone or in combination. An example of several qualitatively different options: lower price, better payment terms, no delivery charge, and bulk discount. Don't write "$1,000, $1,100, $1,200 . . ." as separate options; those are just quantitative variations on a single option. Here, you're looking for fresh ideas that let you satisfy Interests creatively if your first idea fizzles. (Don't worry: you'll create numerical ranges later in the *T* of the mnemonic.)

As we've seen, it's wise to include silly ideas that foster creativity. For example, readying for talks with a noisy business next door, you might list "helicopter lift factory a mile away" . . . which might inspire you to think of a useful Option: help the neighbor move.

Think of Options that at least help you satisfy your side's Interests: "Which Options could help me provide more for my family? Which could help them improve their cash flow?" Get help from a trusted friend or colleague and ask interviewees for suggestions. It's also wise to list Options that serve the other's Interests.

As we've also seen, once you've listed as many ideas as you can, it's wise to group them into topics. Seek six for each topic you wish to negotiate, because having many qualitatively different Options lets you be, as I often exhort my students to be, *powerfully, pleasantly persistent.*

Don't critique the ideas you brainstorm until you've generated six per topic. Later, you'll cherry-pick the best.

Rapport, Reactions, and Responses. Set a good tone, and get ready for hard resistance.

Here is where you plan to speak thoughtfully, and cope well with tough talk. Think first about the tone you want to set by noting what you'll say at the start of the conversation. Usually, it's best to say things that are constructive, optimistic, and genuine. You can jot down the gist of things you'd like to say as brief phrases. (For example: "Greetings. Glad to meet. How are you? Looking forward. Hopeful. Satisfy both. Let me listen.") Or you can write specific sentences that feel real to you. Don't treat it as a script—just speak the ideas. (That's how many of the best teachers and extemporaneous speakers get ready.)

Then prepare for resistance. Let your fears out here. Imagine the hard things the other side might say, and consider how you might respond to each. In other words, roleplay (something we'll explore more later, 🎭 [Chapter 5]). Don't feel you have to write a play or try to anticipate everything—just write down a few separate pairs: "If seller says, I will say." For example:

> **If Seller says:** "We never negotiate price. That's our policy."
> **I will say:** "Let's talk about what's possible. Do I understand correctly you offer a bulk discount?"
> . . . .
> **If Seller says:** "You're being totally unreasonable!"
> **I will say:** "I know we both want to be fair, so let me share what I've learned from an industry benchmark . . ."

Seek responses that channel the conversation toward constructive discussion, not argument. You can often find inspiration in the rest of your I FORESAW IT plan. For example, in the first pair above, you drew on Factual Research and a creative Option. Or you might share Independent Criteria, as you did in the second pair.

Empathy and Ethics. Express the other's feelings, and spot moral traps.

First, put yourself in your counterpart's shoes. Speak or write a paragraph about the situation in the other's internal voice. What problems does your counterpart have? Why do you, dear reader, seem difficult? What hang-ups are you bringing to the negotiation? How would you like to be treated if you were in your counterpart's place? If you are working with someone from another culture, try learning about her culture and history.

Empathizing with a negotiating counterpart may feel like a waste of time. It isn't. It's arguably the single most important preparation task, because it can illuminate almost every other part of your plan. It can help you build trust by seeing her humanity. And it can reveal other insights too, like the validity of the other's concerns. ("You're right to be concerned about X. Since I thought you might be, I did some learning and found a way to help us deal with it . . .")

If your counterpart is part of an organization, try too to empathize with her political situation by considering who the hawks and doves are—that is, the players on her side who are hostile to you, and the players there who are friendly.*

Then consider the ethical and spiritual dimensions. Ethics helps you spot practical, legal, and political traps early. (For example, what if they ask you to help them avoid paying taxes, or conceal something from the government?) So, what likely ethical dilemmas will you each face? Write them down in list format. How will you deal with yours? What ethical limits will you set? Is there something you're missing that could anger someone important?** Add the answers to your list. If you're so inclined, it may also help (perhaps in ways that have nothing to do with money) to pray or meditate for patience, for strength, and for the other person, especially if relations are strained. In a crisis, simply taking a few seconds to breathe before you plan fully—perhaps with the help of meditation or contemplative prayer—can calm the reptile brain and create space for purposeful, compassionate thought. This part of the mnemonic can remind you to do that.

Setting and Scheduling. Plan where and when you'll negotiate.

Where will you negotiate? By phone? Email? Video conference? In person? Where are you each more comfortable? If you meet, where, specifically? Your place? Theirs? A neutral place? The golf course? Why?

The medium matters. A message shared by text is different from the same content shared over coffee or on the golf course. As Harvard Business School professor Kathleen Valley found in one study, face-to-face talks tended to end in impasse 19 percent of the time, while email negotiations without prior verbal talks tended to reach impasse 50 percent of the time. As she observed, "When the

---

* For example, during the Cuban Missile Crisis in October 1962, John Kennedy and his advisers worked hard to understand what pressures Soviet premier Khrushchev faced from hardliners and doves (if any) within the Kremlin. Doing that led former Soviet ambassador Tommy Thompson to advise Kennedy not to invade Cuba to remove Soviet nuclear missiles there, and so risk nuclear war. Instead, Thompson recommended offering a deal that would help Khrushchev save face with hardliners. That advice was one of the keys to ending the crisis peacefully. As Kennedy's Secretary of Defense Robert McNamara later said, "Now that's what I call empathy."

** To the point: In the opening story of the trapped airline passengers, Dr. Barsky's solution raised an ethical dilemma no one considered: is it fair to pull strings to leapfrog ahead of dozens of other planes that have been waiting longer? That question might have prompted Dr. Barsky to at least call back the president's wife after she'd helped him and ask her for more help for the planes ahead of his. Or it might have prompted him to call the president of another airline with a plane trapped on the tarmac. Or the mayor. Or the governor. Or a TV news producer.

interaction is purely electronic, people are more willing to escalate conflict—to get downright rude, even." And she added, "When people talk over the phone, the most frequent outcome is that one party takes the greater share of the profits; it's asymmetric."[3] That doesn't mean you always have to negotiate in the same room—email and phone can be much more efficient, and each can have other advantages too. So can video. It does mean be intentional and aware.

Separately, will you meet in private or public? (Negotiating in the public eye often makes it harder for each side to make concessions without losing face.) Write your choices down. Have a change of setting in mind in case you reach impasse—often this can help change the result.

Setting can also include any discussion ground rules you'd like to introduce.[*] So jot discussion rules down here too.

Then ask: When will you negotiate? Before something else happens? After? Why? Timing can be crucial. If there are several parties, with whom will you meet first? Then whom? What time of day will you negotiate? (Avoid negotiating when you're tired or drunk if at all possible, a surprisingly common experience in several parts of the world where people expect you to stay up late and drink while you're doing business. Can't avoid it? Consider going with a teammate who brings a face-saving reason for serving as the "designated driver"—and the sober negotiator.) What, if any, deadline will you set or face? Jot it all down here. Knowing the deadline can concentrate the mind wonderfully, helping you manage time and strategize. Scheduling also can mean any sequence of talks you envision, an idea we'll explore later ⊗⊗ [Chapter 6].

Often, Setting and Scheduling are valuable preliminary negotiable issues. If, for example, you face a tough deadline, then winning a day, a week, or a month more may improve the situation. If you have only one offer, buying time can help you find another offer, improving your leverage. Conversely, if you need quick resolution, negotiating for a shorter deadline may help. And the venue and ground rules can also be worth talking about up front.

---

* For example, you can foster more creativity and lower the odds your counterpart will try to "nibble" you late in the talks if you suggest at the outset, "Let's agree nothing is agreed till everything is agreed." We'll explore the power of simple discussion rules later 👥 [Chapter 11].

In fact, negotiating Setting and Scheduling is so important in high-stakes matters that diplomats routinely take time before talks begin, sometimes weeks or months, to hammer out these and other preconditions.

One young negotiator was anxious about negotiating job terms with his future boss, fearing he'd look greedy. Then as he thought about Setting and Scheduling, he realized that instead of a tense meeting with her in her office at 9:00 A.M. Monday, he could suggest a congenial lunch that day at a nice restaurant, build Rapport, and then, over dessert, warmly invite conversation about the terms.

Alternatives to Agreement. List choices you each have if there's no deal.

Put down the different possible Alternatives to Agreement separately for each side. For example, if you're negotiating to buy a neighbor's used car and you can't agree with him, what exactly will you do instead? Take the bus? Buy a new car you saw at the local dealership yesterday? Buy a very similar used car you saw for less nearby? List at least five possibilities.

Five may seem like a lot—but often, your first or second answer isn't the best one. For example, "I'll sue!" often seems like a good idea, but as an attorney I can tell you it's often a last-resort nuclear choice, and that other, less obvious Alternatives to Agreement are often better. Try to improve your Alternatives to Agreement with research and creativity; doing that can reveal surprising sources of power. Which is your best? By definition, that's your Best Alternative to a Negotiated Agreement, or BATNA. BATNA is a term of art—a tool, really—coined by the authors of *Getting to Yes*. It's a negotiator's best available choice if she must walk away from the talks, the choice that best satisfies her if she *doesn't* do a deal with the counterpart. For example, if cost and independence matter most to you, and the neighbor's final price for his car is very expensive, your BATNA would be the less expensive but similar nearby used car.

Knowing your BATNA is important, so much so that in a survey, 150 of my former students reported that BATNA was one of the most powerful ideas they'd learned in our negotiation course. That's because it helps you know when to say no. When a final offer doesn't serve your interests as well as your BATNA does, it's time to walk away. Knowing that one idea made it easier for them to spot bad offers, ask for better, and, if necessary, end the talks.

Then list at least five possibilities *the other* has so you don't overestimate your strength (or the other's). What is her BATNA? Knowing each party's Alternatives to Agreement can reveal who has more leverage, something that can strongly influence the talks.

It's also wise to identify your and your counterpart's respective Worst Alternative to a Negotiated Agreement (WATNA), the biggest worry or danger you each face. While a negotiator's BATNA may look attractive, a BATNA can sometimes prove illusory, vanishing even as they grasp it. For example, in our used car illustration, the seller might think they can sell it to someone who outbids you, but what if that buyer has little cash and bad credit? Winding up with a bad offer (or no others) could be the seller's WATNA. Meanwhile, your WATNA might be that you have to take the bus (and so lose a lot of independence, not to mention time and comfort). Knowing your WATNA can sober and warn you not to overplay your hand, and perhaps remind you to firm up your BATNA first. Factual research might reveal your neighbor's WATNA is quite possibly "no buyers for months" since it might take a long time to sell the car at anything close to that price, perhaps arresting his ability to use the money for something else you learn he badly needs. Tactfully noting this risk may encourage him to say yes, an idea we'll explore later ❝❞ [Chapter 9].

Who. List who else can influence the outcome of the talks.

Who's support (or opposition) could affect the talks? A spouse's? Customers'? Regulators'? Name them. Who does each negotiator answer to? Who are the hawks and doves? Who else should you involve in the process? Should you use agents? Mediators? Is there someone else who would be better to deal with instead? Are there allies you can form coalitions with? Other coalitions you need to block? And will your negotiation have a good or bad impact on other stakeholders? If so, list them here too—they may have added resources to bring to the bargaining table. Think about involving them.

How critical is Who? Clarence Avant, known among top celebrities as the "Black Godfather," is a celebrated negotiator who won pivotal deals for people like Barack Obama, Hank Aaron, Quincy Jones, Lionel Richie, Jamie Foxx, P. Diddy, and a host of others. A key to his success: "I don't have problems—I have friends."[4] His ability to network and talk to anyone made him a powerful advocate for many people who were overlooked or underpaid.

Independent Criteria. List fair, trustworthy benchmarks.

That is, what objective standards can you appeal to so the other person sees your offer is fair and reasonable? Look for something the other person is likely to trust that's out of your control. (Some examples: Blue Book estimates of fair market value, *Consumer Reports* ratings, a jointly chosen accountant's appraisal, industry statements about standards and practices, verifiable precedent, existing contract terms, or a fair decision rule such as "I cut/you choose.") Independent Criteria let you say, in effect, "Don't take my word for it; let's turn to something we both trust." They are more persuasive than saying, "I'm making you a very fair offer." And they're a good way you can test for fairness.

You might ask, "Is the category Independent Criteria a subset of Factual Research?" It is; we break it out as a separate item because benchmarking can be unusually persuasive and grounding.

But what if you can't find a criterion you both trust? What if one party says, "That's a fake source; we never listen to them." That's why you want to list several (thus the plural *criteria*) so you can reply, "OK, just to be sure, I also found this second source." But what if your counterpart keeps vetoing your criteria? You can ask them to propose a benchmark you might both respect, making sure it isn't skewed toward them. Disagree with their suggestion? You can treat the question itself—"What standard should we use?"—as a negotiation you want to pursue constructively: "I know you want to be fair, and so do I, and it looks like we're not finding something suitable yet. Let's dig in together to find it." Good thing you anticipated their Reaction ("That's a fake source!"), thought about their Interests, Empathized, and Researched other sources they do tend to listen to that you're comfortable with too. Can't find any? Think more widely: Consider *people* you both respect, like, say, an expert in the field or even an arbitrator or consultant. Or consider using a fair *process,* like a formula, or even a random coin flip, or a widely accepted *norm* like basing a used car price on the Blue Book.

Topics, Targets, and Tradeoffs. Create a glance-and-go play sheet.

Finally, create a focused one-page summary guide to the talks that distills many of the key insights you've learned from the rest of the I FORESAW IT mnemonic. That grid helps you ready for both the competitive and collaborative sides of the talks ahead. We'll explore the TTT grid in depth later 🗂 [Chapter 4].

I FORESAW IT serves as a mental checklist, helping you walk around the challenge and see it from different angles. Often the letters work together synergistically; many negotiators have found, for example, that the mnemonic can reveal nonobvious, evidence-based, mutually satisfying deal terms—and revolutionize a situation. Like Diego, many negotiators report feeling more confident in negotiations once they've gone through the I FORESAW IT mnemonic. They are more willing to listen to their counterparts because they have less reason to feel threatened; they've done their homework. This confidence and openness can make a difference in their ability to deal with intimidation, to respond effectively to claiming tactics and threats, to listen for hidden agreements, to disarm, to relate with compassion and creativity, to learn something, to know when to walk away, and to craft surprisingly satisfying agreements. It doesn't always go so well, but luck favors the prepared.

The Power of I FORESAW IT in Deeply Emotional Conflict

I FORESAW IT can give you poise even when it seems impossible. It can equip you to act effectively even when your world seems to be falling apart, and even when you're dealing with a deeply emotional conflict. Usually when we face sorrow or anguish, it can seem as if we have a Hobson's choice: lash out, or give up. But even then, I FORESAW IT can help give you a better third choice.

On January 12, 2010, Mike's fiancée died in the Haitian earthquake, and his life spiraled into darkness. A few months later, workers recovered her body, but Mike had no legal rights to anything about her; everything connected with her body, her burial, and her estate was under the control of her father, Brian, and as far as he was concerned, Mike didn't exist. What would you have done at a moment like that?

I know I would have found it almost impossible to get out of bed in the face of such anguish. But Mike decided, despite his grief, to treat the matter as an occasion for loving and principled negotiation, and so he prepared an I FORESAW IT plan. Because he considered Empathy and Ethics, Mike came to appreciate that, contrary to his early raw impression, Brian wasn't a bad person; Brian was a grieving father. Because Mike considered Setting and Scheduling, he realized it was crucial to talk with Brian where Brian would feel safest and where they could connect more fully: at Brian's house on a quiet Saturday afternoon. So Mike reached out to Brian by phone and won Brian's reluctant invitation to come by. When they met there, Mike was able to begin with a note of compassion as he'd planned (Rapport), saying, "Brian, how are you doing with all this?" And hesitantly at first, Brian began to share a bit of the sorrow he was facing at the death of his daughter. After listening a long time, Mike said, as he'd planned (Responses): "Brian, thank you. You were such an excellent father that you raised to adulthood a woman I admired and adored. You did so well that I wanted to spend the rest of my life with her. And," he continued, "I need to talk with you about a few other things." Then, gently, Mike raised a number of Topics, as planned: information about the circumstances of her death and the disposition of her remains, his wish for some mementos from their time together, and even his wish to buy as a keepsake the small boat she had owned and that they'd frequently sailed on together. Mike felt more confident than he expected because he was ready with different Options that might serve Brian's Interests if Brian was reluctant, and good Factual Research and Independent Criteria to reassure Brian that Mike was being reasonable. Though it helped knowing he had them, Mike was pleasantly surprised to find he didn't need to use the Options and Factual Research, or even to Respond as he'd planned to tough Reactions. By the end of the conversation, not only had Brian agreed to everything Mike had requested, but he invited Mike to be with him when they dedicated a small reading room at his daughter's school in her honor, and they began a relationship. In all likelihood, the compassion, respect, and poise Mike was able to muster through his preparation spoke volumes to Brian, who reciprocated, even in his grief.

How do you do something like that—overcome a tsunami of pain and powerlessness and transform alienation into connection? Mike's preparation seems to have helped him channel his feelings into constructive forethought, and gave him the freedom to speak from his heart, knowing he was ready to care for himself as well as for Brian.

Not that you always have to negotiate in the depths of heartbreak. Sometimes it may be better to have someone you trust negotiate for you, perhaps drawing on the I FORESAW IT mnemonic and whatever other help you can muster. Just know the mnemonic can help when you need it.

No Need to Memorize I FORESAW IT

Neither Diego nor Mike needed to worry about memorizing I FORESAW IT; simply knowing its power and having a prompt handy was enough. So, you'll find an I FORESAW IT plan form in Word format at Professorfreeman.com that you can use as a prompt and preparation guide. (You'll also find a copy of the form in Appendix III.) I highly recommend you get the form onto all your electronic devices so that when you need it you've got it at your fingertips.

A Map, Not a Script

I FORESAW IT is not a script; it won't just tell you what to say. That's because scripts don't work in negotiation; the process is too dynamic for that. Rather, I FORESAW IT is like a map, showing you the destination and much of the terrain before you arrive at it, so that whatever the other side does, you'll be ready to steer toward your goal.

That said, how *should* you start? While we'll explore answers in Part II, here's one frequently wise approach: get (re)acquainted, spend time on personal matters, set a constructive tone, ask some simple questions, and listen. You can prompt yourself to do these things in the Rapport section. For major talks, it may also be wise at some point to suggest a simple agenda, as we'll explore later 🗗 [Chapter 4].

The Downside?

Is there any downside to using I FORESAW IT? Potentially. While systematic preparation is a key to negotiation success, when less experienced negotiators first do it, they sometimes feel so invested that they find it harder to walk away from the talks, even when the other side's offer is bad. Experienced negotiators avoid this trap, not by avoiding preparation but by using it *more,* testing each offer against their Interests, their best Alternative to Agreement, the Independent Criteria—in short, by using I FORESAW IT to also help them decide whether to say yes. (We'll explore how to do that 🔯 [Chapter 13]).

But What If You Have No Good Alternatives to Agreement?

I FORESAW IT can help you level the playing field in several ways when you feel weak. But what specifically should you do if you have no Alternatives to Agreement and the other side is big and powerful? Later we'll equip you with several tools to improve your Alternatives: Who I FORESAW ⚙ [Chapter 6], Targeted Negotiation ◎ [Chapter 6], and Notional BATNA ⊖ [Chapter 12]. But here are three ways to cope:

1. ***Work the mnemonic harder.*** Spend more time seeking good answers to each of the other parts of the mnemonic, perhaps with the help of teammates. Power comes in many forms and the mnemonic is good at revealing them, especially with others' support. Typically, negotiators listen to rumors or gut fears or headlines and assume all is lost. But often that's not true. Do your homework; you'll know better what is and isn't possible.

2. ***Make it better for Godzilla and you.*** Even if the other party is a Godzilla who can dictate terms, offering her a deal you both like better can sometimes save the day, as Diego's story illustrates. Imagine your biggest customer tells you that most of the terms are fixed, and you know you don't have any other prospects. Good preparation may reveal hidden Interests your customer has, Options that would help you a lot at little cost to them and vice versa, others Who you could recruit to help you both, additional Topics that *are* negotiable, and so on.

3. ***Don't negotiate.*** If your I FORESAW IT work reveals that you are at the other's mercy, or if you have every reason to believe you're facing a juggernaut, then use the mnemonic to help you find ways to *avoid* negotiating for now, such as buying time, scheduling a postponement, politely declining to engage, or reaching a relatively inconsequential deal that you can renegotiate when you're in a better position to do so. Temporarily leaving the negotiating table can give you better Alternatives to Agreement and better Options—an idea we'll explore in detail later, ✪⊛ [Chapter 6].

Can You Use I FORESAW IT in the Face of an Urgent Emergency?

But what if you face an urgent emergency? After all, Diego and Mike each had a few days to plan. What if you only have a few minutes? As many have found, even then you can deploy I FORESAW IT to help save the day. Travel crises, for example, are a frequent occasion where in-the-moment I FORESAW IT planning can be surprisingly effectively.

To the point, Myra, an EMBA student, was checking in when she learned her flight from JFK to LAX was canceled due to a bomb threat. Desperate to see her child, she asked for the airline's manager. As she waited for thirty minutes, she used the time to develop an I FORESAW IT plan. Among other things, she spotted some of the manager's hidden Interests she could appeal to, including satisfying a customer, Myra, who had many classmates who traveled regularly by plane. Also, she saw she could empathize with the manager's plight of having to deal with hundreds of angry passengers. In all likelihood too, the process helped her channel her anxieties into constructive effort and calm down, meaning she didn't speak to him sharply and impatiently as so many others surely did that day. When they did speak, she appealed to his Interests, and pointed out that it would help the airline's reputation if he could do something to help a mother reach her child. It would also give Myra a strong incentive to recommend the airline to her classmates. Also, she noted, many passengers might be more willing to be bumped because they'd be glad to stay longer in New York during the holiday season.

To her amazement, he actually took her points seriously and told her he'd look into what he could do to help. While he checked, she did further Factual Research and learned about a partner airline that had a flight that day. When he returned and said there was nothing he could do, she reported this new information as an Option to him. Clearly impressed, he smiled, praising her for her tenacity and resourcefulness. He then got her on the flight at no extra cost and even let her stay in the executive lounge. To her surprise, Myra got home sooner than she'd originally planned. Being prepared with I FORESAW IT had both calmed her and given her specific, valuable ideas to politely offer.[5]

Myra is not alone; others have used I FORESAW IT in even less time to handle travel disasters. Here's an augmented example of an I FORESAW IT plan a student created in fifteen minutes with his family when they arrived at an overbooked hotel.

I FORESAW IT Plan for the Alpha Hotel Case

(Based largely on the student's work during a fifteen-minute planning session. I've added a few other ideas (*) for teaching purposes.)

My family's interests
Comfort
Affordability
Peace of mind
Convenience
Respectable treatment

Alpha's interests
Maintaining a positive reputation by keeping customers happy
Abiding by the law (not being allowed to evict guests)
Encouraging repeat customers
Minimizing costs

Desk clerk's interests
Impressing her boss
Keeping customers happy
Minimizing the cost of relocating guests
Keeping her job

Common Interests
Fair outcome*
Swift outcome*
Avoid a scene*

Factual and Financial Research

- I talked with another woman online who mentioned that she works for a different hotel chain. She had made her reservation through one of the Alpha's General Manager's friends, but she too was being relocated. I asked her if she was familiar with the nonevict law for hotels, and she confirmed there is such a law.
- Through a phone call to the Beta Hotel, we found out that their rooms cost $159.00 per night and that they are located directly across the street from the Four Seasons.
- A travel agent I called reported that it is an industry standard for a hotel of this class to offer one to two nights free at a comparable hotel.*

Options (Each is a separate, novel idea. It's *not* a list of complete package offers but a list of separate suggestions the negotiator can offer in different combinations.)

Rooms

- Similar room at Beta
- Two double beds at Beta
- Two king- size beds at Beta
- Suite at Beta
- Two rooms at Beta
- Adjoining rooms at Beta

Compensation*

- Alpha pays for room(s) for both nights
- Alpha pays extra cost of room(s) for both nights
- Transfer to Beta
- Complimentary stay at any Alpha hotel
- Free breakfast coupons
- Complimentary dinners at restaurant

Things We Can Offer*

- We agree to join Alpha's Frequent Guest Stay Program
- We promise to recommend Alpha on social media
- We promise to recommend registration clerk to her boss
- We agree to late check-in
- We agree to waive maid service
- We apply for hotel credit card

Rapport, Reactions, and Responses

*Hi!

*Tough night?

*Confident we can figure it out

If she says: "I'm sorry, sir, but I can't approve your request."

I will say: "I understand. You've been very kind to listen to my suggestion. Since it looks like we may have gone as far as we can in this conversation I wonder if we could speak with your manager? Perhaps he can approve it."

If she says: "No, it's against policy."

I will say: "I certainly don't want to make you violate the hotel's policy if we can avoid it. Can you tell me more? I wonder what else we might do? One possibility might be to . . ."

If she says: "I don't have authority to give you this."

I will say: "I see. I wonder if you can tell me what authority you do have?"

Empathy and Ethics

- Empathy

"Everyone is screaming at me about a situation over which I have no control. I'm just not in a position to negotiate terms with customers. I have to keep everyone happy, but I also want to dispose of the customers as tactfully as possible. Diffusing their anger is probably my biggest challenge. If I handle this wrong, I risk losing a customer, getting yelled at by a customer, or getting in trouble with my boss—and maybe losing my job."

- Ethical Dilemma

How far is it appropriate for me to press a clerk who clearly isn't at fault here?

Is it right to ask for more than others are getting?

If the hotel has promised a room what is their obligation here if they can't keep that promise?

Setting and Scheduling

Face-to-face with the clerk, preferably out of earshot of other customers so she doesn't feel forced to take a hard line. Keep parents away so they don't get angry and spoil the negotiations.

Next few minutes. [There was a time limit on the negotiation because in two hours we had a dinner engagement so we had to do the negotiation in the next hour.]

Alternatives to Agreement

Ours

- Stay at another hotel without Beta's help.
- Complain to CEO
- Stay with relatives*
- Complain to popular travel website
- Complaint on social media*
- Complain to visitor's bureau

Alpha's

- Obey non-eviction law and refuse us*
- Lose us and others as customers*
- Rely on other customers to show up if/when current occupants leave*
- Social media complaint that goes viral (WATNA)
- Publicize high demand for hotel

Who

- Hotel clerk
- Manager
- Upper management
- My family
- Other customers*

Independent Criteria

* Unafilliated Travel agent: 1 to 2 free nights at nearby peer hotel is industry standard compensation

*Frommer's: 1 free night is a reasonable compensation for being walked

*Visitor's Center: most 4 stars give travellers 1 free night at a nearby peer hotel if a hotel can't keep a reservation

Topics, Targets, and Tradeoffs

Topics	Targets		Tradeoffs	Tradeoffs w/i
	(Best)	(Worst)	b/w topics	topics*
Alternate room	2 rooms	1 room at the Beta with a double bed a single bed and a cot	1	Suite Two double beds
Compensation	Free room(s)	Alpha covers $ difference	3	Meal coupons Future free stay Taxi to Beta
How long?	Both nights	Saturday night only	2	Late check-in Sunday Option to stay put

That I FORESAW IT plan (which I've augmented for the sake of learning) helped the student negotiate well. Unlike other guests, he convinced the clerk and manager at Hotel Alpha to agree Alpha would cover the additional cost of *two* nice rooms for *both* nights at Beta, a nearby peer hotel. That meant he got a $1,200 value for the original $350 price, a just and fair result. And the plan helped him negotiate in a way that was kind and respectful to the clerk and the manager.

Seven Ways to Use I FORESAW IT Under Time Pressure

Pick a few letters. Sometimes in a crisis I like to use *IFO* and *A*. In others, I "go to IOWA." Or you might prefer to go right into a Topics, Targets, and Tradeoffs grid with some Factual Research. While full preparation is considerably more powerful, any cluster of letters can help in a pinch. I find it's best to mentally browse the mnemonic and grab three or four parts I can quickly work on. That said, Factual Research is usually one of the parts I grab. Dr. Barsky might agree. (Just don't make a habit of always going for the quick and dirty approach—excellent negotiators set aside time for full preparation. That's a big reason they're excellent.)

Ask friend(s) to help you plan. You can divide and conquer the task by asking friend(s) or colleague(s) to handle specific parts of the mnemonic while you handle others. Or you can ask them to work I FORESAW IT with you, letter by letter, so you come up with more and better ideas in the same amount of time. If your team is stressed and unfamiliar with the concepts, you'll need to be less ambitious and give more-focused requests. Later we'll discuss this idea in more detail ✈ * [Chapter 3].

---

* I envision a day when Siri, Alexa, or another bot will be able to help you verbally create an I FORE-SAW IT plan: "Siri! Let's plan for my negotiation with the desk clerk about my canceled flight!" "OK, what are your Interests? For example, you can say things like 'get home soon,' 'avoid a layover,' or 'respect.'" "*W, X,* and *Y*." "OK, *W, X,* and *Y*. Do you want to consider *Z* too?" "Yes." "OK, *Z* too. What are the airline's and the clerk's Interests? . . ." [Later] "OK, what Factual and Financial Research do you need to do? Would you like to hear about airline industry norms for compensating passengers for canceled flights?" "Yes." "OK, I found a website that says . . . " [Later] "OK, here is your plan

(continued)

Teach others I FORESAW IT. To give your team the best chance to help in future crises, teach them I FORESAW IT now (or give them this chapter to read). That way when the crisis comes, you'll have a common language, they'll better understand the advantages of systematic preparation, and they'll be better able to fully help the cause. (And as we'll see later, there's an extra benefit for you: one of the best ways to master a tool is to teach it.) We'll explore more ways to use I FORESAW IT with a team later ✈✈ [Chapter 3].

Treat I FORESAW IT as a set of interview questions. Call someone who's an expert in the field your crisis involves and treat I FORESAW IT as a set of questions to ask her. First, ask a broad question to get her overall wisdom: "Minyi, you've worked in a travel office for years. Here's our situation. What wisdom do you have for us?" Then get more specific, asking her about little-known Interests, important Facts, creative Options, and so on. (You don't have to cover everything in order; *I,F,O,* etc. And you don't have to cover every letter—you can cherry-pick the letters that seem most important to ask about.) Work your way through as much of I FORESAW IT as you reasonably can. Doing that can accelerate your planning and make best use of your time talking with your adviser.

Save, reuse, and revise old plans. Since many negotiations are similar, keep your written I FORESAW IT plans so they can help you jump-start your thinking about a new negotiation on the same subject.

Use I FORESAW IT in your head. You're driving to a crisis meeting. You're running down a hallway to your boss's office. You can't stop and write things down but you need to get ready. What to do? Summon I FORESAW IT from your memory and mentally run through it letter by letter, thinking about

---

with all the answers you've developed. I've highlighted some of the Options that may best serve the Interests . . . " Alternatively, I can envision this interaction: "Alexa! I need to negotiate with an airline desk clerk in five minutes about my canceled flight and I need a plan!" "OK, you need a negotiation plan right away to negotiate with a desk clerk about a canceled flight. Here's a basic plan; I've highlighted some of the Options that may best serve typical Interests. You can modify the plan if you like. For example, you can tell me about different Interests someone has here. Would you like to change something?" One thing: too much support can be a mixed blessing; like having a friend practice the piano for you, you may find you're less ready to perform if you're not actively engaged in readying yourself. That said, negotiators have long found that having a teammate can help them discover more/better/different insights. And by the way, "hagglebots," which rely on artificial intelligence, are becoming more adept at helping, or filling in for, negotiators.

the Interests, brainstorming Options, listing people Who could be influential, and so on. To be ready to do that, you might want to keep a list of the words the letters stand for by your desk, in your car, on your phone, and so on. The Professorfreeman.com website has a list you can download or print out. And a list of those words also appears below under Tool in Brief.

Whisper "I FORESAW IT." As one student found, simply whispering the phrase "I FORESAW IT" in a crisis can activate the higher reaches of your brain, prompting you to visualize the upcoming conversation and possible outcomes, which can trigger useful thinking.

The Alchemy of Preparation

British prime minister Winston Churchill reputedly said, "Let our advance worrying become advance thinking and planning." I FORESAW IT lets you do that; it lets you perform alchemy on your fears, turning them into poise, power, and readiness.

But now that you know I FORESAW IT, you may know more than you know. Next, we'll see several different ways you can use it to handle an array of advanced challenges better than before.

Tool in Brief

I FORESAW IT: Interests, Factual and Financial Research, Options, Rapport, Reactions, and Responses, Empathy and Ethics, Setting and Scheduling, Alternatives to Agreement, Who, Independent Criteria, Topics, Targets, and Tradeoffs.

The 20-Minute I FORESAW IT Challenge. This week, think of a moderately important conflict, need, problem, or negotiation you'd like to handle well. Set a timer and take twenty minutes to work through as much of I FORESAW IT as you can. Then go negotiate.

CHAPTER 3

Get More Help Than You Expected

> ## THE TOOL: I FORESAW IT (AGAIN)
>
> **Use this tool when you . . .**
> - need to negotiate with bureaucrats
> - face sharp bargaining tactics
> - need help mentoring and counseling someone
> - need to help a team solve a big problem but lack authority
> - need to give better gifts.
>
> **Use this tool to do all these things.**

In a pivotal sequence of the movie *The Karate Kid*, seventeen-year-old Daniel asks Mr. Miyagi, his building's handyman, to teach him karate. Daniel asks because bullies have used karate to beat him up, and Mr. Miyagi is a karate master. Mr. Miyagi reluctantly agrees, and for his first assignment, he tells Daniel to wax his car, moving the cloth a certain way. For his second assignment, Mr. Miyagi tells Daniel to paint his fence, moving the brush a certain way. For his third assignment, Mr. Miyagi tells Daniel to sand his floor, moving the sandpaper a certain way. Finally, Daniel protests, shouting that none of these tasks has anything to do with karate. Then Mr. Miyagi tells him to repeat each move he's learned: "Paint the fence!" "Wax the car!" "Sand the floor!" And as Mr. Miyagi calls for a move, he tries to hit Daniel. But Daniel finds his muscle memory of each move lets him fend off the blows. To Daniel's amazement, he's unwittingly acquired the key defensive moves of karate. Equipped with new skills, he has the first building blocks he'll need to overcome his nemeses.

That sequence illustrates a key point: once you've learned something, you may be more powerful than you realize. Similarly, now that you know the basics of I FORESAW IT, you're readier than you may realize to put it to powerful use. Here, we'll see how it can help you negotiate with bureaucrats, mentor or counsel someone more wisely, lead a team, and defend against sharp bargaining tactics.

Negotiate with Bureaucrats

Years ago, I got a thrilling invitation to teach in China, but it would require me to reschedule one class, and my business school's new dean had just set a strict new policy: "Professors *cannot* reschedule classes." To try to solve the problem, my wife and I worked through I FORESAW IT, but at first I saw little hope. Then, as we reviewed the first four letters, my wife noticed something: "I'm looking at your schedule under your Factual Research. It says you have an exam date at the end of the semester, but you never use it—you give a take-home final. So instead of asking the dean to *reschedule* a class, what if you pointed out that you have one too many meeting dates and ask her to *cancel* the one that conflicts with the China trip?" Wouldn't that be hair-splitting? I asked. "Not to your dean," she said. "It will meet her Interest because you won't be *rescheduling* anything." Skeptical but desperate, I asked my dean. "Sure!" she said. "Cancelling the extra session makes perfect sense to me. We can cancel any date you want." And so I got to go to China.

Administrators and other bureaucrats often *can't* agree to creative Options, precisely because the ideas are too creative, and bureaucrats understandably have strong Interests in being consistent with the policies they administer. So, a naive effort to use Interest-based bargaining with a bureaucrat often backfires. But as the China story illustrates, I FORESAW IT can help in several ways.

Learn to speak their language. To do this, do Factual Research about the organization's policies, schedules, terminology, mission statements, and mandates. The idea is to look for "magic words," terms and phrases you can use to show your request fits their rules. Or to demonstrate that your request *doesn't* trigger a magic word that requires them to say no. (That's how I got to go to China, by taking my wife's advice to show my request *didn't* trigger the magic word "reschedule.") In the process, you'll learn the bureaucrat's orders, which can help you satisfy her Interests. Many of these sources, such as policy manuals, precedents, laws, and regulations, are Independent Criteria you can use persuasively. And as you learn, you can better Empathize with the administrator's mandate, a kind of understanding an administrator rarely gets but strongly values. You can identify Options that fit their mandate and their magic words.

For example, the HR executive at your new organization may insist that since you are, say, a "G7" (the bureaucratic box they've put you in), you must get the same treatment every G7 employee gets. But by learning to speak his language, you can reply, "The thing is, I see from the policy manual that technically I'm a G8–New York, as my supervisor reminded me to mention. I see the manual says G8s get special treatment."

Speaking bureaucrats' language is so powerful that there's an entire profession that devotes much of its work to it: lawyers. As lawyers will tell you (and as my China story illustrates), words matter. Even a seemingly trivial language difference may give an administrator leave to change things in your favor, and I FORESAW IT can help you spot subtleties like that.

Learning to speak their language can help you understand and deal better with bureaucrats when at first their behavior seems inscrutable. As Jeswald Salacuse notes in *Seven Secrets for Negotiating with Government: How to Deal with Local, State, National, or Foreign Governments—and Come Out Ahead*, government bureaucracies (and, we might add, many others too) face constraints on how they act: boxes. If you understand those constraints, you can reduce the power difference you face. For example, imagine you think a certain agency should use your office equipment repair services because you can help it save a lot of money, but it seems oddly uninterested and stops corresponding with you. Then your Factual Research reveals the agency's rules require it to favor suppliers that meet certain standards of environmental sustainability—a hidden Interest. Your research also reveals that, unlike your competitors, you can readily meet that standard by switching some of the fuel you use to green energy—an effective Option. You get back in touch with the agency, which becomes more open to your services.

"What do you have authority to do?" There's a related way I FORESAW IT can help you negotiate with bureaucrats. When the registrar, the nurse, or the county clerk tells you, "I'm sorry, I don't have authority to do the thing you're asking me to do," the mnemonic has several suggestions. Focusing on your Interests and Options, you can ask, "OK, I wonder what you do have authority to do that might help?" Focusing on Who, you can ask, "OK, I wonder if you can refer me to the person who does have authority?" Most important, perhaps, is Empathy, treating her with the respect she deserves but, in all likelihood, rarely gets. But, before you do any of these things, careful Factual Research can pay valuable dividends. For example, if the bureaucrat is near a sign that reads, "No admission without a certificate from HQ," you can do some quick learning to see what "admission" means and if there are other ways to get where you need to go without being "admitted," such as visiting, touring, or even going to the bathroom.

Find the right person. Yet another way to work with bureaucracy with I FORESAW IT's help is to do Factual Research to understand how the organization is set up and also by talking with people like you who have dealt with that bureaucracy in a situation like yours. Then use that learning to find the office where help awaits, the official there Who can do what you want, Who else must say yes, and in what Schedule or order should you speak with them. Then prepare for the meeting(s) using the rest of your I FORESAW IT plan.

Avoid the wrong person or the wrong word. Because officials can have strict mandates and because words can have special meanings to them, it's easy to blunder by sharing the wrong information with the wrong person. For example, many people, unaware how the law works, overshare with police officers, thinking they're proving their innocence when they're actually incriminating themselves. Similarly, someone on welfare who innocently volunteers to a social worker too much information about her child's absent other parent could trigger the social worker to investigate for possible welfare fraud.[1] For these reasons, it's important to do Factual Research to learn the words and rules the administrator lives by, identify Who is safe to talk to—and perhaps talk less or to someone else.

You can put all these ideas together by preparing an I FORESAW IT plan before you engage with a bureaucrat, looking for one or several strategies that may help you win the day.

Defend Against Sharp Tactics

Think of I FORESAW IT as your first response kit when you face sharp tactics, those ethically questionable, manipulative, or high-pressure moves people sometimes use to get over on you. Sharp tactics are high-risk, high-return maneuvers; they offer short-term payoffs, which makes them tempting, but they can backfire badly, especially if used against someone who knows how to cope with them. Soon, that will be you.

Most people don't use sharp tactics, so don't be alarmed—but do be ready in case someone does. Here are examples of sharp tactics and how I FORESAW IT can help you respond well:

Limited authority. "I can't give you that; my boss won't let me." The speaker himself is usually speaking quite truthfully; it's the organization, not him, that may in effect be using a sharp tactic by asking you to deal with someone who can only say no. (The Soviet Union was so infamous for negotiating this way it became known as a part of "Soviet-style bargaining tactics.") Responses include:

Who. "Who does have authority and may I speak with that person?"
Options. "What *do* you have authority to give?"
Alternatives to Agreement. Politely signaling you're able to walk away often discourages the practice, especially if you combine it with Options: "While I may have to walk away and take another offer, I'd love to make this work. What if . . . ?"

Bluff. Lies, extreme puffing, serious omissions, and misleading claims. Responses include:

Factual and Financial Research. Gather information that tests the claim. As top sports agent Bob Woolf put it, "You have to establish the reputation for being smart and honest. I learn everything I can before a negotiation."[2] One way to use this sort of research is to politely ask questions you now know the answer to to test for honesty. John Kennedy did just that, early in the Cuban Missile Crisis, to discover Russia's ambassador was lying about Soviet missiles in Cuba. In business talks, a supplier may tell you they must have cash up front. If your research tells you they frequently give up to sixty-day payment terms, you might be wise to reply, "I see. Tell me, please, do you ever make any exceptions?" If they say, "Never!," you probably have spotted dishonest dealing. What then? Be ready with Reactions and Responses.

Reactions and Responses. When you do spot likely lying (that is, a dubious Reaction), the idea isn't to respond like a prosecutor— "Aha! Isn't it true that . . . !"—because humiliating them might produce a pyrrhic victory. ("OK, you're right. Happy? Now get out.") Sometimes you may not even want to immediately reveal you know they're lying because you haven't worked out yet how you want to proceed. Kennedy thanked the ambassador and politely ended the meeting, then privately talked with his aides about how best to deal with dishonest adversaries. In other cases, you may want to be ready to call out the apparent lie, in part to signal you're smart and honest and won't be easily fooled, and in part to rebut the claim. But since you *may* still be interested in working with them, and since it *may* not be a lie but something else, it's usually better to raise the point in a way that gives you (and them) face-saving cover. For example, "Hmm, I'm confused. This says X. What am I missing?"

Options. Offer a face-saving choice that lets the other quietly drop the bluff. "I'm sorry to hear weather delays will require extra time to deliver our order. What if you lent us one of the display models while we wait?"

Alternatives to Agreement. Being able to walk away is a face-saving way to call someone's bluff: "I'm sorry to hear you'll have to hire costly new staff to produce these widgets. It may be this isn't a good match. While I do have another offer elsewhere, I'm also happy to explore other options with you. What if we . . . ?" Or: "I'm surprised to hear you say the warranty isn't your responsibility since my research says you own the warranty company; I hope I won't have to bring this matter to the attorney general's attention . . ."

Who. Negotiate with someone in the organization who's less inclined to bluff.

Independent Criteria. "Hmm, I'm sorry to hear you never offer a guarantee. The benchmarks I'm finding say it's market practice to offer one. Here's a copy of three of them. Since I so respect your firm as a leader in this market, I wonder if a two-year guarantee makes sense?"

Good cop/Bad cop. One negotiator on the other side acts tough, the other nice, but each presses you to agree to the same bad deal. Responses include:

Independent Criteria. "Since my attorney reminds me the law is clear that this isn't even a crime, I can't agree to a four-year plea deal. I'll let her discuss any further questions with you."

Interests/Factual Research. Test the offer against your Interests and your Factual Research, not your gut feeling about the other negotiator.

Alternatives to Agreement. Walk away if the offer is worse than your BATNA.

Killer question. A question you answer at your peril, like, "How much did the last supplier charge you?" "What other offers do you have?" and "How much are you willing to pay?"

Reactions and Responses. Politely decline to answer and change the focus. "With respect, we find it's best to focus on market rates and creative options. So, I wonder what would make sense in this market? One possibility..." Notice you will be able to do this better if you've done Factual Research and found Independent Criteria. Alternatively, you can plan to postpone discussion, saying, "Let's wait until we each know more. Can you tell me more about your organization?" A third possible response: if it feels appropriate, you can tactfully name the elephant in the room: "I know we don't want ask each other awkward questions; would it make sense, then, if we agree not to ask each other about things like other prospects we each have?"

Commitment tactics. The other claims she's so constrained herself that she can't back off her demand: "I promised I'd quit if I agreed to a price a penny higher." Same as limited authority. Also,

Responses. Ignore the claimed commitment and keep negotiating the point for a while.

Mentor and Counsel

I FORESAW IT lets you help others help themselves. That's because it gives you powerful questions to ask rather than advice to offer. Typically, the other negotiator is the expert about the problem and can develop good answers herself; it's the questions that help most.

In his book *Humble Consulting: How to Provide Real Help Faster,* top consultant and MIT professor Edgar Schein writes that the best consulting work he's done has often taken less than an hour and has depended on his ability to ask simple questions as he and his client walked around the problem together. I FORESAW IT lets you do just that.

To use I FORESAW IT to mentor or counsel someone facing a conflict or a business problem, simply let the mnemonic prompt you to ask questions. For example, it never ceases to amaze me how much it helps students seeking my advice when I ask them, "What do you really want here, and why? What are your concerns?" That is, when I ask them about their Interests. In a fifteen- to thirty-minute conversation, you can naturally jump around from one letter to another. Don't worry about covering every letter; just a few can be a big help. At the end, ask, "Has this conversation helped you?" Typically, the other person will say, "Yes. This gives me some excellent ideas and insights." Best of all, when she works out her problem later, she can truthfully say, "I did it myself," which is the best kind of help you can give someone.

For example, imagine a friend comes to you with a problem: his brother wants their elderly father to stop driving.

"Let me just listen," you say. And for some time you do just that.

"What do you think I should do?" he finally asks.

"What do you want here? What are your concerns?"

"Those are good questions," he says. After a moment, he tells you his real concern is that his father will be grounded and that his quality of life will be miserable.

"And your brother's interests?"

"To keep Dad safe as his memory fades."

"And your Dad's?"

"Driving means self-respect."

"Anything you all long for?"

"We all want Dad to feel as much autonomy as he can safely have."

"Tell me more about transportation where your father lives."

"I'm not particularly clear about that, but I can find out with a quick Internet search," he says.

"Good idea," you say. "I wonder also what your father's financial situation is and what he could afford if he sold the car." Your friend thinks a minute.

"I can probably find that out by asking his sister Alice," he says. The next day your friend reports what he found: "Dad's not rich, but he does have a fair amount of discretionary retirement income and selling the car would give him more. And there are five car services, a ride-sharing service, and a neighbor of his who shares his love of bowling and seems to have a car herself."

"I wonder what options might address your concerns about your father's autonomy and quality of life given what you've learned." Your friend comes up with seven or eight possibilities based on his research.

"Are there others?" you ask. He comes up with several more, including an idea he'd never thought of before: ask his father to drive on quiet, familiar roads, but to hire a taxi or carpool for longer or more complicated trips. You're not done yet, but already for the first time, your friend is starting to feel hopeful.

"Say," your friend says, "this is helping."

"But I haven't come up with a single idea," you say. "Everything you've come up with is your suggestion."

"True," your friend says, "but you ask really good questions."

By asking them, you're helping your friend walk around the problem and see it more clearly and deeply, so that whatever he decides will be tailored to the situation he faces.*

But I FORESAW IT can do more than help you help others; it also can help you deal more effectively with an often difficult counterpart—your team.

Lead a Team Using I FORESAW IT

As Diego's story about I FORESAW IT ✈ [Chapter 2], suggests, that tool can help you and a group. First, if you're like Diego and many of my negotiation students, you'll produce better, richer plans with better ideas and insights when you work together with at least one other person. Second, because I FORESAW IT helps you walk around a problem, it can help a team think and, like Diego's colleagues did, see hidden hope when they didn't see much hope before. It can also help the team spot hidden problems sooner, and deal with them.

---

* Notice this example doesn't complete the story or reveal what the right choice is. As I FORESAW IT reveals, there's more to think about: How will the brother React to a given idea? The father? Are there Ethical issues? Is any driving the father does dangerous to pedestrians? What Alternatives to Agreement does each person have here? Can the brother simply take the father's keys away? Any problems (WATNA) with that? What do experienced counselors (Independent Criteria) advise? And so on. But asking the questions can illuminate the problem for the one you're helping, like turning the lights on in a dark room.

At a meeting, your knowledge of I FORESAW IT can help prompt the right kinds of questions: "What are our Interests here? What are theirs? Any Common Interests? What Facts do we need to learn? What Alternatives to Agreement do we have? Who is influential here?" That's how Diego did it.

Alternatively, you can bring your team members in on the exercise, explaining up front about I FORESAW IT, how it works, and why you feel it can help the team. Your team might then spend a fixed amount of time on it, and treat the results as a framework for discussion, posting team members' answers to each part on a whiteboard or a flip chart.

A still richer way is to actually teach the team I FORESAW IT in depth (or share this book with them). In fact, my students routinely teach negotiation to their students (my "grandstudents"), often with I FORESAW IT, and we are usually quite pleased how well it goes. Once your team understands the mnemonic, you can circulate copies of the I FORESAW IT template (from the Professorfreeman.com website) and invite them to fill it out separately. Then you can either have them submit their plans to you or have them bring their plans to a meeting and have everyone share ideas together, one letter at a time. Or you can set up a Google Docs page with an I FORESAW IT template and have them contribute there.

You can also circulate previous I FORESAW IT plans, or a draft plan you've developed, and invite them to suggest revisions or additions. Or, as we saw with ✈ in Chapter 2, you can divide up the mnemonic, giving one part of the team lead responsibility for the first few letters, another part for the next few letters, and so on, then having the team convene (or post) to share what they've developed. If time or team members' attention spans are short, you can limit the time or do selected letters.* Regardless, emphasize it's about thinking together systematically to discover insights (and power) you'd otherwise miss.

Later, we'll discover another tool that can help any discussion go more easily and harmoniously 👥⓪ [Chapter 11].

---

* Speaking of time, I don't usually recommend that each teammate should fill out a full I FORESAW IT plan, since melding all of them together can be time-consuming and confusing. That said, a two-person team might benefit from doing so as a way to backstop each other.

Versatility Plus Focus

The first nine letters of I FORESAW IT make it a versatile tool. The last letter, *T,* lets you distill your preparation into a single page so you're focused and ready in the moment. We'll see how next.

Challenges

The Bureaucracy Challenge. The next time you need help from an administrator, use I FORESAW IT to learn to speak their language, develop requests they can agree to, identify what authority the administrator has, identify Who can help you, and spot words (and people) to avoid.

The Sharp Tactics Challenges. The next time you anticipate someone will use ethically questionable gambits in negotiations, take the five minutes you'd spend on Rapport, Reactions, and Responses and use them to (1) anticipate the sharp tactic(s) and (2) summon other parts of the mnemonic to help you craft good responses. Caught off guard by sharp tactics in a negotiation? Call a time-out and mentally run through your I FORESAW IT, thinking about good responses, or end the conversation for now so you can go prepare fully.

The Leadership Challenge. The next time you find your team needs help readying for talks or solving a serious problem involving people— whether it's a project team, a department, or a group facing a travel crisis— use I FORESAW IT to raise good questions, focus discussion, give effective assignments, or create a thoughtful plan.

CHAPTER 4

Get a Glance-and-Go Play Sheet

THE TOOL: TOPICS, TARGETS & TRADEOFFS GRID

Use this tool when you . . .

- feel unsure how you'll stay focused, think, or stay poised in the talks
- think you may have trouble keeping the details of the talks straight
- fear you'll either create too little wealth or claim too little wealth
- wonder if your negotiation team will act like a herd of cats
- lose the forest for the trees in the talks
- find you lose track of the status of talks from meeting to meeting
- aren't sure what your mandate is
- need help negotiating a single issue competitively.

Use this tool to . . .

- get glance-and-go readiness
- stay focused and poised
- create and claim wealth well
- insure the team is on the same page
- manage many issues
- track talks through several meetings
- work out a clear mandate
- prepare to negotiate a single issue competitively.

Watch an American football game and you'll inevitably see a coach on the sidelines consulting a laminated play sheet. It's how the coach copes as the pressure builds, the crowd roars, and the game hangs in the balance while millions watch at home. Each coach uses his play sheet to help him quickly get his head together and call the right play. College offensive coordinator Matt Kalb says a customized play sheet "can be a coach's best friend in tense game situations." Dick Vermeil, a former NFL coach, explains why: "Things happen so fast." As former Baltimore Ravens coach Brian Billick says, "You need the help."[1]

Astronauts need that help too. If you search online for "iconic photo of Buzz Aldrin walking on the moon," you can see his arm is crooked. The likely reason: he was looking at a checklist sewn into his sleeve.[2] Similarly, before veteran astronaut Chris Hadfield got into a spacecraft, he always made sure he brought a homemade "one-pager." To create one, Chris took everything he'd learned about a critical spacecraft system and boiled it down into a cheat sheet. His one-pager readied him to deal with a crisis. As Chris puts it, "You've got to be able to solve your problems in one breath."[3] The one-pager gave him his best chance to do that under extreme pressure, and also reduced his anxiety.

Astronauts and coaches aren't alone. Doctors use glance-and-go decision tools extensively, to great effect. As Dr. Atul Gawande found, checklists helped his fellow surgeons cut deaths following operations by 47 percent. Medical students too found reference cards so improved their practice and lowered their stress that 76 percent were still using them months after they first got them. U.S. military commanders rely on a glance-and-go decision card too: a Decision Support Matrix. It helps them cope with the fog of war. And in aviation, veteran and new pilots alike routinely use checklists, both before takeoff and during crises. Even when pilots have only seconds to make critical decisions after an engine flameout, they immediately refer to emergency checklists to help them make key choices and prepare for landing.

Checklists, one-pagers, and play sheets ease the cognitive load people face when they're under tremendous pressure. But oddly, negotiators lack that kind of help. You need it—especially when you face high-pressure talks. Thus, the Topics, Targets, and Tradeoffs grid, the last part of I FORESAW IT. The TTT grid is a negotiation tool valued by everyone from high school students to seasoned business leaders. It's a simple but powerful way to distill your other preparation for high-stakes talks. Like a play sheet or a one-pager, it improves your situational awareness, eases your mental burden, and quickly gives you guidance and choices that can improve your results. And it can help you improve the other side's results too.

The TTT grid summarizes much of your I FORESAW IT work into a simple chart that guides you in the moment. By design, it captures many of the keys to successful negotiation. If necessary, you can prepare one in just a few minutes.

That kind of readiness is especially vital when you feel stressed or weak going into a tough negotiation. The TTT grid reveals promising opportunities you might otherwise miss. It helps you gather and focus power, much like David's slingshot. And it can instill you with confidence, especially when you feel overwhelmed.

Top dealmakers swear by it. "Frankly, we use it a lot on key deals," says Gaurav Mittal, then a global senior vice president of Corporate Development at MasterCard.* In that role Mittal led a deals team that negotiates several dozen acquisitions and investments worth a couple of billion dollars each year. "I find it's incredibly helpful. In business things are moving very rapidly. It's often easy to lose sight [of] what is really important on a given deal." The grid, he reports, helps him and his team quickly master and manage talks more effectively.

Similarly, novice negotiators report that the TTT grid helps them feel more calm, confident, and in sync with teammates when they simulate intense talks. That may be because, as we've all experienced, negotiation can often feel overwhelmingly stressful, and stress makes it harder to think clearly and act rationally in the moment.

Whether you're experienced or new to negotiating, you can improve your performance with a TTT grid.

How it works. The basic TTT grid is a simple chart with four column headings:

Topics | Targets | Tradeoffs Between Topics | Tradeoffs Within Topics.

Think of it as a device that can help you bake a larger pie and cut it well. The last two columns help you expand the pie creatively, and the Targets column helps you divide it favorably. The first column, Topics, is the mold, if you will, the part that shapes the rest of the task.

Here's a simple example to see how it works. Imagine you represent a com-

---

* Guarav has since been promoted to CEO of a MasterCard subsidiary.

puter parts supplier negotiating a contract with an important new buyer. There are just two issues: you want an excellent price, and you also need to discuss a money-back guarantee the buyer has floated. Both issues matter to you, but price is more important. Your TTT grid might look something like this:[4]

Topics	Targets	Tradeoffs between topics	Tradeoffs within topics
Price/unit	$100 - $80	1	Most Favored Nation Rebate Quantity discount Discount select items
Money-Back Guarantee	2 years- 5 years	2	Replacement Repair Credit toward new purchase

Opening offer: $110 + 2-year money-back guarantee

Worst acceptable offer: $80 + 5-year money-back guarantee

Creative offer: $100 with a discount on selected refurbished items + 5-year guarantee granting credit toward another purchase.

Notice it's a grid, like a calendar or a spreadsheet, with four columns and, here, two rows. (The offers are separate.) Much of the power comes from laying it out in table form, which helps you visualize everything more easily, rather than in one big list, which doesn't.

We'll look at each part a bit later. But first, let's see the grid in action. How might you use this one in the thick of actual talks with the buyer?

Imagine the buyer begins the talks with an aggressive demand: "We must have a seven-year money-back guarantee, and we want to pay $70 per unit." Afraid of losing business, you might be tempted to agree. But you glance at your TTT grid and immediately see the problem: the buyer's demands are worse than you can accept. The Targets section reminds you that your boss wants a price of *at least* $80, and can barely tolerate a five-year guarantee. So, she will not be happy with this deal. The Targets section also reminds you that a substantially higher price, and a shorter guarantee, are reasonable.

So, you politely make a strong counteroffer: $110 per unit and a two-year guarantee, adding, "We're flexible, as long as we've served our key concerns well. What are your priorities here?"

The buyer tells you they care more about the guarantee. Glancing at the Tradeoffs Between Topics column, you remember that you care more about the price. So, you suggest a trade: "If the guarantee particularly matters to you, we might be able to lengthen the guarantee if you can do better on price." The buyer is intrigued and offers $85 and four years. That's an improvement, but as you glance again at your Targets, you see you're still far apart. What now?

You take another moment, glancing at the last column for creative ideas. Then you say, "We're making progress. We're still far apart, but I'm confident we can still reach a deal that satisfies us both well. I know this will sound like a dumb question, but since higher prices are reasonable in this market, can you tell me why you want such a low price? What are your concerns?"

The buyer tells you they want to be sure you don't give better prices to their competitors. Glancing again at the last column of your grid, you say, "OK, what if we offered you a most favored nation clause so that you'll always get the best price we offer?"

The buyer likes this. "In that case," she says, "we could live with a price of $90." You think, That's good. But how can I do better for my boss?

So, you glance again at the last column and notice the phrase "discount select items." That reminds you that your boss especially wants a high price on new parts—your highest-margin products—to improve cash flow. So, you say, "Thank you, we're making more progress. To make more, I might be willing to charge $93 on selected refurbished parts if you'll agree to $100 on new parts." The buyer likes this idea enough to discuss it, and after further talks, you both agree to $92 on selected refurbished parts, $99 on new parts, and a three-year guarantee. You breathe a big sigh of relief.

Your buyer is pretty happy; she's won concessions, a partial discount, a most favored nation clause, and a substantial guarantee. Your boss is *very* happy; you won terms close to your Best Targets, substantially improved your cash flow, did particularly well on your top priority, price, and did it all in a way that's left the buyer feeling good too. You smile and think to yourself, How did I just do that?

The answer lies in the grid. Here's how each part works.

How Each Part Works

Topics. Here you create an agenda. What will you discuss? Diplomats often spend months before talks working out matters like the agenda, in something called pre-negotiation negotiation. Seriously. Why?

First, it helps you shape what you will and *won't* discuss. When someone tells you, "Price is nonnegotiable," they are hoping you will agree to their demand on price without discussion; if you do, they've won on that issue before the talks even begin.

Second, the agenda helps you both manage time well. So for both reasons, it's often wise, when appropriate, to email the other(s) saying, "I enjoyed our get-acquainted conversation yesterday, and I'm looking forward to our meeting next week. I thought it would help us use time more efficiently if I sent a list of things we probably want to cover. Let me know if you have any suggestions." This way, *you* shape the agenda, so the talks include things you want to discuss, and things you don't want to discuss are less likely to come up—and you also help everyone manage time better.[*]

Third, it readies you to think about the other parts of the TTT grid.

Fourth, if you're working with a team, it gets everyone on the same page. That reduces the risk a teammate will bring up something you *don't* want to talk about, or that you'll forget something vital.

Last, agreeing on an agenda reduces the odds your counterpart will nibble you, asking for extras just when you think you've got a deal. In one infa-

---

[*] It's probably not necessary to send an agenda before an informal, get-acquainted conversation. In fact, it may be inappropriate. Better to suggest an agenda as you enter more formal talks.

mous case, a German plastics manufacturer's agent nibbled an ill-prepared Oklahoma materials supplier for over a year on a pivotal multimillion-dollar contract. The agent punctuated seven consecutive meetings with the phrase "there's just one more thing." The result: the Oklahoma supplier may have wound up with the kind of deal that can ruin a company.[5]

So, in our sample TTT grid, we've listed price and money-back guarantee under Topics. Any way you order them is fine.

Targets. Here you start to get ready for the competitive side of the negotiation. Success here hinges on two tasks: (1) setting a range and (2) setting a first offer. In this part of the grid, we focus on the first task. Later, we'll tackle the second.

You'll negotiate much better if, for each issue, you write down a specific *range* of well-researched goals. That is, write down your Best Target on the one hand and your Walkaway on the other.

Wandering into talks without knowing your range can be devastating. In 1964, a twenty-six-year-old record store manager from northern England named Brian Epstein found himself managing the most popular musical act of all time, the Beatles. Brian deserves high praise for discovering them, but alas, he had almost no idea how to negotiate. Understandably, he was eager to conceal that fact from the hundreds of business executives who were deluging him with offers. One day, a Hollywood executive and a director came to his office to discuss a possible movie deal. Brian entered the room, sat at his desk with great formality, and, speaking in his most proper English accent, immediately told them, "I think you should know that the boys and I will not settle for anything less than 7.5 percent."[6] The filmmakers looked at each other, then quietly agreed to Brian's demand. The movie, *A Hard Day's Night,* became a global hit earning millions. Only later did Brian learn that the industry norm was for stars like the Beatles to get up to 25 percent, which the Hollywood people had been willing to pay. By not knowing these best and worst acceptable rates—his Best Target and his Walkaway—Brian asked for far too little. He lowballed himself. He probably should have asked for 30 percent and settled for ~25 percent. By winging it, Brian cost the Beatles a fortune—perhaps $200 million between this and other negotiations.[7] It's vital to know your range. And the terminology matters.

Best Target. A Best Target is your ambitious but realistic goal; it's the result you actually hope to get. In our story, your Best Target on price is $100; your Best Target on the guarantee is two years. Each is an outcome you'll strive for. A Best Target is not a wild guess, it's grounded in evidence. In our example, imagine you found a top industry journal report that the best price sellers are getting is ~$100. Imagine another reliable source reports the shortest guarantee a seller is giving is ~2 years. So, you've plugged $100 and 2 years into the grid as your Best Targets.* Nice going.

(Notice your Best Target is *not* your first offer; your Best Target is what you *want*. Your first offer is often a more aggressive number you'll initially *request*. But don't worry about crafting a first offer just yet; that's coming soon.)

Walkaway. Your Walkaway is the worst outcome you can accept. It's not a wild guess either; usually, it's your BATNA.[8] In our example, imagine you find you'll lose money if you get a price less than $80. Or you find the best offer you have from another buyer is for $80. Agreeing to a price of less than about $80 would be unwise, so that's your Walkaway. You then do something similar for the other Topic: guarantee. If, say, the other buyer's offer is for five years, that's your Walkaway. Negotiators who know their Walkaway don't allow counterparts to push them into bad deals; the Walkaways make it clear when to say "Stop!"

People often tell me they wished they'd known about Walkaways and Best Targets much earlier in life. Consider the experience of Kai. Long before I met Kai, his boss offered him a promotion, a better title, a juicier expense account, and a $10,000 raise. Honored and shocked, Kai quickly accepted, only to find the new job turned him into a road warrior with punishing hours that crippled his physical and emotional health. Then, one day a few months later, his new peers told him over coffee they were surprised he'd accepted the offer. "Why?" asked Kai. "Because," they said, "everyone knows you're much better than the executive you replaced, and we don't know if you realize this, but both she and we are making $50,000 a year more than you are." A few minutes of research might have revealed Kai's range, and made it clear the raise his boss offered was pitiful.

---

* We'll later refine your ability to set a wise Best Target later by using a mini tool called the 5 Percent Rule of Thumb, ▮⁵ᐟ [Chapter 7].

Tradeoffs Between Topics. Here you rank your priorities. This is key; it readies you to create value by swapping things you care less about for things you care more about. It's how many kids handle lunch in school: "I'll trade you an apple for a bag of chips." Tradeoffs Between Topics can make both parties in a negotiation happier, and is often better than settling for a mediocre "split the difference" deal on each issue. In our earlier example, you've determined that price is your first priority and guarantee is your second, so you note it here. Now it's easy to trade one for the other.

Gaurav Mittal of MasterCard notes that creativity like this is essential, but it's not something you can easily do if your mind is flooded. "One condition for creativity to flourish," he says, "is your mind has to stop running around and to really know what's important to you." He adds that clear structure with a ranked list helps you focus and keep your eyes on the prize: "The key thing is identifying what your priorities are. There could be dozens of issues, but if you know what your top five or seven are, you can focus on those." Also, ranking priorities helps you negotiate better even when dealing with unfamiliar technical issues. "Developing the TTT grid can help a novice figure out some of these technical items—what is this? How important is this? . . . I may not know all the details of the technical issues, but I at least know their relative importance and range of acceptable outcomes."

Ranking priorities also helps you win when you feel tiny. If you've ever received a long draft contract from a big counterpart, you may well have felt (1) it's not OK to change it, (2) you don't have any power to change it, and (3) it's too complicated to try to change it. None of that is necessarily true. Consider the advice of Joseph Bartel, a business attorney with long experience handling David and Goliath contract talks:

> Almost always, I'm David's negotiator. But I always find Goliath has a weak spot. It can be very hard to deal with him when he makes his first push and expects you to submit, but when I act as if I'm a peer and look at how reasonable the offer is, I discover you can force Goliath to explain himself, and you actually get somewhere. (It helps too if you've decided you're not willing to make a bad deal.) Almost invariably they'll give in.

You can't assume up front that you're weak, and they're strong. They're counting on you to just fold. I know that happens because they often say, "No one ever asked before." Often even *they* haven't read the contract.

But how do you take such a bold yet reasonable approach? It starts, of course, with excellent preparation (often including excellent legal advice). When you have that and then rank your top priorities, you can often successfully negotiate some of your key concerns with giants, much the way Joe does.

Just because one Topic is a high priority doesn't mean you have to give away everything else just to satisfy it. You don't have to trade your spleen for a $1 price increase. At some point, you'll sense you're paying too much. There's a bit of art to this, but most negotiators are pretty good at knowing when the cost of getting that last bit more of their favorite Topic is too high. You can also rehearse: "What if he offers me a penny more for a five-year money-back guarantee?"[9] *

How you talk about your priorities matters. Don't trivialize anything, saying, for example, "We don't care at all about the guarantee." Your counterparty may think it's worthless to you and expect you to give it away. Similarly, don't signal desperation: "We'd do anything for a higher price." You may tempt your counterpart to hold you up and demand top dollar for it. A better approach might be: "While everything is important to us, price is a top priority."

Why not just say, "Everything is important to us"? Sounds savvy, but it usually backfires: it makes everything a "split the difference" battle and kills your ability to trade for more of the things you prize.**

Tradeoffs Within Topics. But what if your counterpart won't budge? Is

---

* You could go further. Borrowing from economists' advice, you could assign and jot down in this column a granular point value for each additional portion of a given Topic to reflect its relative value, like so: "A money-back guarantee of 5 years would be worth 50 points to us, 4 years would be worth 75 points, 3 years would be worth 90 points, and 2 years would be worth 100 points. A price of $80 would be worth 90 points, $90 would be worth 120 points, and $100 would be worth 130 points." (Here and often, there are diminishing returns to a better and better result.) Then seek a trade that produces the most points. In practice, I find most negotiators can't be that precise, including me, and I have an economics degree. But if you can do it, it may help.

** What if you can't rank your Topics numerically? Try at least to rank them high, medium, and low so you still can spot some good trades.

all hope lost? Not at all. You can overcome impasse and create a lot of value by focusing on creative Options for a given Topic, Options that satisfy someone's underlying Interests. Drawing on the creative Options you listed earlier in your I FORESAW IT preparation and picking the best ones to put into your TTT grid can turn a frustrating discussion into a more satisfying one.

During the 2008 recession, a national survey of HR executives found that most were making low offers with few concessions on salary, to the dismay of candidates. But the HR execs were open to offering other perks. Like what? Longer vacations, later start dates, more moving expense money, and even better benefits if their candidates would ask for them. But their candidates, for the most part, didn't.[10] If only the candidates had had a list of these possibilities. The Tradeoffs Within Topics section gives you that very kind of list.

Why list two to four good creative options per Topic? More than that can make the grid unwieldy; fewer leaves you with little hope of overcoming the impasse. The point is to put your best ideas here where you can glance and find a cool solution when you feel discouraged. (You can find others if needed by checking the Options section of your I FORESAW IT plan.) As we've seen, having several cool ideas helps you become *powerfully, pleasantly persistent.*[11]

Package Offers

Once you've got your TTT grid, the last step is to use it to create packages: a well-cushioned first offer, a worst acceptable offer, and a creative offer. A package is a group of terms that cover all the Topics. Research shows the special magic of packaging. It fosters conversation about creative trades that make you both happier.[12] Counterintuitively, going issue by issue breeds one battle after another. Did you get that? It's usually a mistake to simply negotiate one Topic at a time, even though it seems so efficient. Why? Because it kills your ability to spot trades you'd both prefer and encourages isolated fighting over each point.[13] (Sure, you can tentatively agree on one issue, but it's wise to leave open chances to trade.) So, if you hate negotiating because it can become so argumentative, you'll like packaging because it reduces arguments. That's why the bottom part of the TTT grid is there to help you package. Creating three packages can ready you to (1) set the tone in your favor, (2) spot unacceptable counteroffers, and (3) creatively break impasses. Here's how to do it.

Opening offer. As we said, to do well competitively, skilled negotiators create a well-cushioned first offer. Here's the place to create one and write it down.

First, mentally note your Best Targets in the Targets column.

Then add a cushion to at least one Topic. Picture cushioning this way:

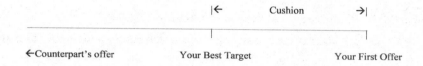

Why cushion? Because most negotiators need a concession to help them feel respected and fairly treated. So, if you start the talks saying, "Our price is $100," your counterparty will probably expect you to make concessions and may resent it if you hold firm: "Who are *you* to dictate terms?" (There are exceptions. In some cultures and industries, cushioning and bargaining are less common. As a study by Travelex found,[14] haggling in bazaars is almost universal in China and India, but rarely done in Japan or Brazil. But in most significant matters, the Dance of Concessions is normal.) Thus, if you start the talks by asking for your Best Target, you usually won't get it. To get your Best Target, you'll need to make a cushioned first offer so you can make concessions.

It's especially wise to cushion your favorite Topic(s), so you can make concessions and still reach your Best Target(s) on the thing(s) you care about most. (You *might* cushion every Topic, but there's a risk/return thing to consider: the more items you cushion, the more aggressive you look.) So, how big a cushion should you add? Briefly, you can cushion a lot and concede quickly, or a little and concede slowly. (We'll discuss the question further later, 🏆🏆 [Chapter 7].) Here's one example of a cushioned first offer: $110 plus a 1.5-year money-back guarantee. Another: $101 plus a 17 months guarantee.

Worst acceptable offer. To know when to say no, you next identify a "bright line test," that is, a least tolerable deal. To do that, you go to the Targets section and note your Walkaways. Together, they become your worst acceptable offer. For example, $80 + 5-year money-back guarantee. Usually, it's wise to reject any offer that's worse.*

Creative offer. Here you get creative and put together at least one package using your Tradeoffs Between Topics and your Tradeoffs Within Topics. The idea is to be ready with a bundle you can offer that serves you both well and that can inspire creative problem-solving if you hit resistance. For example: $100/unit with a discount on selected items + 5-year guarantee granting credit toward another purchase. The final deal may well be quite different; the key is to use the offer to foster collaborative thinking.

And that's it. You're now in a stronger position because you've got a map for the journey. Or, if you prefer, a play sheet.

But What If You Only Want to Negotiate Competitively?

Sometimes all there is to negotiate is a single issue, like price. How do you get ready then? Just use the Targets section of the grid for that one Topic (e.g., price $100–$80). Then, set a cushion (e.g., $110).

Change the Scope, Change the Power Balance

One way to survive and thrive when you feel powerless is to change the scope of the negotiation by narrowing or broadening the agenda—that is, by changing the number of Topics. Narrowing can protect you when the other side wants the moon, the stars, and the sun. For example, imagine a huge buyer wants to negotiate a comprehensive supply deal that would commit you to provide all your products for years, all at low prices, with a slew of unattractive terms. You might want to limit the agenda to just one or two products, protect-

---

* An exception: If an offer is worse than your Walkaway on some issues and better on others, you face a harder choice. If that offer gives you little for your top-priority issues, it's probably best to reject it; if it gives you little for your low-priority issues, it *may* be wise to consider it.

ing most of your product line. Conversely, broadening the agenda can help you when the other side focuses on one or two big demands. If a powerful landlord insists on a hefty rent increase, you might want to expand the agenda to cover the renovation work the landlord promised you under the current lease but that you haven't received yet. One young tenant did so and turned a demand for a 10 percent rent increase into an agreement to waive the renovation work in exchange for no rent increase. She might also have asked to talk about the length of the lease, seeking a two-year lease for little additional rent.

You can even narrow *and* broaden the agenda by making *when* you'll negotiate a key Topic. If you're in a weak position now, but know you'll be stronger when you get a significant loan, investment, regulatory approval, offer, or degree, you may want to make *timing* a key agenda item. One way is to seek a limited deal now (such as a product trial) and a broader deal later (such as a full sale). (Just notice if you agree to an unfavorable price up front, you'll have trouble improving the price later.) Another way to negotiate timing is to seek an option, such as an exclusive right to negotiate during the next sixty days, or simply negotiate the postponement of a looming deadline. Just changing the deadline can often make a big difference.

Separately, making *where* you negotiate a preliminary Topic can make a difference. For example, in 1949, when UN mediator Ralph Bunche convened peace talks between Israel and Egypt, he intentionally chose the Grand Hotel of Roses on the Mediterranean island of Rhodes. Conditions were primitive, the food was terrible, and all the participants suffered from dysentery. As fellow diplomat Lawrence S. Finkelstein recalled, Bunche "intentionally used his prerogative as chair of the meeting to keep all the parties negotiating nonstop until they could no longer resist agreement." That, said Finkelstein, was how Bunche said he won the Nobel Peace Prize.[15]

"Nothing Is Agreed Until Everything Is Agreed"

As you've seen, the TTT grid also reminds you not to negotiate one issue at a time but to think and talk about several things: discussing packages and swaps across issues to create value. You can reinforce the idea by suggesting a discussion ground rule as talks begin: "To help us explore creative possibilities together, let me suggest we work with the principle that nothing's agreed until everything is agreed. We can certainly agree tentatively, but let's give ourselves room to edit before we sign off, so we find a deal we're happy with. OK?"

Mandate and Coordinate

Your TTT grid is especially handy when you represent someone because it helps you work out your mandate. How much latitude and creativity does your principal want you to have? Often, it's the difference between trying to read your boss's mind and actually knowing; between driving blindfolded and seeing clearly. You can use the TTT grid as an interview tool to draw out from your boss what you should and shouldn't negotiate, how much room you have to maneuver on each agenda item, what your boss most cares about, and what creative possibilities are acceptable.

And the TTT grid can help you *negotiate* the mandate. For example, would you prefer broad authority with broad Targets and several Options, so you can negotiate like a king or a prime minister? Or would you like narrow authority with narrow Targets and few Options, so you're little more than a mail carrier?

When you are part of a team of fellow negotiators, the TTT grid helps you stay well coordinated. Gaurav says he and his team members feel more aligned and confident knowing they've got a TTT grid they've worked through together. "It helps bring everybody on a common page," he says. "It helps establish a greater degree of trust and reliance on team members, so there is no confusion on our positions. We find the tool quite important for fostering this trust based on the complexity, volume, and size of the deals we interact with." Students discover the same advantages.

(For those leading several negotiations at once, Gaurav notes yet another advantage: "It is sometimes hard for me to recall deal specifics for every deal underway, so having a common reference to keep us aligned when negotiating several deals simultaneously is wonderful.")

One way to harness the TTT grid for group work is to use it as an interview tool with them, asking each team member in turn about Topics, Targets, priorities, and so on, posting the answers on a whiteboard or Google Docs. (You can find a template at Professorfreeman.com.) Then massage it together until you form a consensus. That's an especially valuable thing to do if you're representing a group and different members have different views about the talks ahead. The grid can help build consensus—and group members tend to trust a representative more if they feel fully heard.

Help for a Negotiation Team in the Age of Video Conferencing and Beyond

If you've ever tried to work with partners on a video call, you may know the sinking feeling you get when a partner starts to make bad suggestions, and you have no way to get his attention and get him to stop. That's why sharing a finished TTT grid with your team prior to video talks is particularly valuable. As Gaurav notes, "When you don't have the ability to look at everybody's expressions (if some folks are off-camera) . . . and study body language or nudge somebody under the table, this sort of tool becomes incredibly important. We avoid stepping or speaking over each other in the time of Zoom to clarify what somebody on our team meant because we've taken the time to clarify it beforehand using this."

But whether or not you use video, sharing a TTT grid with your team can help them negotiate better. First, circulate it before the talks and ask the team to review it, so everyone knows the plan. Then meet beforehand to roleplay, assign roles, and answer questions, so everyone's ready together.

Help Managing Highly Complex, Lengthy Contract Talks

While the TTT grid can help negotiators handle relatively small matters well, it only grows in value as a subject becomes more complex. Gaurav emphasizes, "In a contract that's several hundred pages long, it is extremely important to have a TTT. Because the first thing the TTT helps you do is identify within those hundreds of pages what are the three, five, seven issues that really matter. Because that's really the key. And across those five or seven issues, where do you want to concede, where do you want to press the point, and what is the point you're trying to make?"

Focus like that can turn an ocean of issues into a manageable pond; without that focus, it's easy to feel overwhelmed and silenced. Years ago, as a junior attorney, I helped handle aircraft lease deals. The contracts for these deals were hundreds of pages long. One Friday, I sent a hundred-page draft to our client, a Norwegian bank, asking for comments by Monday. Monday morning, I asked my contact at the bank if he'd received and read the draft. "Yes," he said. Did he have any comments? "No," he said. Neither he, nor I, nor any of my colleagues had thought to help identify his priorities or suggest ones he should focus on; we'd just thrown him into a sea of legal documentation and asked him to quickly find his way back to dry land. Lost, he could have used our help spotting possible high-priority issues. Having a TTT grid would have helped us do that.

Does complexity require a super-long TTT grid? Gaurav says no: "I don't think you need [one] that's five, ten, fifteen pages long, frankly. [Maybe] two to three pages, depending on the level of the executives involved. If you have a CEO involved and it's longer than a page [it's] probably too long. If you've got the operating team, then two to three pages is probably appropriate. If you've got a bunch of detailed lawyers and real detailed operators in the room you might have a slightly longer one, depending on the nature and the context of the negotiation." Instead of being overwhelmed by a massive document, negotiators with a TTT grid find they can follow the action more easily. They can navigate the issues with a clear overarching sense of strategy and perspective. They also develop a granular ability to handle specific sets of issues more powerfully.

An Ongoing Guide Star Over Several Meetings

Most high-stakes talks don't end in one sitting; often, there might be dozens of meetings over weeks, months, or even years. So how do you remember what you're striving for? Seasoned negotiators find the TTT grid helps them do just that; they simply compare it to the latest proposal. Without it, if the other negotiator makes a series of offers, it's easy to focus on her last concession and forget what your original objectives were. Studies find[16] it's easy even for seasoned negotiators to get "anchored," meaning that they subconsciously shift toward an extreme offer. A TTT grid helps negotiators resist this bias by giving them a clear guide star. The grid also makes it easier for one negotiator to hand off to a colleague; it serves as a reference tool and offers clear guidance to the new negotiator to draw on for the remaining talks.

Harmonize Several Negotiations

You can also use TTT grids to harmonize several related or similar negotiations. The MasterCard deals team has found they can use one TTT grid as a model for another, saving everyone time and helping them spot ideas they otherwise would have missed. Over time, the team has created a small library of grids they can borrow from, much the way lawyers use model contracts.

Quick and Dirty versus Fuller Prep?

In a crisis, you can whip up a TTT grid a few minutes before a conversation, using it to prompt you to do some quick research and think creatively. Of course, a quick and dirty TTT grid is better than just winging an unavoidable negotiation. But fuller preparation usually is a wise time investment offering excellent returns; if you're making a habit of quick & dirty TTTs, you're probably shortchanging yourself, especially if you're just guessing about your targets. Better to make it the summation of your I FORESAW IT work. Can't? Consider asking teammate(s) to help prepare one for you, then review it together.

———

Critical Fail-Safe Reminders

It's common for even experienced negotiators to belatedly discover that they have forgotten to ask for something, or that they've exceeded their limits, or that they've failed to mention a creative idea that could have finessed a critical problem. Having debriefed thousands of business negotiators, I have seen first-hand how easily stress and time pressure increase the risk of a mistake like that. A TTT grid helps negotiators avoid these sorts of critical errors.

The Power of Creating the Other's TTT Grid

Imagine discovering your counterpart's secret internal memo about his preferences in upcoming talks with you. That knowledge could help you create and claim wealth even better. You can kind of have that knowledge by also creating a separate TTT grid *as if you were your counterpart*. Start doing it provisionally before the meeting, using research and guesswork to fill it out as much as you reasonably can. Then in the meeting, you (or perhaps better, a teammate) can listen and ask questions that help refine it, asking, for example, "What are your priorities here? What matters most to you? What's next most important?" (Just be careful to take his statements about his ranges with a grain of salt.) Skilled negotiators strive to learn the other's perspective so well that they can at least partly do the equivalent of filling out the other's TTT grid, which can reveal valuable trades. To the point: it is standard practice for U.S. State Department officials to assign a team member to identify the priorities of counterparts before talks.[17]

The Lawyers' (and Clients') Special Reason to Use a Variation of the TTT Grid

I started this discussion of the TTT grid highlighting many fields where people rely on well-crafted glance-and-go play sheets, but, sadly, my own first profession doesn't. I practiced corporate law for years, and perhaps for that reason, I have a special feeling of bafflement and dismay when I see how transactional lawyers often negotiate contract language. If they bring a guide to the talks at all, they might bring something called an Issues List, and here I must confess to you, dear reader, that it drives me crazy. The Issues Lists I've seen have four columns: Topic, Counterpart's Position, Our Position, and Our Suggested Talking Points. It's more like a legal brief than a TTT grid, and almost by design, it invites argument.

Rarely if ever do corporate lawyers explicitly set ranges, rank Topics, or write down creative Options. They're rarely *powerfully, pleasantly persistent.* As a result, lawyers have little idea how much value they are creating or claiming in many corporate transactions. More than one partner at a top law firm has told me that they mainly just document the deal—that is, make sure the legal papers say what the client means, avoid needless legal risk, and are legally enforceable. Valuable things to do, to be sure. Yet, when I asked an investment banker friend about this approach, he winced, shook his head, and said, "Yep, that's our biggest frustration with our lawyers—that's all they think we want."

The idea that lawyers can create wealth for their clients (and counterparts) is so important and unappreciated that Harvard law professor Robert Mnookin cowrote an entire book about it: *Beyond Winning: Negotiating to Create Value in Deals and Disputes.*

What else, then, *should* clients expect their corporate lawyers to do? I recommend lawyers create a Lawyer's TTT grid, a slightly adapted version of a basic TTT grid that I've specially designed to help them negotiate contract language. Using it can help lawyers and clients produce more satisfying contracts and do it more quickly—and know they've done it. The Lawyer's TTT grid may be particularly attractive to lawyers because it helps them manage talks and discover ways to overcome an impasse in less time.

And there's another reason to create one: it makes it easier to automate the contract process. Increasingly, artificial intelligence is enabling lawyers to draft or revise contracts automatically. Most contract AI software requires you to tell it many of the very things a Lawyer's TTT grid already holds. So, if you've created a Lawyer's TTT grid, you can even further accelerate the contract negotiation process.[18]

Here's what a Lawyer's TTT grid looks like. This one is for a lawyer negotiating a loan agreement for a borrower:

Topic	Lender's Draft	Borrower's Mark-Up	Borrower's Best Target	Worst Acceptable	Priority	The Firm's Suggested Response
Covenants See §____	Cross default provision for any default >$500; minimum net worth of $500,000.	No cross-default provision and no minimum net worth provision	Cross-default for debts >$1M; and minimum net worth of $1,000	Cross default for debts >$10,000; minimum net worth of $25,000	1	Borrower needs latitude to handle trivial and passing cash shortfalls without creating a needless house of cards scenario. Borrower should not be required to sustain an unrealistic net worth given the projected ups and downs of the business plan. This should not be an issue for the lender. This point is of particular concern since the lender is permitted under §____ to raise the interest rate in the event of a technical breach un-remedied for three days. OPTIONS: • Right to inspect financials quarterly • Right to request further assurances • Immediate notice+ Technical default begins 120 days after breach
Remedies See §____	No cure period	21-day cure period	14-day cure period	5-day cure period	6	Make the case 2+weeks is market OPTIONS: • Cure for most events of default • Right to further assurances w/i 5 days

Corporate lawyers, my former colleagues, I love you, but you've got to get it together, and the Lawyer's TTT grid can help. (A sample also appears at Professorfreeman.com.)

Astronauts, Football Coaches, Pilots, and You

I picture a day when it's as common and essential for negotiators to use TTT grids as it is for astronauts and pilots to use checklists and coaches to use play sheets. That will be a day when negotiators enjoy more collaboration and prosperity than they do now. But, till then, think of the TTT grid as a competitive advantage as well as a collaborative one, a simple tool that can help you and your team make negotiation more satisfying in several ways, especially when the pressure's on.

We've now developed several tools to help you mentally prepare and thus reduce your anxiety. But what can you do if you still sense that head readiness doesn't give you *heart* readiness? What if you understandably feel your nerves will flood you when you talk with the other person, crippling your efforts? You're not alone. And there is another tool that, by design, can help you deal with that challenge too, overcome it, and triumph.

> ### Tool in Brief
>
> **Topics, Targets, and Tradeoffs grid:** A four-column grid capturing the agenda, ranges, priorities, and best creative Options, together with sample packages.

Seven Topics, Targets, and Tradeoffs Grid Challenges

How, then, can you put the TTT grid to use this week? Seven separate suggestions:

Quick Practice Challenge. Take less than fifteen minutes and jot down a TTT grid for an upcoming or past negotiation, just to see what it feels like to whip one up on the fly. Practice using it with a friend. (Next I'll give you more ideas about how to roleplay 🎭 [Chapter 5].)

Full-blown TTT Grid Challenge. Take more time to create a serious, well-researched TTT grid for your next significant negotiation and bring it to the talks.

Unify Your Team Challenge. Ask your boss or your team to help you put together a TTT grid before a significant negotiation so you're literally and figuratively on the same page.

Give Everyone a Copy Challenge. Give a copy of a completed TTT grid to everyone on your team who's accompanying you to the talks, brief them on it, and ask them to refer to it as the talks unfold so they're on the same page.

Counterpart's TTT Grid Challenge. Prepare (or ask a teammate to prepare) a provisional TTT Grid as if you were your counterpart to better spot possible trades and offers you'd be happy to make that the counterpart might accept. Refine it as you learn more.

Regroup Challenge. Review your TTT grid after a round of negotiation to see if you've missed any Topics, to see how close you are to your Best Targets, and to see what Tradeoffs you could suggest to make further progress later.

Teach Someone Else Challenge. Since one of the best ways to learn is to teach, sit down with an interested friend or colleague and teach them how to create a TTT grid to help ready them for a mildly significant negotiation and debrief them to help you both learn.

CHAPTER 5

Rehearse Your Dance with Godzilla

THE TOOL: ROLEPLAY

Use this tool when you are . . .

- worried emotions will overwhelm you in talks
- worried you'll forget what to say under pressure
- unsure how to respond if the other is tough or mean
- worried you'll say the wrong thing, or cave.

Use this tool to . . .

- manage your emotions
- ready yourself to perform well under stress
- know better what to say and what not to say
- safely practice using other tools in real time.

At the height of the Cold War in June 1961, John Kennedy flew to Vienna for his first and only summit meeting with Soviet premier Nikita Khrushchev. Brilliant but emotionally unprepared, Kennedy entered the meeting confident his charm and intelligence could sway Khrushchev, a surviving underling of Joseph Stalin. Ninety minutes later, Kennedy emerged so shaken that his aides were shocked. "Is it always like this?" Kennedy asked his ambassador.[1] Later, talking with a *New York Times* reporter, Kennedy said it was the "worst thing in my life—he savaged me."[2] This from a man who had nearly died in World War II, who had suffered such crippling health problems most of his life that twice he was given the last rites, and who had endured the death of his older brother. How could a conversation with a man in a room be *worse*?

I've been badly shaken in a negotiation too. Years ago, I received an invitation from a large bank to return and give a negotiation training similar to what I'd given the previous year. "Fine," I said, "I'll send you an updated version of the one-page letter agreement we used last time, and we can take it from there." A brief pause. "Yes, about that," said my contact, "we're using a new contract now with our vendors, so let me have one of our lawyers send it to you." When I got it, I discovered it went on for twelve pages and made a slew of extraordinary demands, including this one: I was to indemnify this $100 billion company against any claim by anyone for any amount forever. My financial life flashed before my eyes. So, I contacted the bank's lawyer, Amanda, and said, "Thank you for the draft. I'm confident we'll work out a contract that makes everyone happy. I do have a few things I need to discuss with you, and I—" Amanda interrupted me and said, "Look, let me explain to you what a contract is. It's a binding agreement. This is the contract. If you have questions for me, I will answer them for you, but this is the same agreement we use with hundreds of other vendors, and we certainly aren't going to change it for someone like you."

When my wife saw me a few minutes later, she says she almost didn't recognize me; I was so angry I was shaking with rage. I have only splotchy memories of the rest of my conversation with Amanda; I mostly remember that I had instantly gone ballistic. *"Let me explain to you what a contract is?"* I immediately lost every vestige of good negotiation practice and started to splutter and shout, interrupting her and hearing almost nothing she said. If you had seen me then, you would have been dismayed: "I thought you were a negotiation expert. But you were terrible!" I was. Only after did it dawn on me that in the last ugly minutes of the call, she'd actually offered some concessions. Only later too did it dawn on me that there were creative Options that could have finessed the biggest issues. I did not return to the bank.

Around the same time, a student told me he'd tried to negotiate a job offer, only to feel dumbstruck when the employer had aggressively pushed back. My student too had lost all his negotiating form. Humbled and chastened by his report and my own experience with Amanda, I realized something: I and my students *and even John Kennedy* all needed something more than we'd brought with us to our talks. We needed something to help turn the tide and cope with emotional flooding.

Here we'll explore a tool I've since discovered that can do just that. It's helped me, my students, and seasoned negotiators, and it relies on practices similar to those used by a host of professionals in other high-stress fields. It's a simple process that can give you more confidence, effectiveness, and emotional readiness whenever you feel like you're Bambi about to meet Godzilla.

What Helps You Cope with Stress?

Years ago, an accounting firm asked negotiation experts to train its accountants on the eve of talks with clients about their annual auditing contracts. Audits are the most lucrative and important service most accounting firms perform, and yet the firm's accountants were going into these talks with little negotiation training or experience. The negotiation experts ran an experiment. They gave a third of the auditors basic training centered on unrelated simulated negotiations, about purchasing something, like a house. They gave another third basic training on how to prepare systematically. But it was the final group that outperformed all the others; their counterparts were happier and more satisfied, and yet the deals those auditors reached were more favorable than any of the others'.[3] What was the additional skill they'd learned?

Here's a clue: watch Olympic athletes—skiers, gymnasts, skaters, and others—in the moments before they perform, and you'll often see them with their eyes closed, gyrating as if they are performing the routine in their heads. They are. They're *visualizing,* a standard practice for elite athletes in most sports. I've met high-level athletes who visualize in swimming, hockey, mixed martial arts—in fact, I've never met an elite athlete who *didn't* visualize. Why? Because it prepares them emotionally and physiologically; studies find the act of visualizing confers benefits similar to actually performing the task.[4] The athlete feels calmer and readier; they enter the arena feeling more at ease: "Been here, done this already. I got this."

You'll find a similar power at play on the eve of a political debate, when politicians recruit a skilled ally to play the role of the opponent and other aides to play the debate questioners.[5] Similarly, soldiers simulate battle conditions when they war game, sometimes even using live ammunition to help them capture the emotional reality of combat.[6] Astronauts and mission controllers rehearse continually; when Neil Armstrong and Buzz Aldrin landed on the moon, it was only the last of hundreds of "landings" they'd previously practiced in a simulator in Houston. And pilots routinely use the same inflight simulators. The simulators are so realistic that the FAA will credit a pilot with one actual flight hour for every hour she spends in the simulator.[7] Many pilots experience sweating and constricted breathing there; some even vomit, so realistic is the experience. They do it to prepare for the most harrowing situations they could face in actual planes.

Roleplaying

So what was the additional negotiation skill the auditors used to outperform others? Roleplaying: they rehearsed with each other the very talks they were about to enter in with clients. Like them (and like presidential candidates, Olympic athletes, soldiers, astronauts, and pilots) you as a negotiator can draw big benefits from roleplaying. How best to do it?

Søren Malmborg is a Danish negotiation scholar, political adviser, and an expert on roleplaying. Malmborg has studied and championed a simple way to harness the power of roleplaying on the eve of high-stress talks. Here's how he recommends you do it:

1. You find an ally and ask her to prepare as if she is the counterpart you'll encounter in the talks ahead while you prepare as usual.
2. You and your ally meet in character and begin roleplaying the negotiating.
3. After five minutes, you pause, and your ally critiques your performance, *in character,* and offers suggestions.
4. You resume the roleplay for another five minutes.

5. You pause, and your ally again gives you a critique and suggestions.
6. You resume and roleplay for another five minutes.
7. You conclude with your ally critiquing the entire performance in character and offering concluding suggestions.

Or, to put it succinctly: *Roleplay, Review, Resume.*

Malmborg and other roleplay experts emphasize that preparation is crucial. As Paul Schoemaker,[8] a leading consultant, puts it, it's as crucial as the roleplay itself: "garbage in = garbage out." Roleplay isn't a substitute for preparation any more than visualization is a substitute for athletic practice; it enhances and perfects preparation.

Before a successful roleplay, it helps if you and your ally have each already created separate, abbreviated I FORESAW IT plans, skipping Rapport, Reactions, and Responses and Empathy and Ethics since the roleplay will naturally illuminate those parts. For the same reason, you can even dispense with thinking about the other's Interests and Alternatives to Agreement; the other roleplayer will identify those. Malmborg and I call this method I FORESAW IT 2.0. Regardless, encourage your ally to play the most difficult realistic version of your real-life counterpart, and let your ally know what the counterpart is like: Is he loud and neurotic? Sullen and taciturn? Professional and sweet but busy and ungenerous? The better your ally and you prepare, the more realistic the emotional experience.

How do you treat a roleplay seriously? I've witnessed thousands of simulated negotiations and I know it's not uncommon to giggle together about play-acting in the first moments. Sometimes all it takes is to agree beforehand, "Let's meet in the conference room and take it seriously from the start." Or simply roll with the awkwardness, knowing you'll naturally inhabit your roles as the intensity of the exercise grows. In fact, sometimes simulations come to feel so real that participants have to decompress afterward.

Roleplaying is especially valuable when a negotiator is about to meet a Godzilla, an intimidating counterpart. Some Godzillas are friendly, avuncular people who simply happen to have a *lot* of power. Others are holy terrors, purposely obnoxious, bullying, or manipulative. Soviet diplomats were particularly infamous Godzillas, renowned for throwing papers, shouting, banging tables, throwing furniture, stalking out, repeatedly saying, "*Nyet, nyet, nyet,* I have no authority to do this," and making eleventh-hour ultimatums. And these were the nicer things they did. In 1960, Nikita Khrushchev modeled Soviet-style bargaining practice at the United Nations when he repeatedly banged a shoe on his desk while another diplomat spoke. Watch it on YouTube and remember as you do that this was one of the two men in the world with a nuclear arsenal, and you'll have some idea what John Kennedy faced in Vienna. There, Khrushchev interrupted Kennedy, warned him Russia might invade West Berlin, and if the U.S. tried to stop him, it would mean nuclear war. Shocked, Kennedy said, "A nuclear exchange would kill 70 million people in 10 minutes." Khrushchev stared at him. "So what?" he said.[9]

You may never have to face someone quite like that, but hostage negotiators routinely do: they deal with people who are threatening to kill a child or an ex-girlfriend. To cope with emotional stress like that, they routinely roleplay crises, such as one where a hostage taker is threatening to kill someone in sixty seconds unless they get exactly what they want. "Roleplaying is critical and necessary," says Dr. Jeff Thompson, a research scientist, crisis counselor, and former law enforcement hostage negotiator who's trained thousands of crisis negotiators around the world and who's studied their work closely.[10] When Dr. Thompson debriefs a crisis negotiator, they often say of the skills they'd roleplayed, "Oh, wow, that really worked!"

The secret: preparing for distress. To be effective, Dr. Thompson notes, the roleplay has to be as authentic as possible, putting you into an uncomfortable experience, so you get used to it. Ideally, that means using someone as your practice counterpart who really understands what you're about to face. To foster that kind of realism, Dr. Thompson would have a trainee's practice counterpart use the actual language a hostage taker, a suicidal person, or a terrorist used in a real-life incident: "I WANT A CAR IN SIXTY SECONDS OR SHE DIES!" He'd further intensify the pressure by having trainees perform in front of dozens of others. "It's about stress inoculation," he says, by "purposefully creating a similar level of stress in a place where it's safe to make mistakes." Studies, Dr. Thompson notes, including one by the FBI, find roleplaying helps crisis negotiators to be measurably more effective.[11] "Knowing the skills doesn't make you effective," Dr. Thompson says. "It's your ability to use them through practice." Do veteran hostage negotiators outgrow the need for roleplays? No, Dr. Thompson says. "It doesn't stop; roleplays are part of the carousel," the ongoing cycle of practice and performance that even the most seasoned negotiators need.

But what if you can't find an ally who can prepare well? Here are three alternatives:

Find an experienced ally. Suppose your ally doesn't have time to prepare but she knows your actual counterpart or she has done similar tough negotiations before. In that case, she may still be able to roleplay with you without preparation and do it well enough to still give you substantial benefit. For example, before I spoke to Amanda, I might have called a fellow negotiation professor who's negotiated training assignments with large companies and asked him to roleplay with me on the phone for a half hour. Similarly, my student might have asked a career adviser or a friend in an HR department. And John Kennedy might have asked Tommy Thompson, an American diplomat who had lived with Khrushchev, to roleplay with him. (As we've seen, later, during the Cuban Missile Crisis, Thompson's experience gave him insight about Khrushchev that helped Thompson give Kennedy pivotal advice that deescalated the crisis.[12])

Roleplay alone. I sometimes find it helps a lot to verbally playact both sides of the conversation myself once I've prepared, picturing myself on the phone or in the room with the counterpart, speaking as myself and then speaking as my Godzilla, then responding, and so on. Essentially, it's the verbal equivalent of preparing the I FORESAW IT's Rapport, Reactions, and Responses section. Though I'd prefer a full roleplay with an ally, I find that even roleplaying alone helps make the actual encounter more familiar and less stressful. It may seem odd to talk to ourselves like this, but when we do, we're in good company. Alexander Hamilton used to walk the streets, audibly rehearsing speeches to juries and legislatures. So much so that once, a shopkeeper who didn't recognize him thought Hamilton was a crazy man blathering outside the store. He wasn't; Hamilton was perhaps the greatest advocate of his age.[13]

Record yourself. Listening to yourself in character can give you new perspective on your tone and choice of words. This benefit is why some negotiation instructors require their students to video themselves in simulated negotiations and then review the tape. "I said *that*? That's how I come across?!" Getting feedback like that *before* the meeting can make a big difference.

A Change of Mindset and Heartset

Roleplaying is a powerful way to ready your heart, just as the Three Little Words, I FORESAW IT, and the TTT grid are potent ways to ready your head. It helps you change from being in a state of residual fear to a state of understanding and visceral readiness. But what if your preparation reveals you're quite weak and that entering full-blown talks now will go badly? We explore next a preparation strategy that can help you overcome.

> **Tool in Brief**
>
> **Roleplay:** You and a teammate each prepare, then Roleplay, Review, Resume.

Challenges

The Roleplay, Review, Resume Challenge. This week, as you look ahead to a difficult encounter with a Godzilla counterpart, prepare (perhaps with the Three Little Words or I FORESAW IT), and then brief an ally and ask him to Roleplay, Review, Resume with you for less than twenty minutes.

The Team Roleplay Challenge. This week, ask your negotiation team to roleplay with you with some playing your side, others the counterparty's side. Before you do, decide which roles each teammate will play at the talks, such as lead, subject matter expert, notetaker, etc., and roleplay in those roles. Then see if you want to make adjustments.

CHAPTER 6

Trade Up and Up—or Drill Down and Down

THE TOOL: WHO I FORESAW*

Use this tool when you . . .

- feel weak and your counterpart looks far too strong to influence
- find you have no leverage, no choices, and may have to go with no deal or a bad deal
- sense you need help from others.

Use this tool to . . .

- build momentum and magnify your strength through a series of deals
- become more attractive and powerful
- give your counterpart a reason to be concerned about your BATNA
- gain powerful information you can't find on your own
- find an ideal counterpart who is likely to agree to an excellent deal
- and more.

*Can be used too for Targeted Negotiation

One day, David Ortega, a sixteen-year-old in Scottsdale, Arizona, got a free used pair of headphones from his brother. Twenty months later, David had turned the headphones into a Mercedes coupe he drove to his senior prom.

Who in his right mind would think you could do something like that? Imagine David sees the car sitting in his neighbor's driveway, wants it, and knocks on the owner's door. When the owner comes to the door, David says, "I see you own that Mercedes." The owner says, "Yes, I do." David replies, "I own this used pair of headphones. Want to trade?" Pause. The owner says, "Kid, get off my porch." But instead, David did something so astute that when he *did* knock on the owner's door, the owner warmly welcomed him and gladly traded over his Mercedes. How?

David made a series of moves *away* from the table that made him more powerful *at* the table. Over several months, David traded the headphones first for an external hard drive, then traded the external hard drive for a series of motor scooters, the last motor scooter for a desktop computer, the desktop for a high-end golf cart, the cart for a motorboat, the motorboat for a used Chevy Silverado, and the Chevy Silverado for the Mercedes.

David's success illustrates the wisdom of something sixteenth-century thinker Francis Bacon wrote, which I'll paraphrase slightly into modern English: "In all difficult negotiations, you can't expect to sow and reap at once, but must prepare business and so ripen it by degrees."[1] So, how can you use that wisdom when you feel powerless as you face a difficult negotiation or conflict, perhaps with a Godzilla?

One key strategy is to choose *not* to negotiate with them immediately but instead to first turn to other people; to make moves away from the table like David did. That can mean making one or more deals with others that improve your position. It can also mean finding advocates who can persuade your Godzilla—or, to paraphrase one big-city mayor, to "find the guy who can talk to the guy who can talk to the guy." Kids know well how to pull this off: "Sis, can you ask Dad to get us new bikes? You're older; he'll listen to you." Making moves away from the table is a strategy that's saved powerless activists, prime ministers, presidents, and small business owners. And you can harness the approach by using a familiar tool in a different way.

Building Strength Away from the Table with Who I FORESAW

> I don't have problems. I have friends.
> —Clarence Avant, the "Black Godfather"

I FORESAW IT is a valuable tool, but there will be times when merely preparing for direct talks won't be enough. Indeed, working through I FORESAW IT can reveal more clearly that you need more leverage and that negotiating now may be dangerous. Fortunately, you can discover paths to additional power by using a slight variation, a tool called Who I FORESAW. Using it can reveal allies, sources, trading partners, influencers, and protectors, among others, and, critically, the sequence of meetings you have with them. In essence, the tool shows you how to sing, along with the Beatles, "I get by with a little help from my friends."

First, create a rich list of potential helpers by asking more deeply, "Who can be influential or helpful?," using most of the other letters to help answer. Specifically:

Whose **Interests** complement mine? Whose are the same as mine? (*Allies*)

Who knows valuable **Facts**? (*Sources; experts*)

Who of my potential allies can I negotiate with for attractive **Options** I can offer my Godzilla? (*Trading partners*)

Whose **Reactions** to my efforts may be hostile? (*Adversaries*)

Who can **Respond** for me, i.e., advocate for me? (*Influencers*)

Whose involvement might raise **Ethical** dilemmas? (*Off-limit figures*)

Who might raise **Ethical** concerns about my efforts? (*Critics*)

(Skip **Schedule** for now.)

Who of my potential allies can I negotiate with for valuable **Alternatives** to Agreement I can use if I can't reach a deal with my Godzilla? (*Protectors*)

Who else? (*Other players*)

Even answering just a couple of these questions can help; answering all of them can help that much more.

Second, pick from your list the people who seem most important to talk with.

Third, **Schedule**: sequence conversations in a way that builds your strength. That is, decide in what order you should talk to people on your list. Sequencing meetings can help your power snowball as one conversation better equips you for talks with one or more allies or trading partners, which better equips you for talks with a protector, and so on. This schedule doesn't need to be rigid; it's fine if you wander from chat to chat using serendipity along with planning. That's normal and natural. But having specific people and a rough sequence in mind can help you build power, to "prepare business and ripen it by degrees."

Fourth, prepare to negotiate with each party you want to talk to.

Fifth, time permitting, test your strategy by reviewing your original I FORESAW IT plan for Godzilla, asking, "If the negotiations I do away from the table go well, will the results strengthen me at the table with Godzilla? How?" Use your answers to refine your strategy.

Sixth, execute: negotiate with one player, then another, and so on, until you're ready to talk again with Godzilla.

Who I FORESAW in Action: Hannah's Warehouse Project

Let's see this idea in action. Imagine a hypothetical entrepreneur named Hannah wants to start her first venture: a new warehouse in a redevelopment zone of Tacoma, Washington. She's already signed contracts with several midsize customers, mainly firms in the aircraft parts and integrated circuit industries. She's also made progress on other fronts: a local landowner has agreed to give her an eighteen-month option to build on his land, the town government has agreed to give her a nine-month option to develop it, and a bank has given her a twelve-month commitment to lend her the money to build it. But key to the plan is winning as a major customer Bening, a top aircraft manufacturer, which is renowned for negotiating aggressively. Sure enough, Bening's representative demands a one-sided deal and seems in no rush to sign. Hannah fears the venture will fail. After all, her other deals expire in a few months. Worse, if Hannah loses Bening, she will have no major customer to replace it. She prepares an I FORESAW IT plan, but it reveals she's quite weak. What to do?

To answer that question, Hannah deploys Who I FORESAW.

First, she identifies Who has Interests that complement hers or that they share. She then considers who else knows valuable Facts, with which key players she can negotiate for valuable Options, who presents Ethical issues, who can be an attractive Alternative to Agreement, and so on. This work produces a richer list of players than she'd seen before: her bank, the town government, other major customers, a rival of Bening called Skyward, the landowner, an influential columnist named Dan Archer, a large prospective customer in the adult film industry called Passion, and the Tacoma Developers Association (TDA).

Second, she reviews the list, asking Who seems most important to talk to. She cuts Passion on ethical grounds and TDA because she learns it has little to offer.

Third, she Schedules meetings with the surviving players she's listed.

Fourth, she prepares to negotiate with each.

Fifth, to test her strategy, she asks how her I FORESAW IT plan with Bening will improve if she gains something useful, as planned, from each of these prospective meetings. Will she be in a markedly stronger position to negotiate? Probably.

Sixth, reassured, she launches her strategy. Using one of several sequencing methods we'll explore shortly, she starts with the town government.

Early in her meeting with government officials, she points out, as she'd planned, that the city needs jobs and real estate tax revenue. And it needs to prove to the public the redevelopment zone is starting to work: all Interests her warehouse can satisfy. The warehouse, she adds, would be more likely to launch if the city gave her zoning waivers and air rights, things she's learned the mayor had promised developers in several recent speeches to local chambers of commerce. She adds that she's learned a key Fact from a highly respected journalist: mayors in nearby Seattle, Vancouver, and Portland are moving to promote the recent successes of *their* redevelopment zones, and Tacoma has few projects to tout. So, she asks for a waiver, larger air rights, and a six-month extension on her option to develop the property. The city agrees. Score one for Hannah.

She goes to the landowner and tells him that the deal with the city means she can make his land more valuable now. She points out, as planned, that the warehouse will be more likely to launch if he gives her a lower rent and a longer option. He does. Score two for Hannah.

Winning the rent cut and the rent deferral enables her to go to the bank and make a compelling case: the warehouse will be less risky and more likely to thrive now, thanks to her recent deals with the city and the landowner. She adds that she needs a lower interest rate and a longer commitment to help her negotiate well with Bening (or another major customer). The bank agrees. Score three for Hannah.

Winning these things, she then goes to Skyward, an aerospace company and a strong competitor of Bening, and makes her case: she has a warehouse project Bening is quite interested in, and she has now made the project more attractive. She proposes terms to Skyward that cut out Bening, terms that are also better for her than the ones Bening has been demanding, and Skyward expresses serious interest. Score four.

Winning that interest, she holds a conference call with several of her mid-size customers. There she tells them she is close to signing a major customer. Thanks to deals she's recently struck, the warehouse is looking more likely to launch and thrive, and she can offer them lower rents than before. In return, she needs them to each give her more latitude to make concessions to the major customer. Almost all agree. Score five.

Along the way, Hannah has an off-the-record conversation with Dan Archer, an influential newspaper columnist who has previously criticized other developers for environmental recklessness. Anticipating his concerns, she shares that she's included in her construction budget money for green features she's learned a well-respected professor of ecology recommends. Impressed, Dan strongly hints he won't criticize her work. Score six.

Now Hannah returns to Bening, far more confident. She has less deadline pressure, better economic support, and more choices. She presents Bening's representatives with a compelling message: the warehouse is now more attractive and less risky. And, she adds, she's received strong interest from one of Bening's competitors. Hannah's new proposal makes some concessions to Bening but not others. If they agree, she adds, Bening will get an excellent, state-of-the-art green warehouse; if not, they may lose it to a key competitor. Also, Bening's other choices may not be as green, risking criticism. Impressed, and eager to block Skyward and avoid a bad environmental reputation, Bening reduces its demands, and Hannah secures the deal on excellent terms.

Hannah achieved all this success by harnessing insights crystallized in Who I FORESAW: thinking about complementary and Common Interests, she spotted allies, trading partners, and protectors. Among other things, this part of the work helped her discover people she could talk to away from the table who could help her create more value for Bening, and more concern too. Speaking with others, like a leading journalist, revealed a persuasive and little-known Fact. With each key player, she negotiated attractive Options. She was careful to avoid talks with players who posed Ethical problems, like Passion in the adult film industry. And she anticipated and defused an important critic, Dan, who might have raised other Ethical concerns. Another player she did appropriately contact, Skyward, became a strong Alternative to Agreement. She Scheduled a series of well-sequenced meetings and after prepping for talks and testing her strategy, won deal after deal. Her power snowballed, giving her both the ability to negotiate a more mutually satisfying deal with her Godzilla and the ability to live without it. Merely preparing for bilateral talks with Bening would not have helped as much; her breakthrough came from using Who I FORESAW to see beyond the Bening negotiation to a larger field of play.

Ways to Sequence

Notice that one of the keys to Hannah's story was her ability to sequence moves. How do you do it? There are several possibilities.

Take your easy shots first. One way to sequence is to "take your easy shots first," speaking with those most likely to help, then parlaying their help to win over other, more challenging people. For example, Hannah might have asked herself, "Which party is most approachable and most likely to give me a valuable deal I can build on?" This method may work best if the most important player on your list seems pretty unapproachable now; that player may be easier to reach if you've already won some other good deals first so you'll have attractive things to offer. David Ortega in effect used this approach.

Move the boulder from the stream. Another way to sequence is to "move the boulder from the stream"—speak to the most important player first, hoping that the others will easily follow if you win a good deal from it. Hannah might have asked herself, "Which party is the turnkey here?" That might have been the bank. (One way to finesse a turnkey deal early is to get a contingent agreement: e.g., "*If* you can get a rent reduction, we'll cut your interest rate.") This method may work best if the most important player on your list is influential but fairly approachable and if you have reason to believe you can interest them immediately.

Map backward. A particularly compelling sequencing strategy is to map backward from your Godzilla, picturing a chain of deals. That's what Hannah did. In effect, she thought, "Who are the key players here? OK, then, to get Bening to strike a better deal, I can offer it a better, less costly warehouse. To get a better, less costly warehouse, I can negotiate for interest rate concessions (and more) from the bank. To get bank concessions, I can negotiate for lower rent (and more) from the landlord. To get landlord concessions . . ." and so on until Hannah had identified her first move. It's easier to map backward when you have a map first, a picture of the several players who inhabit the landscape. Who I FORESAW can help you create that map. This method may work best if you can clearly envision each negotiation.

The Power of Moves Away from the Table

Hannah's story illustrates a business truth: entrepreneurs routinely practice building strength away from the table. They have to. One definition of entrepreneurship is "creating something out of nothing." So, much of entrepreneurship is a continual process of negotiation, where each deal becomes a link in a chain. Each deal leads to another until the organization is ready to fly.

Consider Bob Reiss, an entrepreneur who once created a board game company, with little more than a desk, a chair, a phone, and a secretary—a company that in eighteen months produced $2 million in profits. How? By sequencing a series of deals, starting with a famous magazine, then a lead investor, a game designer, a manufacturer, and a sales team. Only then was he ready to negotiate with stores. Each earlier deal made him attractive enough to win the next deal, and then the next.

Building strength away from the table can turn around a seemingly hopeless challenge, creating even greater wealth, and even saving a presidency.

To the point, Steve Perlman was the founder of a startup venture called WebTV, a precursor of Netflix. Selling the venture to a big firm like, say, Microsoft was one quite attractive exit strategy Steve had. But his firm was still unproven, so trying to interest Microsoft would have been like David Ortega offering a pair of headphones to a Mercedes owner. Substantial financing from a top venture capitalist (VC) would have helped interest a firm like Microsoft, but most VCs were skeptical. Backing from a firm like Sony would have made VC support easier. But how to win a deal with Sony? Sony needed to overcome declining sales and compete with firms racing into the online media content space. But Sony was ambivalent. Fortunately, Steve was able to win the backing of one or two early investors, which enabled him to strike a deal with one of Sony's competitors, Philips, an electronics manufacturer that wanted access to the technology WebTV held. Steve entered a nonexclusive contract with them, then used the agreement to help strengthen Sony's interest. Winning a deal with Sony, he now had the credibility to quickly win the financial support he needed from a leading VC and several corporations. That backing made WebTV attractive enough for Steve to sell it to Microsoft for $503 million, just twenty months after WebTV began.[2]

The important point from a negotiator's perspective is the way one deal turned the key for the next deal, then the next—a task you can do intentionally.

Even a small part of Who I FORESAW can transform a desperate situation. A day after becoming president following John Kennedy's assassination, Lyndon Johnson discovered the Senate was scheduled to vote, three days later, on a treaty the administration favored—a treaty everyone knew the Senate would reject. No one but Johnson realized the vote was pivotal: if he lost it, the Senate would see him as a lame duck, he'd get no legislation passed, and he'd never win election the following year. He also knew senators resented having a president tell them what to do, which meant he had no direct leverage, little time, and little hope. What to do?

Two days later, at the gravesite of John Kennedy, Johnson had an epiphany: all fifty governors were there too, and Johnson knew senators listened to governors. So Johnson told aides to round up as many governors as possible and have them attend a speech he'd give them that evening. Thirty-five came, and there Johnson appealed to them to contact their states' senators and urge them to support the treaty as a vital show of national unity. Two days later, the treaty passed overwhelmingly, establishing Johnson as a power to be reckoned with. The vote paved the way for Johnson to win passage months later of the 1964 Civil Rights Act and a massive landslide in the 1964 presidential election. What made the difference? Finding others whose Interests Johnson could appeal to and who could persuasively Respond to the seemingly unmovable Godzillas Johnson faced.[3]

In contrast, the failure to make moves away from the table can kill even the best ideas.

Many management experts have noted the importance of forming alliances when you need to influence an organization.[4] Without an alliance, even the best ideas can die. To the point, consider the story of Charles Kettering, the resident genius of General Motors who, among other things, developed the automatic transmission, electric ignition, safety glass, shock absorbers, and Freon refrigerant, the foundation for refrigerators and air-conditioning.[5] As one coworker put it, Kettering was "one of the gods of the automotive field, particularly from an inventive standpoint."[6] So, in 1920, when Kettering proposed an air-cooled automobile engine, he had good reason to expect GM would back him. It was a brilliant idea; four decades later, Volkswagen had a breakthrough hit in America with its famous Beetle, a car that relied on an air-cooled engine inspired by Kettering's work. But GM never took him up on it. Why?

Because even though the idea was brilliant, Kettering did little to cultivate allies in GM at the division level. Perhaps he thought his record so spoke for itself that he no longer needed to do the hard work of lobbying. Or perhaps Kettering had had more leverage earlier under the previous CEO, who'd used a more freewheeling organizational structure that arguably didn't require as much lobbying. (Under the brand-new CEO who took over that year, Kettering was isolated in his own research and development department.) Whatever the reason, opposition emerged quickly. As one historian put it, "[b]ecause the air-cooled design had been developed by GM's research labs in Dayton, rather than within the divisions, division managers regarded it as experimental and untested."[7] Kettering thought the project's chances were good when GM's board assigned the project to the Chevrolet division. But K. W. Zimmerschied, the division's head, jealously guarded Chevy's autonomy and resented the board's ordering him to pursue Kettering's project. Organizational problems immediately arose. Zimmerschied, afraid GM was gambling his division's future on a risky new invention, trashed it in conversations with his engineers, who quickly grew skeptical about the project. Chevy's staff treated typical early design problems as proof the air-cooled engine was a bad idea, and rumors of problems multiplied. Like a child complaining to a teacher about classmates, Kettering took a top-down approach to overcome this resistance, asking GM's board to order Chevy to fully commit to the project. By then, the board had witnessed such resistance that it refused to support him. Brilliant at invention but baffled by GM's new politics, Kettering eventually quit the project, effectively killing GM's involvement with the air-cooled engine.

What should Kettering have done? As management experts note, among the keys to winning organizational battles like Kettering's are (1) forming and negotiating key alliances with people who have at least some power to decide, fund, and implement, (2) building enough alliances to create a snowball effect as the number of people who back the idea grows, thus pressuring adversaries to give up, and (3) using that momentum to win more concrete support—money, staff, incentives, policies—from those in authority.[8] In other words, to, in effect, make moves away from the table. Using ideas baked into Who I FORESAW could have helped him do that.

Kettering's failure was not technical—it was political. He didn't give enough attention to the people dimension. Things might have been different if Kettering had asked himself questions Who I FORESAW suggests. For example, Whose Interests complemented his own? While division heads were cool to the idea, he might have found other allies, such as influential dealers, suppliers, engineers, and junior executives. And since division heads had an Interest in avoiding risk, Who could reduce the risks they'd be running? Perhaps younger leaders of smaller units might have been open to experimentation, which could have then showed wary division heads the idea would work. And who knew valuable Facts? Facts such as likely consumer demand, competitive pressures, and the like. Industry journalists, people in the finance department, and staff who'd worked for competitors might have had valuable insights. And so on, working through Who I FORESAW. In short, Kettering needed to think and learn about people even before he got too far into the engineering task itself.

As powerful as building strength away from the table can be, there is an alternative way to "prepare business and so ripen it by degrees," a way to turn weakness into power that relies on a reverse strategy. It's helped the lovelorn find marriage, helped a charity win tens of thousands of dollars in donations, and depends on the same approach used widely by entrepreneurs, marketers, purchasing agents and recruiters. To harness it, we'll deploy the same tool, Who I FORESAW, just in a slightly different way.

Targeted Negotiation with Who I FORESAW ◎

Imagine you are involved in a lawsuit, and by some strange turn of events, you can pick every juror. Suddenly your chances of winning the case soar because the jury, by design, will be the people who are most sympathetic to your arguments. While you can't do that in a litigation, you can, quite ethically, do it for a negotiation. That is, you can pick your *counterpart* so well that there's a strong chance you'll reach a mutually satisfying deal. To do that, use a second strategy, something I call Targeted Negotiation. Like David Ortega's work trading upward, you make a series of moves to improve your chances of getting an excellent, unlikely yes. But unlike trading up and up and up, with Targeted Negotiation, you cull, and cull, and cull. Trading up builds what you have to offer; Targeted Negotiation identifies someone who would *love* what you already have to offer.

Here, we'll use Who I FORESAW not to create a large list of people who can help you with a Godzilla you think you must face, but to *cull* a large list of people to find someone you want to face. Instead of expanding your power with many helpers, you narrow your focus to find one great counterpart.[9] Targeted Negotiation is especially helpful when you have many prospects but few good ones. That frustration often happens when you're seeking key customers, donors, lenders, vendors, partners, or clients—and so you sense you'll have to face an unattractive, demanding counterpart.

The idea is to first ask, "Who in this universe has one Interest that meshes with mine?" using your answers to first assemble a long list of prospective counterparts, perhaps thousands. Next, you cull them by adding one filter after another. For example:

"I now have three thousand prospective counterparts who have one Interest that meshes with mine . . .

"And of these, who also has a second Interest that meshes with mine?

"And of these, who also has a third Interest that meshes with mine?

"And of these, who survives a few basic Factual or Financial Research questions (e.g., sales greater than $3 million)?

"And what does Factual Research reveal most speaks to my target counterparts?

"And who of these I've identified would be interested in the Options I most want to offer?

"And of these, with whom will I likely find it easy to build Rapport and Respond to likely Reactions?

"And of these, who presents few or no Ethical issues?

"And of these, who can I likely Schedule at an opportune time?

"And of these, who will likely have few or weak Alternatives to Agreement?

"And of these, who will I likely have contacts with Who can introduce me?"

So, after beginning with, perhaps, several thousand prospects, you might wind up with just a few highly qualified counterparts and contacts who can help you reach the right person there. You don't have to cull using every letter of Who I FORESAW; just treat each letter as a possible useful screen.

Targeting sometimes has an additional advantage. It may help you connect with more excellent prospects than you first think: your Factual Research about what best attracts your target prospects can give you a better chance of actually reaching many of them. That result, in effect, further increases your choices.

Targeted Negotiation in Practice

Here's an example. An international charity practiced something called patient capital; it sought to do social good by investing in select start-ups in impoverished places, seeking a modest profit as its start-ups created much-needed products like mosquito nets and drip agriculture tubes, using local employees and fostering local prosperity. It had special programs for majority-world women who struggled to raise money for the charity from New York–based corporations. Each season, it hosted a dinner for executives at a renowned restaurant, but after two years, the charity had little to show for its efforts. These weak results were odd because New York was home to many top firms with active philanthropic departments.

So, a team of volunteers decided to take a Targeted Negotiation approach. One team member researched and identified 2,500 potential donor firms in New York. Of these, he found ~1,100 did business in countries the charity worked in. Of these, he found ~700 had given money to charities devoted to helping majority-world women. Of these, ~500 passed simple Factual and Financial tests for size and creditworthiness. Of these, ~300 said they preferred to give money to charities that empower people (rather than charities that gave away products and services). Of these, all passed a basic Ethical screen. Of these, ~75 had never given to a competing patient capital charity—they weren't "taken" yet. Another team member found that of these firms, the charity's board members had personal connections with at least one board member of ten of them. Of these ten, the charity had the best connections with three firms, one of which, MetroBank, had the most prestige; if MetroBank said yes, others would likely follow.

Using its connections, the team lined up a twenty-minute meeting with MetroBank's chief philanthropic officer and an executive vice president, then carefully prepared a ten-minute slide deck. Five minutes into the presentation, the EVP stopped it, saying, "OK, we're sold. Would a $40,000 donation the first year work for you?"

Targeted Negotiation is a bread-and-butter feature of supply chain management. Professor Kate Vitasek, a world-renowned expert in the field, refers to it as funneling.[10] When, for example, a customer is seeking a vendor to partner with, it often starts by putting out a request for partners, then screens the candidates for a particular set of capabilities, then whittles down the list from there, culling the pool from, say, sixty bidders down to five or three. Then it negotiates, knowing each is highly suitable and interested.

Even in the realm of love and marriage, targeting can be revealing and powerful. To the point: even if you live in a city with eight million people or have access to twenty million people online, there may just be a few dozen people who are serious marriage prospects once you cull for specific requirements (like sex, age, marital status, physical attractiveness, education, values and beliefs, desire for children, and the odds of meeting within, say, a year). Fortunately, you only need one. That said, if you use targeting wisely, you may find a larger pool of prospects than you might have expected.

In *Data, a Love Story: How I Cracked the Online Dating Code to Meet My Match,*[11] my New York University colleague Amy Webb, a digital strategies expert, describes how she overcame chronic dating heartbreaks. She did it by bringing a kind of Targeted Negotiation to the online dating market. Her work deserves praise and study as an example of the power of targeting. First she listed her many requirements for a mate. Doing this is akin to the kind of filtering one does with Targeted Negotiation by listing one's Interests, a task that here narrowed the field from millions of prospects to dozens. Then, she Factually researched the kind of women's profiles that attracted the men she'd targeted. As we've seen, Factual research is a key early step for further filtering the field, and learning too what your most desirable targets respond to. Using this targeting work, she posted her own revised profile. Unlike past online attempts, her new profile spoke just to her targets' Interests. Then began the deluge: dozens of men wanted to meet her, men who actually met her requirements. Among them: her future husband. What I particular like about Amy's story is the systematic approach she took to understanding both her Interests and her dream date's Interests, and using those insights to cull accordingly. Doing that can help one find a proverbial needle in a haystack.

Targeted Negotiating is closely related to niche marketing, a time-honored approach to business. It's based on the insight that you'll be more attractive, competitive, valuable, and effective if you focus narrowly on a specialized area where you can shine instead of trying to reach everyone and be all things to all people. The difference between niche marketing and Targeted Negotiating is that Targeted Negotiating isn't about selling to a few hundred or a few thousand customers; it's about finding a handful of counterparts—or maybe even just one—with whom you can strike an excellent deal. In the process, it allows you to avoid Godzillas—or discover you're highly attractive to one or two of them.

You now have the negotiation tools to help you do better by *preparing* better. Fine, but what do you actually do and say when you're there in the thick of it? That's what Part II is about.

Tools in Brief

Who I FORESAW: To deal more effectively with a Godzilla, identify key players by asking "Who?" as you review most parts of I FORESAW IT, then schedule a series of moves away from the table to obtain more valuable things to trade, to gain more independence, and to gain more leverage.

Targeted Negotiation: Find ideal counterparties by starting with a large pool of candidates and culling them using Who I FORESAW.

Challenges

The Build Strength Away from the Table Challenge. Identify a Godzilla who seems to be thwarting your efforts. Using Who I FORESAW, make a list of people who could be influential, cull, and then sequence a series of well-planned conversations/negotiations, each of which helps you become more and more attractive or independent, until you are well positioned to deal more effectively with your Godzilla. Then prepare an I FORESAW IT plan (and perhaps role-play). Then meet with your Godzilla.

The Do a Deal with Your Dreams Challenge. Identify someone you would love to do a specific kind of business deal with (or build an important business relationship with), but who seems *somewhat* out of your league—perhaps someone fairly renowned in your sphere who is three degrees of separation away, or a decision maker at an organization that's financially ten times bigger. Using Who I FORESAW, make a list of people who could be influential, then sequence a series of conversations/negotiations with some of them that each helps you become more and more attractive, until you are well positioned to reach out to your dream counterpart. Then, prepare an I FORESAW IT plan (and perhaps roleplay) before you meet your dream counterpart. Then go negotiate.

The Targeted Negotiation Challenge. Identify a deal you would love to enter with a counterpart-to-be-named-later, preferably in a realm where many potential counterparts exist. For example, identify a dream deal with a hypothetical ideal customer, donor, lender, vendor, or client. Using Who I FORESAW, collect listings or find a data set of potential prospects in that realm till you have many dozens, hundreds, or thousands of names. Then use the tool to filter the list (and learn) until you have just a few excellent prospects. Then pitch a couple of your best prospects first (perhaps using things you learned about how best to reach them). When a prospect shows strong interest, prepare an I FORESAW IT plan (and perhaps roleplay) so you're fully ready to negotiate.

PART II

Meet

Do Good for Them,
Great for You:
**Win Warmly
Recipe Card**

Deescalate:
***Exactly!* Challenge**

Be a Boss Whisperer:
APSO

Unify Your Group:
**Common
Interests Hack**

Help Meetings Work:
Golden Minute

Talk Good:
Reframe

Many years ago, when I was young and foolish, I had a job interview in which the interviewer began by asking me why I'd chosen the school I was attending. "Well," I replied, "it's got a good reputation, and it's not cutthroat like some others I might have attended." To which he replied, "Oh really, like which one?" Great—now I had a chance of inadvertently naming the interviewer's alma mater, insulting him, and killing my chance of getting the job. I hemmed and hawed and finally named another school. BINGO! The very one he'd attended. I never heard from him again.

One of the biggest challenges we face in negotiation is managing ourselves in the heat of the moment. Under pressure, we can get tongue-tied, confused, and overwhelmed, blurt out a serious gaff, or miss saying the very things we intended to. Then, after, we replay the experience, wondering, What *should* I have said? Part II of this book gives you the tools to handle these situations in the moment, instead of ruing them in hindsight.

You'll discover there are simple templates that can help you say things that are hard on the problem, soft on the person. They can equip you to speak to a Godzilla or a boss in ways that can often turn bad to good. It's not about insincere scripting or false playacting. Quite the opposite. It's about translating what you want to say, so you express it genuinely, wisely, and winsomely. That's worth emphasizing: the goal is to speak so the other person can *hear your point and appreciate it.*

Often now, when I coach a student, client, or family member as they prepare for a tough conversation, I'll offer sample language, and they'll say, "You said it the way I wish I could say it! You must be naturally good at this." Nope, it's just that after putting my foot in my mouth so many times, I learned the tools in this section.

As we'll see, one brief recipe can help you win warmly when you need to, helping you say something simple and powerful that enables you to create and claim wealth well. As we'll also see, you can use a simple tool to answer rage and intimidation in a way that so deescalates conflict that it's the response hostage negotiators rely on. There's a third simple tool that, in a moment of crisis, helps you respectfully and safely correct a boss. A fourth enables you to help make a meeting more constructive in a single golden minute. Some simple templates, including ones built on just a couple of words, can help you speak persuasively when it seems nothing will help. And another is so powerful that leaders from Churchill to Mandela have relied on it to help change the course of history.

To learn a foreign language, one must master the simple structures that make up sentences, like subject-object-verb. *Er hat einen Apfel gegessen*—"He has eaten an apple." Once you do, you can convey thousands of different thoughts more easily. *Sie hat einen Kuchen gebacken*—"She has baked a cake." The tools here work in a similar way, giving you effective structures you can use in the moment, so that you can avoid pitfalls, and know that *du hat das Richtige gesagt*—you have said the right thing.

CHAPTER 7

Win Warmly

THE TOOL: WIN WARMLY RECIPE CARD*

Use this tool when you . . .
- fear you will do poorly compared to your counterpart
- fear talks will leave your counterpart feeling resentful
- don't know what to say to avoid these traps
- need a valuable and favorable deal.

Use this tool to . . .
- truthfully reassure your counterpart you want them to do well
- speak to create a "good for them, very good for us" deal.

*And the 5 Percent Rule of Thumb.

Picture three executives, Abel, Baker, and Charlie, who are informally vying for the same promotion. Their boss separately asks each to negotiate a deal with similar key customers. "I need you to do well for the firm," the boss tells each one; "and bring back $15,000 in revenue." Abel returns with a deal that would give the firm $9,000. "Wait," says the boss, "$9,000 is very low." But Abel pushes back, saying, "You don't understand; I got them *way* up from $6,000, the fee they were demanding to pay. And besides, $9,000 is slightly better than the worst deal we've ever settled for." The boss grimaces. The next day Baker returns with a deal. "It's creative," Baker explains. "I estimate it created $20,000 in combined revenue for the two firms, thanks to some inventive Options I proposed." The boss asks, "And how much did we get?" Baker shrugs and says, "$8,000. But *they love us!*" The boss grimaces again. On the third day, Charlie returns with a deal. "Tell me you got $15,000," the boss says. "Oh, *way* better than that! I got $19,999!" Just as they are talking, the boss gets a text from the CEO of Charlie's customer: "A deal's a deal, but we'll never do business with you again. You bled us dry." The boss groans and mutters, "Can't anyone help me?"

Conventional wisdom holds that when you negotiate, you have a choice. You can focus on collaborating or competing; expanding the pie or dividing it; creating wealth or claiming it. Whole books emphasize one or the other approach. For example, *Getting to Yes* emphasizes creating value and spends little time discussing how to claim much of it. Other negotiation books and experts depict negotiation as something like armed combat and urge you to win as much as you can. At least one instructor I know used to recommend seeking 100 percent of the value of a deal. That's right: he argued you should leave the other side with *nothing*. I hope you'll forgive me for not following in that path.

To be sure, if you're selling a used bike, it *may* make sense to focus mainly on claiming wealth by haggling over price. Conversely, if you're trying to solve an intractable conflict, it *may* make sense to focus on creating wealth by getting collaborative. But often, an exclusive focus on either can be dangerous.

Take hard, win-lose bargaining, or as we call it, competitive negotiating. Studies show that when a negotiator badly "beats" another, the beaten negotiator winds up feeling resentful, uncooperative, and eager to take revenge.[1] That's how Charlie's counterpart felt. Perhaps, like me, you have had a negotiation where you felt taken. How did you feel about the other party, and how eagerly did you want to do business with them again? In fact, if negotiators gain a reputation for being greedy, it can negate their effectiveness. As my fellow negotiation instructors have found, even if you *falsely* believe an expert negotiator is greedy, you will become so defensive that it will kill cooperation and drive you *both* toward impasse or a mediocre deal. In that light, consider the advice of legendary sports agent Bob Woolf, one of the founders of the field of modern sports agency, who, surprisingly, emphasizes the importance of intentionally *not* being greedy:

A successful negotiation isn't one where I get everything and you get nothing . . . I haven't done a single contract that I couldn't have gotten more money on. I always leave money on the table ... [b]ecause it's possible to push the price so far, create such antagonism, that the extra 10% isn't really worth it. If someone feels you held them up, they're going to take it out on your business or ... on you. You have to give the other people a profit margin and let them live. You want them to thrive and grow ... You can't play tricks because you'll probably be going back to these people again—or to someone they know. Your good reputation is incredibly important ... If it really is a one-time deal, then I wouldn't leave as much, but I still wouldn't try for the last dollar ... .[2]

In short, studies and experts warn that in negotiation, greed is *not* good.

But many negotiators definitely *aren't* greedy. In fact, they're so afraid of being greedy that they figure they've negotiated well if they've done a bit better than their worst acceptable deal. Like Abel, they say, "It could have been worse, so I'm content." There's a term for that: "satisficing"—getting an outcome that's only a bit better than the minimum. Now, as we'll see, there are definitely times when it's wise to satisfice. Often, though, people do it out of fear or self-delusion, and so, like Abel, wind up with an unfair, unsatisfying deal.

So, what if you try merely to be creative and collaborative? That can backfire too. Many years ago, my students at Columbia ran a simulated multimillion-dollar negotiation with students they hadn't met before from Bordeaux, France. I'd trained my students for eight weeks; the French students had worked with another instructor for *maybe* a couple of weeks a few months earlier. To my dismay, the French students cleaned out my Columbia students' pockets. But my students assured me they'd done well because, like Baker, they'd gotten creative and fostered good feelings. "We got along so well!" they said.

I'd failed my students. I realized I had to be tougher with them, teaching them a more balanced method—something more, not less, than a collaborative approach, or one day they'd give away whole nations. But how? If greed, satisficing, and naive collaboration can each backfire, what *should* you do?

The Recipe 🏆🏆

It is possible to both create a lot of value *and* claim a favorable portion without being greedy. I call that Winning Warmly, an outcome about which you can truthfully say, "The other side is rightly happy, and my side is rightly very happy."[3] Now, there are definitely times when it's *not* wise to try to Win Warmly; we'll return to that important idea in the last part of this discussion. But often, Winning Warmly should be the goal, because it serves two very frequent interests: the need to serve your side well *and* the need to foster good relationships by truthfully telling the other side, "I really do want this deal to be good for you too."

Intriguing evidence suggests it's possible. One unpublished two-year study of over 250 executive negotiation students explored what effect systematic preparation had on simulated deal outcomes. The study found that, on average, negotiators who systematically prepared produced deals that created 11 percent more value for their side than negotiators who didn't. That's hopeful news: 11 percent more value can mean the difference between profit and loss, survival and bankruptcy for most organizations. But the study found something more: negotiators who systematically prepared also created 6 percent more value for the other side *than the other side would have gotten if the prepared negotiators hadn't systematically prepared.* Something about the way skilled negotiators get ready may measurably help them Win Warmly.

If you've created a TTT grid on the eve of important talks, you're 80 percent of the way toward Winning Warmly. It's the summation of systematic preparation. Here, we want to add a tool that can help you craft a particularly wise first offer and present it in a thoughtful, truthful, winsome way so you can be *both* competitive *and* collaborative. I call it **the Winning Warmly Recipe Card**. And we can write the recipe in three lines:

1. Cushion your first offer,
2. Especially cushion your favorite Topic(s), and
3. Signal a willingness to be creative.

Now let's break that down.

Cushion your first offer. As we saw earlier, 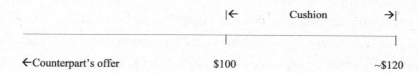 [Chapter 4], it's usually a good idea to cushion your first offer so you can make concessions and still wind up at or near your Best Targets. The idea, you'll recall, is to identify your Best Target for a given Topic and then plan to first ask for something more aggressive. For example, recall our look at your TTT grid, 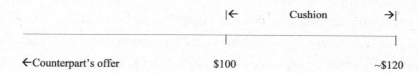 [Chapter 4], when you were a computer parts seller, and your range of Targets for price was $100–$80. Your Best Target is $100. When you craft a first offer, you'll want to add to it, perhaps asking for, say, $110 or $120.

|←   Cushion   →|

←Counterpart's offer $100   ~$120

There is a bit of art and science to cushioning. You can cushion a lot or a little, and each has a case.

Big cushion. One study found that when a negotiator adds a large cushion and then concedes quickly, the other negotiator feels more satisfied than when a negotiator adds a slight cushion and then concedes grudgingly. Thus, store signs that read "50% off!" Conversely, many of us feel uneasy cushioning so much. And yes, sometimes a big cushion can alienate the other person, though studies find we probably overestimate that risk. One way to use a large cushion with less risk is to use a soft offer where you add language to signal you're not crazy or greedy; you're just asking to start a conversation. Thus: "I'm thinking of a price of $120 *negotiable,*" or "*I'm asking* $115," or "I'm looking at a price of *roughly $120 to $100,*" or "The price is $110 *or best offer.*"

Small cushion. Still, you may feel uncomfortable with a big cushion, especially if your research shows over-cushioning will tend to backfire with your counterpart. For example, it's a good idea to talk with peers who have negotiated with your counterpart before, asking them, among other things, "How do they react to aggressive first offers?" If peers tell you, "Well, they'll certainly push back, but they won't take huge offense," then you might consider it. Conversely, if peers tell you, "Whoa, try that and they'll immediately end the talks," then don't. Similarly, a seasoned expert in the field or the culture you're dealing with may be able to tell you what the norm is for an opening offer strategy. Regardless, if you don't want to open with a big cushion, you have another choice. You can cushion slightly by pegging your first offer to the high end of a range of prices reported by a respected Independent Criterion.[4] If you do peg to a benchmark like that, concede slowly. You don't have to match the other's concession dollar for dollar because you're appealing to your benchmark to demonstrate a desire to be fair.

But what Topics do you cushion? That's where the second part of the Winning Warmly Recipe Card comes in.

Especially cushion your favorite Topics. Some Topics are more important to you than others. If you've systematically prepared with a TTT grid, you know clearly which Topics you care most about. In the story we used earlier to explore the TTT grid, □ [Chapter 4], we imagined price is your number one priority. It's particularly important to cushion your top priority items, in part because they're the ones that will give you the most value. It also helps you signal which issues are most important to you.

Should you cushion *every* Topic? I'm not sure. On the one hand, cushioning everything gives you the chance to reach your Best Target on every issue. On the other hand, it can produce an offer that seems so aggressive it may turn off some counterparts. There's a risk/return tradeoff here, one complicated by the culture, the market, and the other person's feelings. The important thing, then, is to cushion your top Topics; cushioning the rest is optional.[5]

Signal a Willingness to Be Creative

One reason many people dislike negotiation is the mixed motives it creates; you're trying to cooperate with someone, yet you each want to do well for yourselves. It's like trying to dance and box at the same time. Your counterpart senses this paradox as much as you do, which is one reason why you're each stressed and wary. As we've seen, there's excellent reason to want good feeling and collaboration. Yet, negotiation, by its nature, can foster cynicism. So how do you signal you sincerely wish to collaborate, want the talks to serve the other well too, and want to together discover creative Options you both like, when you're each aware there's a competition present? How do you truthfully invite someone to dance when you're each wearing boxing gloves?

The third step in the Winning Warmly Recipe Card answers that question. The idea is to plan to speak in a way that signals you genuinely want to be collaborative, to truthfully show that you'd like this deal to be satisfying for both sides and that you have ideas about how to do it. There's no puffery or BS in saying so; you're not saying you want to give away the store or neglect yourself. In fact, you can acknowledge you do hope to do well. Instead, you *are* saying you believe it's quite possible for both of you to be happy, which has the advantage of being true. So, what then do you say?

1. A thoughtful preface and,
2. perhaps, a thoughtful offer.

Let's see what that means by returning to the computer parts contract.

In the thoughtful preface, you frame the forthcoming offer. You say it so the other person begins to see you're hopeful, positive, and constructive, and not greedy, cynical, or myopic. In our example, you might say something like this:

"OK, now that I've listened awhile, gotten a sense of your concerns, and shared some of mine, let me make an offer and see what you think. I'm not wed to any specific numbers as long as we come up with an outcome that serves my needs, as well as yours, and I'm confident we can do that."

No need to memorize this statement—the key is getting the spirit. There are several valuable negotiation practices these two sentences signal. You don't need to cover all these bases in one utterance; the main thing is to plan to convey at least some of these ideas at some point in the conversation before you make the offer:

- You've been going slowly.
- You've been listening for interests.
- You've shared some of your interests.

- You're suggesting, not demanding.
- You're flexible.
- You're firm about your interests.

In short, you're establishing that you are being strong and kind by focusing on Interests, Facts, and Options. You're showing respect, building trust and Rapport, and learning, all by taking time to get acquainted and listen deeply, so you understand the other's needs. You've helped the other person learn something about your needs too, so they're readier to work with you on creative ideas. That doesn't mean revealing *everything*, like desperation (e.g., "If we don't close this deal today, we'll be bankrupt tomorrow."). It simply means you're revealing some things you've decided it's safe and reasonable to share.

You can get ready to make these points by listing them in the Rapport section of your I FORESAW IT plan ✈ [Chapter 2]. You can also practice saying them by roleplaying with a teammate 🎭 [Chapter 5].

Sometimes it's wise *not* to make the first offer, as we saw earlier, 📋 [Chapter 4], as when you sense you know less than the other negotiator does and want to avoid lowballing yourself, but, for some reason, you still must negotiate then. If so, you can use an almost identical preface like this:

"OK, now that I've listened awhile, gotten a sense of your concerns, and shared some of mine, *let's explore specifics*. I'm not wed to any specific numbers as long as we come up with an outcome that serves my needs, as well as yours, and I'm confident we can do that. *What sort of offer did you have in mind?*"

If you do make the first offer, present it as a suggestion, not a positional demand. For example, you might say, "*We'd be open* to a deal for $120 negotiable with a two-year money-back guarantee," or "*We suggest* a contract for $110 with a two-year money-back guarantee." Soon after, you might add, "Everything is important to us, but price is our top priority." That signals a readiness to tradeoff without diminishing the value of a given issue. In contrast, saying, "We care about price, not the guarantee," invites the other person to say, "OK, why don't you just give us a big guarantee?"

As we've seen, research shows what experts know: packaging tends to lead to deals both sides are happier with than ones negotiated one issue at a time.

So, it's wise not to make an offer on just one issue. Instead, tackle some or all of the issues at once. Then you can play with it together, exploring Tradeoffs Between and Within Topics. Your TTT grid will make it easy to do these things. In our first example, you packaged by offering not merely a price of "$120 negotiable" but also a "two-year money-back guarantee." Because packaging invites trades, it's one of several ways you can intentionally do what you say you want to do: satisfy both sides.

The final deal will probably look different from your first offer. But with systematic preparation in hand (including a TTT grid), you can play with the proposals. You can trade off priorities, suggest Options, and concede here and there so that when you're done, you've reached a deal that's close to your Best Targets, and that perhaps includes creative ideas the other person likes too.

Be Ambitious, Not Greedy with the 5 Percent Rule of Thumb ▮⁵%

How can you be ambitious without being greedy? By moderating your ambitions slightly. To do that, set for each of your Best Targets a goal that is slightly, measurably *worse* than you can hope to get. That's right: worse. Why? Precisely because, as we've seen, being greedy can come back to bite you in several ways.

So, how much should you worsen your Best Target? Often a wise answer is to use the 5 Percent Rule of Thumb. The 5 Percent Rule of Thumb is a mini tool I've created, an applet really, that helps negotiators truthfully say, "I don't want to bleed you dry here; true, I want to be ambitious, but I really don't want to be greedy." To use it, you worsen your Best Target by 5 percent; that is, you seek a Best Target that's 5 percent *worse* than the best your research tells you that you could hope to get. So, for example, if you're selling a boat, and research reveals prices range from $70,000 to $100,000, set $95,000 as your Best Target, *not* $100,000. Getting $95,000 is *very* good—and leaving some money on the table is wise, in part because it improves your ability to Win Warmly by saving you from the smell of greediness.*

---

* If it really is a one-time deal it might be sensible to be a bit more ambitious, but not much more.

But wait, didn't we say you should cushion? That's right—cushion your *first offer*. Your Best Target is different; as we've said, it's what you confidentially aspire to wind up with. In contrast, your first offer is the amount you'll first *ask* for, knowing you'll make concessions. In other words, your Best Target is what you secretly *hope* to get, while your first offer is what you'll *open* with. So, for example, in our boat story, you might say, "I'm asking $110,000, and I'm flexible, as long as we serve my key interests well," knowing you're hoping to settle for $95,000, perhaps with creative Options as part of the deal. Thus:

Highest possible boat price (according to Factual Research):	$100,000
Moderate ambition using the 5 Percent Rule of Thumb:	$5,000
Best Target:	$95,000
+Cushion (any of several possibilities can work):	$15,000
First offer:	$110,000

If you are the *buyer*, the 5 Percent Rule of Thumb means you'll worsen your Best Target slightly by seeking a result that's 5 percent *higher* than the best your research tells you that you could hope to get. Here, if the boat buyer's research says $80,000 is the best she could hope to get, her Best Target would then be $70,000 + 5 percent = $84,000.

The 5 Percent Rule of Thumb finds support in several places, including top sports agent Bob Woolf's observation that it's wise to leave some money on the table, and social science research showing greed kills. Another sign: *Consumer Reports* recommends car buyers shouldn't seek a price equal to the dealer's invoice price (for example, $40,000)—the price the dealer paid for the car—but rather a price that's about 3 to 5 percent higher ($41,200 to $42,000).[6]

True, there are times when the 5 Percent Rule of Thumb won't work, like when the market ranges are narrow (for example, in our boat story, $90,000 to $100,000) or you're negotiating for something you can't quantify (for example, a corner office). What should you do then? Lose the rule but keep the principle: moderate ambition slightly.

To get comfortable with the 5 Percent Rule of Thumb, don't take my word for it; try a few negotiations, some where you do deploy it and some where you don't, and see what you think. My humble suggestion: you'll usually like the difference it makes in your approach, your relationships, and your results.

Should You *Always* Be Ambitious?

Now that you have the tools to be creative and ambitious, it's time to ask a question: *Should* you be ambitious? Are there times when it's best not to be? Though it may seem odd in a book about negotiation, often the answer is it's best *not* to be ambitious. Consider several other choices.

Compromise. There are times when an even split is reasonable, customary, and expected, and seeking more can damage or kill your dealings with another. For example, many joint ventures and partnerships start with each party getting an equal cut. As one experienced executive observed in an interview with researchers from Columbia Business School, if his firm had asked their joint venture partner for more than a fifty-fifty deal, the partner would have felt his side was selfish and would have broken off talks. Similarly, compromise is often a simple, clear, quick, reasonable way to settle matters with friends ("Let's split the check."). Sometimes kids get quite inventive about making sure things are fair; the cake cutting rule, "I cut, you choose," is one way to make sure the cutter divides things equally, not knowing what part the other will take. We often find a similar idea in shareholder agreements: "If one of us wants to part ways, that one will propose a stock price and the other can either buy or sell at that price."

Satisfice. Other times, it's wise to seek a deal that's only a bit better than you could do elsewhere, that is, a bit better than your worst acceptable outcome. When you shop for toothpaste or pick a movie to watch, you're often overwhelmed with dozens or even thousands of choices. As Barry Schwartz writes in *The Paradox of Choice: Why More Is Less,* studies show you'll probably be just as happy (and less wearied) if you satisfice: choose something you're OK with instead of wasting time seeking the *perfect* toothpaste, the *best* movie. For many matters, it's simply a waste of time to worry a lot about negotiation terms. When I buy a toaster or a Christmas tree, I promise you I'm not worrying about getting the best terms and conditions, and perhaps you shouldn't either. It may even be wise to satisfice some bigger matters, especially if the terms matter far less than your time or energy. That said, please don't satisfice if your boss, your family, your charity, your firm, or others you serve need you to do well for them; they will not understand if you just tell them to read *The Paradox of Choice* and be content.

To the point: in the late 1950s, Martin Luther King, Jr. came under tremendous pressure to stop agitating for civil rights after Congress passed the 1957 Civil Rights Act, the first such act in a century. Alas, it was a pimple of a reform that did almost nothing for African Americans. If Dr. King had satisficed, he would have let down millions of African Americans who needed help overcoming the cruel injustices of segregation and voter suppression. His response was to quote from the Bible: "No, no, we are not satisfied, and we will not be satisfied until 'justice rolls down like waters and righteousness like a mighty stream.'"[7] He pressed on and helped win passage of the watershed 1964 Civil Rights Act and the 1965 Voting Rights Act. Similarly, one of the most aggressive negotiators I've witnessed was Mother Teresa, who was lionlike in her advocacy for orphans.

Be generous. How do I negotiate with my wife? I will share a secret of my marriage with you. My wife sometimes comes to me and asks, "I forgot to get cash. Can I have $20?" And I will say, "No. But you can have $30." Or she will ask me if I can wait for her for ten minutes, and I will say, "No. But I'll wait thirty." In other words, I try to give her more than she asks me for. Why? Because I love her, and I want to be generous to her. As many have taught, a spirit of generosity is wise. As Wharton professor Adam Grant found in his book *Give and Take:Why Helping Others Drives Our Success*,[8] people who are thoughtfully generous wind up creating better relationships, which, funny enough, improve their career outcomes and lead to greater happiness.

You tend to wind up with what your goal is. If you satisfice, you'll usually get less; if you seek to be ambitious, you'll often get more. Whatever negotiation goal you choose, though, please do *not* simply give away the store and then rationalize it, saying you decided to compromise, satisfice, or be generous when really you just chickened out. Instead, be sure you know how to be ambitious, and then choose your goal from strength, not weakness, so whatever choice you make is truly your own.

Tools in Brief

Win Warmly Recipe Card: (1) Cushion your first offer, (2) especially cushion your favorite Topics, and (3) signal a willingness to be creative with (4) a thoughtful preface and perhaps (5) a thoughtful offer.

5 Percent Rule of Thumb: Moderate ambition slightly by setting as your Best Target a number that's 5 percent worse than the best outcome that research shows you could get.

Challenges

The Winning Warmly Recipe Card Challenge. Before your next important negotiation, prepare systematically (using I FORESAW IT and, perhaps, role-playing and Who I FORESAW). Then use the Winning Warmly Recipe Card to create a thoughtful preface (i.e., talking points) and a well-crafted first offer. Go negotiate. Then, at an appropriate moment in the talks, deploy the thoughtful preface and, soon or sometime later, the first offer. Then use your TTT grid to guide the ensuing negotiations toward a deal that fits the goals you've set, perhaps an ambitious one that lets you Win Warmly.

The 5 Percent Rule of Thumb Challenge. Try a few negotiations, some where you deploy the 5 Percent Rule of Thumb and some where you don't, and see what you think.

The Generosity Challenge. The next time a friend or a loved one asks you for something small or, perhaps, something a bit more than small, see what happens if you offer more than they ask for. For example, offer to wait longer, cover more of the tip, carry more bags, give more to charity than the other even requested. You might also consider trying it, carefully, with a colleague who asks you for help on a project. (Just watch out for a colleague who'll likely confuse kindness with weakness and tend to take advantage.) Offer to do more than the colleague even asks for; or, if that would create a hardship, offer a creative way to unilaterally satisfy the colleague's need, no strings attached, in a way that also lets you protect your needs.

Become a Godzilla Whisperer

In the animated movie *Moana,*[1] the title character, a Polynesian girl, must find the goddess Te Fiti and restore Te Fiti's stolen heart stone. But in the pivotal scene, she reaches Te Fiti's desolate island only to find she must first get past the monstrous volcanic demon Te Ka, who threatens her with fire. Suddenly, Moana realizes something shocking: the horrible Te Ka *is* the goddess Te Fiti. So, Moana simply asks to meet with Te Ka, who races toward her, growing more furious every moment. In response, Moana begins singing, "I know who you really are." Te Ka, stunned, stops, calms, lowers her head, and closes her eyes. Then, Moana places Te Fiti's heart stone in Te Ka's heart, and the demon instantly transforms back into Te Fiti, the beautiful, peaceful goddess, who blesses Moana.

In the face of rage, Moana did not respond in kind. Instead of seeing just a horrible monster, Moana looked into her heart. Instead of fighting or fleeing, she simply stood still and sang a song of deep understanding, transforming the other's rage into a similar stillness.

Can real life mirror Moana's story?

The psychologist Marshall Rosenberg once visited a Palestinian refugee camp to give a talk there during armed conflict between the Palestinians and Israel. One hundred seventy Palestinian men awaited him. As soon as he arrived, the audience began murmuring that Rosenberg was an American. Then, just as he started his talk, a Palestinian man, Abdul, leaped up and started to call Rosenberg a murderer. Others began to shout too, and the gathering quickly turned ugly. So, Rosenberg turned to Abdul and said, "Sir, are you angry because you would like my government to spend its resources differently?" Abdul said, "Damn right I'm angry! You think we need tear gas? We need sewers, not your tear gas! We need housing! We need to have our own country . . . My son is sick! He plays in open sewage! His classroom has no books!" So, Rosenberg said, "I hear how painful it is for you to raise your children here; you'd like me to know that what you want is what all parents want for their children—a good education, opportunities to play and grow in a healthy environment . . ." Abdul replied, "That's right, the basics! Human rights—isn't that what you Americans call it? Why don't more of you come here and see?" This dialogue went on for almost twenty minutes. By then, Abdul and the audience had calmed down. Then Rosenberg asked Abdul if Rosenberg could teach now, and Abdul agreed. After the talk, Abdul came up to Rosenberg, a Jewish American, and invited him to have Ramadan dinner with Abdul and his family.[2]

In the face of rage, Rosenberg did not respond in kind. Instead of seeing just a furious adversary, he looked into the heart. Instead of fighting or fleeing, he simply stood still and did things that transformed Abdul's rage into a similar openness.

When someone seems furious, our natural tendency is to assume they're impossible to deal with. But as the stories here illustrate, there is another way to achieve what shouting, insulting, escalating, or escaping cannot. That's great, but how? What if you're not a psychologist, or a character with magical powers?

What if you fear you'll lose it in the face of an impossible other, or you fear that in a hard moment you'll forget mere principles?* Fortunately, a simple tool can help, a tool that can equip you to become a Godzilla whisperer.

Yet, the same tool can do more. Even if your counterpart is calm, reasonable, and professional, the tool can make your talks go markedly better, in part because it can help lower your counterpart's hidden anxieties, and yours too. In fact, the skill it equips you to perform is so valuable that most expert negotiators rank it as the most important they use in any meeting. So, whether you face a saint or a movie monster, this tool may be critical.

The *Exactly!* Challenge

I know a group of people who routinely deal with others who are way crazier and more hostile than anyone you or I will ever encounter: the New York Police Department's Hostage Negotiation Team. They founded the first program of its kind, and it has become a model for hundreds of similar teams around the world. For decades, they've found a way to get a hostage taker to put the gun down, let the hostage go, and come out peacefully. How? Their secret—the thing that most helps them truly act as Godzilla whisperers—is summed up in their motto: "Talk to me." The key: listening.

Counterintuitively, skilled listening is perhaps the most potent and important negotiation and conflict management skill of them all, and it's particularly effective when you face overwhelming adversity. *Why?* Many reasons:

1. It buys you time and centers you, saving you from blurting when you're overwhelmed.
2. It deescalates the conflict. (Argument and premature fixing tend to escalate it.)

---

* As Rosenberg notes, he used the story to illustrate a "consciousness and intent," and an extensive set of principles he calls nonviolent communication. I share it to illustrate something else: a more learnable task we can crystallize in a tool.

3. It helps you discover the other's interests.
4. It satisfies one of the most universal interests of all, the need to be heard and respected.
5. It fosters feelings of confidence and trust toward the listener: *Here's someone I can confide in, someone who gets me.*
6. It helps you feel and show empathy, humanizing the moment.
7. It invites reciprocity.
8. It lets you respond well even when you don't have a brilliant answer to every question.
9. It costs nothing.

Perhaps for these reasons, my MBA alumni rank deep listening as one of the most valuable skills they learn in a course on negotiation.

Alas, perfunctory listening, the kind we often give each other, lacks most of these benefits, especially in negotiation and conflict, and most especially when we're stressed or afraid. That's first because typical, perfunctory listening tends to be *passive*—we nod as though we've understood, even when we haven't. Worse, we rehearse our comeback while the other is talking, which often cripples our ability to get what the other is saying and what they *aren't* saying. For example:

Annette: How dare you come in here and tell my staff how to spend its budget! Any request for budget cuts has to get my approval first, or there will be hell to pay!

Bob: Look, you don't scare me. I have orders from the CEO herself to get expenses down, whether you or your staff like it or not.

Very soon after Annette began to talk, Bob wrongly concluded he understood Annette's point when he didn't, then began rehearsing his brilliant comeback, further missing what Annette was saying. Bob's tone-deaf reply strongly signaled he didn't understand and didn't care enough to check. Now, Annette feels more unheard, disrespected, and dehumanized, more distrustful, angrier, less interested in listening to Bob, and more eager to escalate. She'll likely raise her voice further, in part to try to get Bob to hear her this time, a tactic that usually backfires, triggering Bob and prompting him to escalate further, and so on.[3] Yet if we asked him, Bob would probably tell us he's a great listener. Many couples, families, and companies live for years like this, fostering a culture of stress and anger.

A key to reversing this dysfunction is to deploy a tool I call the *Exactly!* Challenge. To use it, you periodically repeat the gist of what the person is saying so well that the other person says, "Exactly!" (or words to that effect).

As you may well know, recapping, paraphrasing, summarizing, or repeating the other's words is called active listening, and it is a critical skill excellent negotiators rely on, including hostage negotiators. Here, we're taking the skill one step further by turning it into a tool, a challenge that requires you to repeatedly get confirmation you've understood the other person. Marshall Rosenberg, in effect, used the *Exactly!* Challenge for much of a twenty-minute conversation with an irate audience member, and it gradually transformed an explosive situation. The idea is to check for understanding, occasionally, not constantly, and more frequently if the conflict is intense. Many people I've worked with have been amazed at how well it works. To paraphrase several of them:

"It was hugely useful."

"She seemed to almost faint with relief that I got what she was saying."

"It improved the intimacy between us."

"Just by taking a moment and focusing on what she was really saying let me resolve the dispute."

"As soon as I began actively listening, he relaxed and reciprocated. He just wanted to be understood."

Why does recapping help, especially in conflict? First, because high conflict fosters high stress, and stress, like static, makes listening more difficult. Recapping helps you focus and helps you both see if the stress is defeating communication or if you're overcoming it. It also shows respect and validation, builds trust, buys time, and saves you from blurting. It lowers the pressure, the anger, the speed, the resentment. And it fosters a feeling of space, face, and grace that allows the kind of shift we saw in Marshall Rosenberg's story and Moana's.

How might the *Exactly!* Challenge help Annette and Bob?

Annette: How dare you come in here and tell my staff how to spend its budget! Any request for budget cuts has to get my approval first, or there will be hell to pay!

Bob: Let me first see if I'm getting this. Are you saying you're angry because you don't want to make the cuts?

Annette: No! I'm angry because you went behind my back! You usurped my authority!

Bob: I just want to make sure I hear you. Are you saying it's not the cuts so much that bother you; it's that you want to be the one who communicates the cuts to the team?

Annette: Exactly!

The first few times you take the *Exactly!* Challenge, you may notice yourself increasingly saying, "I'm sorry, I didn't hear what you just said. Can you repeat it, please?" When that happens, rejoice and be glad because you're showing a symptom of improved listening. That's because good listeners notice when they're not getting it; bad listeners often don't.

What can help you do the *Exactly!* Challenge? Here are a few tips:

- Give full attention: eye contact (if culturally appropriate), relaxed body posture, lean in slightly.
- Don't rehearse your comeback. (You'll have time to form a reply later.)
- Visualize the other's statement like you're watching a movie, or, even better, feel what the other's saying as if *you* are saying it.
- Take mental notes of keywords or images.
- Try recapping just fifteen to thirty seconds at a time initially; longer statements are harder to recap.
- Don't worry much about exactness; even if you're mistaken, the other person usually appreciates that you're trying and will correct you if you make a mistake.

You can also practice recapping, so you're ready for your next conflict:

- Practice recapping in the privacy of your own room by listening to an angry movie character's monologue, stopping the video after half a minute, and saying back what the actor said. Then check by hitting rewind and play.

- Practice in a roleplay with a teammate, saying back what your teammate says in character, especially the most aggressive or difficult things your teammate says.

Struggling? Consider bringing in a teammate who can share the task of recapping periodically.

It might seem as if the *Exactly!* Challenge can't work in stressful situations because time is too short and pressure is too intense to permit it. Yet, the reverse is true. It is standard procedure in space exploration to recap what mission control or the astronaut is saying at critical moments. It's standard procedure in commercial aviation to recap what the tower or the pilot is saying. And it's standard procedure for submariners, SWAT team members, and marines confirming an officer's orders; the same is true for stockbrokers taking down securities orders and, increasingly, doctors and nurses in the surgical theater.[4] Put another way, when the stakes and stress are high, you can't afford *not* to actively listen.

Basic active listening works well in most situations. In many conflicts, especially ones where the other person is expressing strong emotions, it can be helpful to also use an advanced version of the *Exactly!* Challenge. Here, you don't recap the words but the emotions, using a simple but powerful method called affect labeling. The idea: say what emotions it sounds like the other person is feeling, perhaps using the phrase "It sounds like . . ."

Annette: How *dare* you come in here and tell my staff how to spend its budget. I can't believe you sometimes! This is so typical; you are *always* trying to undermine me. Any requests for budget cuts need my approval first, or there'll be hell to pay!

Bob: It sounds like you're angry and frustrated; you feel concerned that I've hurt your authority now and before. Am I getting that?

Annette: Exactly!

Research suggests that affect labeling can be particularly good at deescalating conflict.[5] I find too it gives a mix of emotional connection and separation, allowing me, the listener, to step to one side and carefully see the fire hose of feeling race by without being knocked over by it. Usually, the speaker is surprised to be so deeply understood; it's that desire for understanding that often prompted the harsh language in the first place. Basic active listening and affect labeling can each elicit an *Exactly!* I invite you to try both methods. One caution: use affect labeling lightly and in a low-key way; it can sound patronizing if you overdo it. But with a deft touch, it can help. Practice in low-stakes situations first to get the hang of it.

Active listening with the *Exactly!* Challenge is not a substitute for negotiation preparation; it's a complement. You tend to listen better when you're prepared for tough talks because preparation lowers your stress level. By the same token, you can use your preparation more effectively when you slow the negotiation down and tune in to what the other's saying. If you know the talks will be tough, I don't recommend just winging it and deploying the *Exactly!* Challenge. If John Kennedy had merely actively listened to Nikita Khrushchev at the Vienna Summit in 1961, it's doubtful Khrushchev would have backed away from classic Soviet-style intimidation tactics.

That said, if you find yourself in a conflict with a Godzilla, you haven't had a chance to prepare, and you can't just get out of the room, the *Exactly!* Challenge can be an emergency tool to help you stabilize the situation, as Annette and Bob, and Marshall Rosenberg's story, illustrate. Beyond emergencies, it's a go-to skill you can deploy in lots of situations.

Tool in Brief

Exactly! **Challenge:** Actively listen or affect label so well that the other says, *"Exactly!"*

Challenges

The **Exactly!** *Challenge.* During a high-stress conflict or a hard moment in a tough negotiation, see what happens if you actively listen to the other so well that the other person says *"Exactly!"* (or words to that effect) two or three times (or more) during the conversation.

The Home Video Version of the **Exactly!** *Challenge.* Practice your skills by watching a villain's monologue in a highly charged drama or a video of an interview with a political, religious, or controversial figure you strongly disagree with. Then, stop the video after thirty seconds and try to accurately recap what the speaker said. (You might want to record yourself doing it.) Then play the clip again to see how accurately you did it, or have a friend rate you.

The **Exactly!** *Challenge Competition.* This one is a lot of fun. Over brunch, take turns with a loved one trading thirty-second stories about something funny, strange, or weird that happened to the storyteller while traveling. After the first tells a story, have the other recap the factual and emotional content so accurately that the storyteller says, *"Exactly!"* (paraphrasing is fine). Then switch roles. Which of the two of you can more accurately actively listen to the other?

The "It Sounds Like You Feel . . ." Challenge. During a somewhat stressful conflict or a moderately difficult moment in a somewhat challenging negotiation, see what happens if, in a low-key way, you affect label by intentionally naming the other's feeling, using the phrase "It sounds like you feel . . ." Do it so well the other person says, *"Exactly!"* (or words to that effect). Try it once or twice during the conversation; more if you find it's helping a lot.

CHAPTER 9

Speak Softly, Solve Strongly

Tool: Reframe

Tool: If We Agree/If We Disagree

Tool: You're Right

Tool: Positive No Sandwich

Use these tools when you . . .
- find your words often inexplicably backfire
- can't convince the other and need a new approach
- fear saying no will damage the relationship.

Use these tools to . . .
- speak powerfully *and* winsomely
- change a mind
- say no in a way that honors the relationship.

There was a time long ago when I would so often put my foot in my mouth that I would shake my head and mutter, "The less I say, the better!" Perhaps you've had a bit of the same problem, too, now and then. It's a particular problem for negotiators. They often make the kind of clueless, blustering, unpersuasive, needlessly offensive statements that can derail even the most promising talks. Scholars of negotiation call these sorts of crippling bargaining gaffes irritators,[1] and they include such classics as these:

"Look, I'm making you a fair offer."

"I'm being quite reasonable; you're the one who has the problem."

"That's ridiculous. We'll walk first."

"Your offer is totally unfair."

"Ah, you're bluffing."

"Yes, but . . ."

Often negotiators speak these sorts of lines out of fear. Most irritators are aggressive, self-serving, insulting statements the anxious speaker *thinks* are persuasive. In a Hollywood blockbuster, they might be—but in real life, statements like these usually backfire like a dying car engine.[2]

A study of skilled and mediocre negotiators found a stark difference: mediocre negotiators *love* to use irritators; skilled negotiators avoid them like the plague. Mediocre negotiators, the study found, use irritators *five times* as often as excellent negotiators do; the excellent avoid irritators like the plague.[3] Salespeople, diplomats, and hostage negotiators all make the same point: most of the time, self-serving, aggressive language backfires. You don't even need to be hostile to trigger others' resentment. For example, psychologists long thought they were helping alcoholics by pressing them to change, warning them they were killing themselves and speaking with authority about the dangers their patients were running. What effect did that have? Studies found that most alcoholics would drink *more* after such treatment because they felt coerced and disrespected.[4]

What, then, do skilled negotiators do instead?

Reframing TALK ✓

They reframe. Reframing means looking for a thoughtful way to convey any idea in a way that keeps the other person's feelings and Interests in mind. It doesn't require mincing, fawning, lying, or apologizing; quite the opposite. Instead, it's a way to be strong and kind, a way to season powerful messages, so they're tasty too. The idea is to say whatever you need to say in a truthful way that also says, "I respect you; I take your reaction seriously."

Let's take the six irritators I've listed above and see how we might reframe them:

Original: "Look, I'm making you a fair offer."

Better: "Help me better understand your concerns about the fairness of the offer."

Original: "I'm being quite reasonable; you're the one who has the problem."

Better: "I know you want to be fair, and so do I, so I did some research, and here are some benchmarks I found that my offer's based on. Let me know what you think."

Original: "That's ridiculous. We'll walk first."

Better: "While we do have an attractive offer elsewhere, we'd love to work with you if we can, so I wonder if we can do substantially better than that first offer?"

Original: "Your offer is totally unfair."

Better: "Since my research says $X is the market rate, I can't agree to that offer. What if we . . . ?"

Original: "Ah, you're bluffing."

Better: "Can you tell me more about that? Do you have any sources on that? How did you come up with that number?"

Original: "Yes, but . . ."

Better: "You're saying . . . I get that. And . . ."

Each reframed statement is *hard on the problem, soft on the other negotiator.* In each utterance, you're intentionally taking care to avoid saying or suggesting the other person is unfair, crazy, or dishonest. Since even a single word can trigger people, choosing words carefully is key.

In the fifth example, "Do you have any sources on that?" is superior to "Do you have any sources on that *claim*?" "Claim" suggests the other person is making something up, which can trigger defensiveness. Ever have someone lose it in conversation, and you can't imagine why? Chances are the other heard a word that triggered them. And no, I don't mean trigger as in trigger warning, I mean speaking a word that instantly brings up bad associations.[*]

---

[*] Bad writing style can be a valuable way to reframe. The passive voice, for example, can help you help another save face. Compare "You should have told us about these delays" with "We should have been

Trigger words are the booby traps in this work, so an excellent negotiator reframes, with particular care to avoid trigger words. Often, just one mischosen word can undermine a thousand others spoken thoughtfully. But the right word, the gracious word, can give the other person the kind of face and space they need to back down. "I know you want to be fair, and so do I, so . . ." signals respect and good faith, and here lets the speaker introduce evidence of fairness (e.g., a buyer's price guide) in a face-saving way. Grace, space, face. Cool, right?

Mothers know the power of gracious words. "Marcia, wait for this nice man to move before you get off the train." Just the words "nice man" can touch a harried commuter's heart; "Marcia, wait for him to move before you get off the train" doesn't.

The secret of secrets is that it's usually wise to validate the other *person*—not necessarily their offer or behavior, which could be awful, but something you can truthfully honor, such as their dignity, their vision, or their hopes. Nothing about reframing with gracious words requires BS; in fact, truth and goodwill are vital ingredients. True, sometimes you may have to assume facts you haven't established yet if the other person doesn't seem fair or nice, but usually, the other person is better than you think, and there's truth in the saying "Speak to the prince and the prince will appear." It invites reciprocation too. You don't have to reframe every utterance; it's most useful when you have a difficult point to make. Nor does reframing mean you must never be blunt; a blunt statement will have more power if people know you usually speak thoughtfully.

Precisely because it can be hard to come up with the right word—the reframed word—in the moment, it's a good idea to prepare to reframe. Fortunately, you already have tools that can help do just that.

I FORESAW IT. As you'll recall, the R of I FORESAW IT is where you plan to build Rapport, anticipate sharp Reactions, and Respond wisely. It's where

---

told about these delays." The latter, passive version leaves unstated (if implied) who did wrong. Similarly, vague terms (like "this," "that," and "it") can help you avoid trigger words. Compare "How did that screwup happen?" with "How did that happen?" And boring, neutral words can help too. Compare "Let's talk about your negligence and the damage it caused during the storm" with "Let's talk about responsibility for the storm damage." Direct, explicit, plain talk can be vital at times, but because it can trigger, it's very helpful to know how to be subtle too.

you can prepare to Respond in ways that are hard on the problem, soft on the other. So, suppose you expect the other party to drive a hard bargain or bluff or speak harshly. In that case, you can plan to reframe your responses: "If they repeatedly try to lowball me, it will be tempting to say I'm making them a fair offer, but instead, I might say something like this: 'Since my research says $X is the market rate, I can't agree to that offer. What if we . . . ?'" Experiment with a couple of ways to say something, asking yourself, "How does that sound?" In doing so, you're emulating great public speakers, debaters, trial lawyers, ministers, and diplomats, all of whom emphasize the critical role of rehearsal.

Roleplay. You can ask your teammate to roleplay with you by throwing blunt demands and other in-your-face tactics at you to intentionally make you sweat and practice reframing under pressure, then getting feedback: "How did that sound?" Or you can rehearse by yourself, visualizing hard tactics coming at you and practicing reframed responses.

Buy time in real time by taking the *Exactly!* Challenge—or taking a break. In the thick of it, you can also buy time to get centered by using the *Exactly!* Challenge. If necessary, take a break to get your head together and craft a reframed response.

I often rehearse reframing my words for upcoming encounters with challenging counterparts, and it helps me feel calmer and more confident. True, overdone, one can sound canned. The idea isn't to memorize a speech but rather to get a feel for speaking thoughtfully and truthfully and to test word choices. Like a well-rehearsed jazz improviser, I find rehearsing lets me feel freer to safely be in the moment and express winsomely what's in my heart because I'm ready. I'm more relaxed because I've got a reason to know I won't likely put my foot in my mouth.

So, what do practices like this look like?

Consider the case of Stan and the explosive house sitter. One season, Stan's beloved elderly aunt Martha had a house sitter named Donna. Donna was a help 95 percent of the time, but 5 percent of the time, she was prone to inexplicable fits of anger. Asking her to leave was a possibility, but a serious search revealed Martha had no other choices and badly needed Donna for a few months more. On three separate occasions, Stan got warnings Donna was so inexplicably angry it created serious tension for the family or the neighbors. Once, a neighbor called the police on Donna. Everyone who knew Donna thought she was unreachable. What to do?

Each time Donna blew up over some issue, Stan carefully roleplayed alone the conversation he'd have with her, anticipating her toughest Reactions and carefully trying out reframed Responses. Only then would he talk with her. Each time they spoke, he began by practicing the *Exactly!* Challenge. Then he'd gently raise concerns with reframed words that were hard on the problem, soft on Donna, always seeking language to help her save face *even as he clearly signaled they needed to change things.*

That was the approach Stan took when a neighbor named Shelly informed him Donna had gotten into a nasty argument with her. When Shelly had allowed her dog to relieve himself on Martha's lawn, Donna had put a harsh note on Shelly's door, "KEEP YOUR @#$#@$ DOG OFF THE PROPERTY!," prompting the argument. Later, Donna had even gone onto Shelly's property and looked in her windows, attempting to escalate. Soon, Stan got a call from the police about Donna. After hanging up, Stan took a breath and roleplayed talking with Donna using reframed words. Then he called her.

For the first fifteen minutes, he just listened as Donna shouted her side of the story. The *Exactly!* Challenge let Stan give Donna a sense of validation, calming her down some. And Stan learned some things. Shelly *had* been casual about letting her dog wander onto Martha's property. So, Stan could truthfully validate Donna's desire to defend Martha. That further calmed Donna down: here was someone who understood her good motives. And then, gently, as he'd rehearsed, he talked about their shared need as one teammate to another teammate, the need to help Martha stay in harmony with the neighbors. I highlight in *italics* the language he used, as he'd planned:

"Donna, I really honor your desire to protect Martha's lawn. I appreciate your vigilance and your care. And I know as much as Martha cares about the lawn, she cares far more about *handling problems with neighbors in neighborly ways. I know she and you and I don't want the police involved, don't want animosity, don't want to inadvertently scare anyone looking into their windows. I wonder what we can do to avoid friction with them?"*

Put this way, Donna felt ennobled, understood, and safe in the conversation. She began volunteering solutions. "I could avoid talking with Shelly and refer problems to you instead!" That one realization on Donna's part was quite out of character—and golden. Donna promised to do just as she'd suggested. The call ended happily. They never had an issue with the neighbors again.

Now, Stan freely admitted it is *not* good to keep working with someone prone to such reactions. So he regularly checked himself: "Am I helping us manage during this hard season, or am I enabling?" Overall, though, Donna's work was a help to Martha. And when their season together ended, everyone breathed a sigh of relief. But without roleplaying and reframing, he would have either let Donna continue to create trouble, or he would have triggered Donna and escalated crises; with them, he was able to deescalate and draw out the goodness she brought.

But isn't the hard part finding the right word in the moment? Prepared or not, we can all be at a loss for words when we're angry, confused, distressed, surprised: the very feelings we often face in adversity. What then? Fortunately, you already have a tool that can help—in fact, you have two.

Three Little Words. If you go back and review the six sample irritators and their reframed versions, you'll notice something odd: almost every reframed statement relies on Interests, Facts, or Options to express the same idea. For example:

"I'm being quite reasonable; you're the one who has the problem."

Better: "I know you want to be fair, and so do I, so I did some research, and here are some benchmarks I found that my offer's based on. Let me know what you think."

In the better version, you're talking about Interests and Facts instead of just opinions. One more:

"You're offer is totally unfair."

Better: "Since my research says $X is the market rate, I can't agree to that offer. What if we . . . ?"

In the better version, you're talking about Facts and Options.

If you review Stan's words, they rely on the Three Little Words too. So, when you're in an intense negotiation and don't know what to say, you usually can say something effectively if you focus on talking about Interests, Facts, Options.

Exactly! Challenge. Recall another sample irritator:

> **Original:** "Yes, but . . ."
>
> **Better:** "You're saying . . . I get that. And . . ."

Here, in the better version, you're slowing things down, paraphrasing first, affirming that you understand (if not agreeing), then adding something more without directly contradicting—an approach that lets you be hard on the problem, soft on the person. Stan used the *Exactly!* Challenge too.

But what if you can't even remember a two- or three-word tool in the heat of the moment? Then remember just one:

Breathe. When you're flooded and can't even think, do what hostage negotiators do: slow down and breathe in. Research suggests what their experience shows: simply pausing and breathing for a few seconds calms the reptile brain, the fear-driven reactivity that irritators spring from, and makes reframing easier.[5]

Reframing is just one of several ways to use words powerfully and gently, to speak softly, solve strongly. Another is a simple way to change someone's mind when you're dealing with a Godzilla figure who seems unmovable.

If We Agree/If We Disagree 👍 👎

One morning, a student of mine named Keshon rolled out of bed and decided this was the day to fulfill a dream he'd long had. The dream: to be a guest on a live national radio and cable TV show, hosted by a celebrity shock jock I'll call Mack Jackson. Keshon didn't just want to be one of the many callers Mack often talked to; he wanted to come into the studio and be a guest. So Keshon called the show. A screener answered, and Keshon told him he could do over twenty imitations of sports celebrities and wanted to talk to Mack. "OK, let's hear one," the screener said, so Keshon did his impression of LeBron James.

(I've heard Keshon's impression. He's *good*.) The screener said, "Wow! Hold for Mack." After learning from the screener that Mack didn't have any celebrities on that day, Keshon spent his time on hold getting ready to deploy a tool we'd worked on in our negotiation course.

When Mack picked up, Keshon did his LeBron impression. Mack liked it, asked for more, and so Keshon did his routine for several minutes. Then, as Keshon later reported, Mack said, "OK, those were great. Thanks for calling. Bye." Keshon, eager to fulfill his dream, made his pitch to come on as a guest: "Hey, Mack, I'm better in person, and I think your listeners would wait a half hour for me to get to your studio." Mack wasn't enthusiastic about the idea. "Not sure about that, kid. I think we're done." But then Keshon deployed the tool, and moments later, Mack invited him onto the show. Thirty minutes later, Keshon was doing his bit for Mack on live national TV. Keshon hadn't even had time to shave or change clothes. It went so well that Keshon also won an invitation to appear on Mack's other cable TV show, *Strangetoon*. Keshon felt like a champion. How do you do that? How do you wake up and minutes later get yourself on national TV? The answer: Keshon used If We Agree/If We Disagree.

What It Is and How It Works

If We Agree/If We Disagree is a persuasion tool. To use it, you show the other person how agreeing with you will serve their Interests and how disagreeing will hurt their Interests.

One reason If We Agree/If We Disagree works is because it helps you speak the other's language; with it, you are talking directly to both the other's hopes and worries, showing how your idea is the solution. Another: studies show that some people are most persuaded by opportunity—by focusing on the upside—while others are most influenced by fear—by concentrating on avoiding the downside.[6] If We Agree/If We Disagree allows you to simultaneously speak to each temperament, to persuade the eager and the cautious alike. And since many of us are a mix, If We Agree/If We Disagree can speak to both sides of us.

How to Deploy It

Here are the basic steps to creating an If We Agree/If We Disagree statement:

1. List the other's Interests.
2. Learn some Facts and develop attractive Options.
3. List the other's worries—their worst Alternatives to a negotiated agreement that ill-serve their Interests.
4. Using this material, create two lists:
   a. Good things the other will get if the other agrees to your proposal; that is, well-served Interests the other will enjoy if the other says yes
   b. Worrisome things that may happen if the other won't agree that will hurt the other's Interests

So, for example, here's what Keshon jotted down as he waited for Mack:

Mack's Interests: ratings, appeal to sports fans, make people laugh, fun, good radio

Facts: Mack has no celebrities on today. (Keshon asked the call screener. Nice research, Keshon.)

Mack's worries: lame show; people tuning out and shifting to sports talk radio

If I Do Come on the Show, Mack Gets

+Ratings
+To keep sports fans interested
+Profit
+Fun
+Filled time
+Proven, ready talent

If I Do Not Come on the Show, Mack

~Needs to fill the time

~Upsets listeners

~May lose ratings to sports talk radio

Then you deploy If We Agree/If We Disagree by using it in a sentence or two, working it into the conversation when the other party expresses resistance.

With this protocol in mind, consider the conversation Keshon reported he had with Mack and see if you can spot how he turned his jottings into a powerful and persuasive statement:

> **Mack:** OK, nice work. Glad you called. Adios.
>
> **Keshon:** Hey, Mack, I'm better in person, and I think your listeners would wait a half hour for me to get to your studio.
>
> **Mack:** Not sure about that, kid. I think we're done.
>
> **Keshon:** I am nearby, *and you wouldn't want to disappoint your listeners. I know you don't have any famous guests coming on this morning and you need some. I can give you all the celebrities you need right now.*
>
> **Mack:** Are you going to do the same impressions?
>
> **Keshon:** I have different ones that are even better. Look, I love your show. I can be there in a few minutes, you can keep me on for one segment, and then I'll go. Simple as that.
>
> **Mack:** OK, you're on.

The italicized language is where he deployed the tool.

Notice: Tone matters. You must never sound like you're threatening the other person; you're not. The goal is to speak not as an adversary but as a partner, someone who truthfully sees reasons for hope and concern, reasons the other person may have missed. Keshon didn't speak disrespectfully or tell Mack, "If you don't have me on, then your show is going to be the lamest thing on TV." Instead, to borrow a phrase from the authors of *Getting to Yes,* he brought Mack to his senses, not his knees, by making reasonable, truthful statements, showing Mack the opportunity and the problem, and letting Mack draw his own conclusions.

Convincing a boss. If We Agree/If We Disagree can even persuade a seemingly unpersuadable boss where the stakes could hardly be higher. To see how, consider this story about someone you've probably never heard of before: Theodore Roosevelt . . . Junior. The son of the twenty-sixth president, Ted was a brigadier general for the U.S. Army in World War II, and, by all accounts, he was a brave, admired, and effective leader who performed well during the North Africa campaign. But by 1944, Ted was in hot water with the army. A friend of his had made a serious political blunder, and Ted suffered guilt by association. Frustrated that his superiors had sidelined him and given him a desk to command, Ted longed to be involved in the upcoming D-Day invasion. So, he went to his senior officer, Raymond Oscar "Tubby" Barton, and asked for leave to be in one of the first landing crafts to hit the beach at the start of the invasion.

Barton, a no-nonsense leader, immediately turned him down, and who can blame him? Ted was fifty-six years old and walked with a cane from an earlier combat injury; he was hardly fit for the front lines. Also, Ted was in political hot water, so he had little goodwill to draw on. On top of that, both men knew the first wave of soldiers were likely to face severe casualties. Further, no Allied general in any army in any theater of combat anywhere in the world was on the front lines—and Ted also happened to be the nephew of the sitting president, Franklin D. Roosevelt. If Ted got killed, Barton would face enormous political backlash. Undaunted, Ted asked Barton again a few weeks later and got the same answer.

But then Ted wrote Barton a letter, which prompted Barton to summon him. When they met, Barton said he still thought it was a bad idea to send Ted into battle. But, he continued, he couldn't refuse a letter like the one Ted had written, and so he approved the request.

Barton's decision proved to be a good idea. On June 6, 1944, at Utah Beach at Normandy, Ted arrived in one of the first landing crafts, only to discover the military had botched the Utah Beach landing and the troops were arriving a mile or more downrange from their target. Faced with disarray that jeopardized the landing, Ted got his men to regroup, famously saying, "We'll start the war right here!" His leadership proved so heroic and valuable that for it he was awarded the Congressional Medal of Honor. So, what was in Ted's letter to Barton that turned the tide? See if you can spot how he used If We Agree/If We Disagree in this excerpt, which I've slightly paraphrased for clarity:

> The performance of the first troops who hit the beach may decide whether the D-Day invasion succeeds or fails. Since all the troops are inexperienced, every soldier's performance will be shaped by the actions of the first wave. If the first fail, the rest may fail; if the first fight well, the rest may fight well. Also, each new wave of troops will need accurate, up-to-date information as it lands. Similarly, you will need a clear picture of the situation that you can rely on. I believe I can help deliver all these things by going in with the first assault companies. Also, since I personally know both officers and men of these advance units, I believe it will steady them to know I am with them.

Nothing at all in Ted's letter is disrespectful, false, or threatening; rather, it's businesslike (Ted had been an executive before the war) and, above all, written with a clear sense that the writer has thought carefully about the *reader's* needs and cares about them.

Speaking of which: there's another tool to share here that relies on the power of carefully chosen words. Just two words, in fact. It's a tool that's particularly adept at turning resistance around because it helps you speak in a universal language

Two Magic Words

Years ago, a loved one, Marge, an actress, did a star turn for a regional theater company, and the performance went so well that the producer and director assured her they would want her back for the next season's offering. So, you can imagine her surprise when Marge learned through her agent that they didn't want to see her for an audition for the lead. "They love you, Marge," her agent said, "but they just don't think you're right for the part." To actors, who work in a business known for 95 percent unemployment, even kind and appreciative producers are Godzillas. Winning an audition for a lead role is always very hard, and the loss of this audition was deeply disappointing. What to do? Marge went home and wrote a passionate draft email that went something like this:

> Hi Bob and Sheila!
>
> I was so surprised to learn you don't want to see me for the part of Lee in *Tale of the Allergist's Wife*. I don't understand! I thought you loved my work! I know I can do that part. I really think you're making a serious mistake. What am I missing?
>
> Sincerely,
> Marge

Marge emailed me the draft, and we quickly decided it wasn't a good idea to send it. So, we rewrote it and sent the revised version. Twenty-four hours later, Marge got a call from her agent, telling her the producer and director wanted her to come in for an audition. When they met, they warmly hugged and kissed each other. Then the producer said, "You know, Marge, we didn't think you were right for this part, but we changed our minds after we got your email."

You're Right

Marge relied on a simple tool: two magic words that, correctly understood, can turn things around even when you're dealing with a Godzilla: **"You're right."**

The idea is first to appreciate *why* the other person is saying no. What are their Interests? You've already learned to do this with Three Little Words, ⚡ [Chapter 1], and here with If We Agree/If We Disagree, 👍👎 [Chapter 9]. In Marge's case, the producer and director's legitimate concern was to find someone who fit the part of Lee.

Next, *truthfully* validate the other person's concern. This is not about sucking up; truthfully demonstrating you get the other's need is the secret sauce. It's usually easy to do because even if you think her conclusion—"no"—is a bad choice, the Interests are usually understandable. Recall Jamal, the eleven-year-old we met earlier, ⸙ [Chapter 1], who wanted a cat. After he prepared and his father recited the reasons they couldn't get a cat, Jamal wisely replied, "Dad, you're right: those are good things to be concerned about." Plainly, he got *why* his dad was opposed. That one sentence marked a turning point.

"You're right" are magic words first because, as we've seen, everyone needs to feel validated, and when we give them that validation, we satisfy that need. But we do more. We also honor them, surprise them, and quietly pique their interest and respect: "Huh! I thought I was going to get a lot of resistance, but here is someone who gets and appreciates me." It also enhances your credibility: "Huh! Here's someone who sees the merit of my views. She's surprisingly wise. I wonder what else she thinks." Finally, it shows you're tuned in and invites reciprocation. Jamal probably won a hearing from his father because Jamal achieved all these things in two words.

The last step is to show the other person why your idea satisfies the Interest(s) she's rightly defending. That's what Jamal did, showing how he could solve each concern his father had. Instead of saying "Yes, but . . ." you're in effect saying "Yes, and . . ." You're saying, "You have a legitimate problem, *and* I can solve it for you." So do not just say "You're right," as if the idea is merely to be agreeable. The key thing is to show the other that you get their Interest(s) *and* that your idea serves their Interest(s).

So, what was in the email Marge wrote?

Hi Bob & Sheila!

I understand you don't want me to come in for an audition for the part of Lee in *Tale of the Allergist's Wife* because you don't feel I'm right for the part. You're right! If I was casting for the part of Lee and I thought an actress didn't have the qualities of A, B, and C, I wouldn't want to audition her either. It might interest you to know I recently completed a run playing the part of Petra in *A Little Night Music* at Bristol Riverside Theatre, another top regional theater, a part that, as you may well know better than I, is all about A, B, and C. Since I may have exactly what you're looking for, I wonder if an audition makes sense?

Love,
Marge

A Change of Mindset and Heartset

"You're right" is not a trick—it's a change of mindset and heartset. It quickly shifts you from fighting to harmonizing; from resenting and rebutting to appreciating and addressing the other's need in a way that honors yours too.

But now that you have tools to help say things that win yeses, what can you say to help you more persuasively and caringly say no?

Positive No Sandwich ☺◌☺

What do you do when it feels like you can't say no at all, or when you fear saying no will make you seem mean or uncooperative? The tool I want to share here can help. I call it the Positive No Sandwich. As William Ury notes in his book *The Power of a Positive No,* it's often necessary and right to say no, so you can say yes to things you care more about. But saying no is hard; we fear damaging the relationship in the process. So, Ury recommends an approach that buffers a hard message and ends on a positive note.

Building on his insight, I recommend saying no by crafting a verbal sandwich, like so:

1. Truthfully share the Interests you must protect. ("I must care for my sick mother this weekend.")

2. Firmly explain that because you must care for that Interest, you must decline the other's request. ("So, I won't be able to help you move Saturday.")

3. Signal a willingness to say yes to something else that serves the other's need that doesn't hurt yours. ("But if there are other ways I can help, I'd be glad to do it. For example . . .")

If that recipe sounds familiar, it may be because it echoes Wharton professor Adam Grant's insight we saw earlier. As he found, the most successful people are both generous and self-protective, using much the same recipe to care for others, even as they set wise boundaries.

Notice a secret ingredient is truthfulness. The Positive No Sandwich tool won't work well if you make up excuses: "I have to wash my hair that night, so I can't go with you to the prom." Nor will it work well if the Interest you mention is trivial or easily served: "I have to find a pen I lost, so I can't help you move your desk right now." First, because it's insulting. Also, because the other might well reply, "No problem, have one of mine. Ready now?" Last, it won't work well if you make a fake or vague offer to help in other ways because it can breed ill will: "If there's *anything* I can do to help, just let me know." Saying it that way puts the burden on the other to guess what you can do, which fosters cynicism. Better, offer an example of how you can help: "For example, I can help you before the move with some planning details." Doing that demonstrates you're sincerely willing to care in other ways.

You don't always have to use Positive No Sandwich. Sometimes it's best to simply say, "I'm sorry, but no," especially when you have good reason to disengage or when you can't truthfully offer to help in other ways. But in many cases with colleagues, family, or friends, the Positive No Sandwich tool gives you a third choice between no and yes that helps you take care of yourself (and others) and show you also care for the one you must turn down.

But Aren't Carefully Chosen Words Insincere?

The tools here, 💬✓, 👍👎 , 🐎🐎 , ☺🚫☺ , illustrate the power of a few well-chosen words to turn away from dangerous rocks and toward clear water. But couldn't you argue that's bad?

In some cultures, like America's, people so value plain speech that thoughtful words can sometimes seem too artful, too crafty, and, frankly, just dishonest: "Cut the BS and just say it straight!" If you sense the other person may react that way, you'll need to adapt the tool to use fewer, simpler words. Still, even in low-context cultures like America's, where subtlety and nuance are harder to take, the tools here can and do work. That's because none of them are about being flowery or dishonest; they're about choosing words that are respectful, truthful, and powerful. Put another way, they're about saying what you mean to say in a way the other will receive it. And as I've seen working around the world, people tend to appreciate those qualities everywhere, even in my famously blunt native land of New York City.

Tools in Brief

Reframe: Say it in a way that's hard on the problem, soft on the person.

If We Agree/If We Disagree: Show how yes is good for your counterpart, no is bad.

You're Right: Affirm the other is right to care about Interests, prompting a no, then show how yes can serve the Interests well.

Positive No Sandwich: Say no by first truthfully sharing your Interest(s), then declining because of your Interest(s), then inviting a yes that serves the other's Interest(s) and yours.

Challenges

The Reframing Challenge. See what happens if, the next time you're in a heated conversation, you intentionally pause and use gracious words that are hard on the problem, soft on the person—words that intentionally help the other find grace, space, and face. Who knows? Maybe I'll see you in Norway receiving a Nobel Peace Prize. Please remember me in your speech.

The If We Agree/If We Disagree Challenge. The next time you need to persuade someone who seems stuck on a position and you think you're making an attractive offer, see what happens if, instead of saying, "I'm making an attractive offer," you intentionally plan and deploy an If We Agree/If We Disagree statement during the conversation.

The You're Right Visualization Challenge. This week, listen to two people arguing. Imagine being the one you agree with and replay the argument in your head, this time picturing yourself responding to the other with the words "You're right." See if you can get her Interests and articulate reasons why the things your character is asking for serves those Interests.

The Saying No Kindly Challenge. If you find you must decline a request for the sake of a concern you really must favor and you don't see a creative way to serve both sides' needs, see what happens if you say no kindly by using Positive No Sandwich.

CHAPTER 10

Correct a Boss with a Four-Letter Word

👤

THE TOOL: APSO

Use this tool when you . . .
- think your boss is making a serious mistake
- are afraid to speak up
- don't know how to correct without disrespecting
- see no one else can speak up and time is short.

Use this tool to . . .
- correct your boss safely, effectively, respectfully
- honor your boss's authority.

On December 28, 1978, United Airlines Flight 173 left Denver's Stapleton International Airport bound for Portland, Oregon. Flying conditions were good that day, and the captain, Malburn "Buddy" McBroom, was one of the airline's most experienced pilots. The flight was uneventful until the plane reached Portland airspace, when a landing gear problem arose, requiring the plane to circle while the crew tried to fix it. As they worked, the copilot, Rod Beebe, and the flight engineer, Forrest "Frosty" Mendenhall, became aware the plane was running low on fuel. "How much fuel we got now?" Beebe said. "4,000 pounds!" said Mendenhall. But McBroom, understandably focusing on the landing gear, didn't hear them. A few minutes later, Beebe said, "We got about three [thousand pounds] on fuel and that's it." McBroom replied, "OK, on the touchdown, if the gear [collapses] . . ." and continued to talk about the landing gear problem. Minutes passed. Then, as McBroom was about to begin his decent, one of the other crew members said, "I think you just lost [engine] number four, Buddy." No reply. Moments later, Beebe repeated, "We're going to lose an engine, Buddy." For the first time, McBroom responded: "Why?"[1] But by then it was too late; seconds later, the engine ran out of fuel, and then, a minute or two later, another engine did too. Moments later, the plane crashed, killing ten, including Mendenhall, one flight attendant, and eight passengers. Captain McBroom was seriously injured, resigned soon after, and suffered physically and emotionally for the rest of his life.[2] The investigation presented the National Transportation Safety Board with a mystery: How could a plane led by a captain with 27,000 hours of flight experience *run out of gas?*

What the NTSB discovered was so striking that it helped lead to one of the most profound changes in commercial aviation history. The crash wasn't due to mechanical failure or incompetence. It was due to fear, deference, and powerlessness.

In aviation, airplane crews long treated captains as revered figures, the lords of their domains. Their status was reminiscent of the awe people long felt for aviation hero Charles Lindbergh, the "Lone Eagle." On the flight deck, the captain was king; airline culture dictated that the captain was in charge and other crew members were afraid to challenge him even if he was making a serious mistake. In an incident similar to Flight 173, a copilot who raised concerns about dwindling fuel was mocked by the pilot, who told a joke to the flight engineer at the copilot's expense. Many died on that flight too. Researchers discovered the deference problem was particularly serious on board planes from countries like South Korea and Venezuela, where the cultures especially prized deference to authority. Cockpit voice recorder transcripts from a number of crashes revealed that often the copilot was aware of a problem the captain had missed, but didn't know how to communicate it. Often, the copilot would "hint and hope"—say something about the problem as if to himself, like, "Huh! Fuel gauge is low. Sure hope we make it." Or the copilot would speak in such a roundabout way that it veiled the urgency, like "Do you think maybe we should say something about the fuel situation to air traffic control?"

Perhaps you've faced a similar dilemma. You see your boss doing something wrong, maybe something disastrous, but you're afraid that if you say something, you'll offend your boss, get chewed out, and perhaps even lose your job. At times like that, it's easy to say nothing, say little, or say something so awkwardly or indirectly that it doesn't deal with the danger. Somehow, you need a way to show respect *and* urgent concern: to be hard on the problem, soft on the boss. And you need it fast.

Put another way, you need to *negotiate*—to "talk formally with the aim of reaching agreement," as dictionaries put it—precisely because you need a yes, and you can't give an order. While we usually think negotiation means talking about material exchange—"I'll give you a frying pan if you'll give me three watermelons"—it encompasses much more than that. Most hostage negotiation, for example, has little to do with material demands (though there are some) and much to do with meeting psychological needs. Indeed, it might be argued that we create more value in negotiation the more we work up Maslow's famous hierarchy of needs pyramid and address psychological needs;[3] there, Maslow holds that esteem, respect, status, and recognition are some of the highest-ranking needs people have. So, what you can offer your boss is what he most needs—esteem, respect, status, *and* help; that is, both acknowledgment of his authority *and* critical assistance. All you need is regard and safety. The tool here can help you do that negotiation and safely win that critical yes.

Helping copilots talk up to pilots was the challenge the aviation industry faced, and they solved it—so well, in fact, that deaths per million passenger miles flown fell from 8.0 in 1978 to 0.8 in 2008, a 90 percent decline. Comedians in the '70s and '80s made their livings telling airline jokes because people were afraid to fly; by 2008, comedians needed new material. Aviation became one of the safest forms of transportation, a striking achievement given the forces at play. And a key to their success is in a script that airlines taught their pilots and crews to use, a script that forms the basis for a four-letter word you can use in an emergency to save your boss, your firm, and your job.

———

Crew Resource Management and APSO 👥

Drawing on an innovation from NASA, airlines began to introduce something called Crew Resource Management (CRM), a set of principles, tools, and processes for helping crews work together as a team. United was the first, adopting it in 1981, three years after the Flight 173 disaster. At first, veteran pilots resented the change, fearing it would undermine their authority. To their surprise, they eventually found CRM actually enhanced their authority in some ways. It certainly improved their situational awareness, and crew morale. Meanwhile, copilots and flight attendants found CRM let them *safely* talk up to their captains; it gave them a good way to show respect *and* express serious concern under stress. One of the key features of CRM was a simple protocol for talking up to pilots in respectful, clear ways. In essence, it taught crews to say four things:

> **Attention:** Clearly address the captain so he or she knows you want attention: "Hey, Buddy" or "Hey, Captain."
>
> **Problem:** Directly say what you're worried about, including facts and emotions: "We've only got five minutes of fuel left, and I'm worried we may not make it to Portland Airport."
>
> **Solution:** Offer a clear idea about how to solve the problem. "Let's descend immediately, alert the tower, and ready for a possible landing gear collapse" or "I think we should divert to Preston two miles away."
>
> **OK?:** Ask for buy-in or consideration so it's clear the captain has a decision to make: "Does that sound good to you, Captain?" or "What do you think?"

I've translated the protocol into a simple acronym, **APSO**: Attention, Problem, Solution, OK?

Each part of APSO plays an important role. To see how, let's see why Flight 173 suffered without it. (I don't mean to attack experienced pilots under extreme stress; I know I would have failed miserably were I in their place. The goal is learning, not judgment.)

The first mistake the copilot on Flight 173 made was failing to clearly, directly get the captain's **A**ttention. Bosses are busy, especially in stressful situations, and Captain McBroom was rightly concerned about the landing gear. So, a sidebar conversation between the copilot and the engineer about fuel was mere static to McBroom, even though the copilot thought he was speaking urgently, loudly, and clearly about the problem. Later, the copilot did directly tell McBroom, "We got about three [thousand pounds] on fuel and that's it." But he didn't first fully engage the distressed captain's attention, so even that message sounded like a distraction.

The second mistake the copilot made was to not clearly tell the captain the **P**roblem. Stating the specific problem in a clear, succinct way that also conveys its seriousness gives a leader a better chance to deal with it. True, the copilot eventually said, "We got about three on fuel and that's it." But when McBroom didn't respond, it was clear McBroom wasn't getting the problem. The copilot needed to make it clear this was a serious, urgent issue and that he was concerned. He didn't. Notice the focus should be on the problem, not the leader's failings or incompetence. There's no need to say "You're going to get us killed!" or "You are making a big mistake." CRM expressly trains crews to avoid such language because it creates defensiveness. In fact, it actually offers specific phrases team members might want to use to challenge someone without disrespecting them, like "I'm uncomfortable with . . ." and "I'm concerned about."

The copilot also gave no **S**olution to the captain; he merely burdened him further. Offering a solution actually helps—it gives the boss a choice and so makes it easier to lead. And it makes you a fuller part of the team.

Last, since a busy leader may not realize a decision is required, it's important to punctuate the message with a clear sign there's a choice to be made. It also demonstrates deference. Thus, **O**K? As one expert on aviation CRM emphasizes, using only part of APSO and omitting the OK? makes it less effective.

Here's an example of how you can use APSO in a business setting. Imagine you've spotted a serious issue with a loan payment your company must soon make, but your boss waved it off last week, saying it's no big deal and she has more important things to worry about. Things have only gotten worse. So you go to see her and say this:

> **Attention:** LaQuisha.
>
> **Problem:** As you may remember, one of our banks requires us to submit a financial report by Monday at 9:00 A.M.—forty-eight hours from now. We're facing a seventy-two-hour cash flow crisis, and I'm concerned that if we file now, the bank may find us in default, which could trigger a house-of-cards chain of defaults under other loans.
>
> **Solution:** I suggest we ask our contact at the bank now to give us a onetime seventy-two-hour waiver based on our prior perfect reporting record and our strong financial ratings.
>
> **OK:** What do you think?

Notice APSO doesn't just tell you what to say—it channels you away from things you *shouldn't* say. Every syllable is focused on solving the problem, not criticizing the boss, thus making the communication safer for both of you.

APSO at Work in Many High-Stress Settings

The power of CRM in general and APSO in particular has been so impressive that other fields have begun to embrace them. Even when the leader doesn't know about CRM, a tool like APSO can equip subordinates to safely and effectively talk up. For example, emergency medical technicians now train to use CRM, including the protocol that APSO distills. Similarly, the hospital industry has started to embrace CRM and APSO too. In their book *Beyond the Checklist: What Else Health Care Can Learn from Aviation Teamwork and Safety,* Suzanne Gordon, Patrick Mendenhall, and Bonnie Blaire O'Connor discuss how it has helped solve the deference problem that besets nurses with doctors much the way it besets flight crews with captains. Without it, they note, nurses rightly fear a doctor may call them insubordinate and presumptuous if they flag a problem with his approach. Worse, without CRM, doctors and nurses can often act as strangers or even competitors, unsure how to negotiate conflicts over care. Yet hospitals that have embraced CRM (including training nurses how to respectfully talk up to resolve disagreements) have seen dramatic improvements in patient care and doctor-nurse collaboration.[4]

I now train my students to use APSO in normal business life, and they quickly grasp it, finding it helps them feel comfortable talking up to a boss because it equips them to negotiate conflict constructively, even in an emergency. For example, consider what you might do in a situation I routinely throw them into: Imagine you and a colleague are running late driving to a crucial out-of-state business meeting that starts in forty-five minutes. You are on a highway. The boss is driving. You know you are about thirty-five miles away from your destination. The GPS and Wi-Fi died a few miles ago, you can't get a signal, and your phone battery has died. As you near a gas station, you notice your boss, an intense and self-confident leader, is in the right lane getting ready to turn onto a major highway about two minutes ahead, with an exit sign marked "Interstate 495." You have a stab of anxiety, pretty clearly recalling the event is in the other direction, and that the host wrote "take Interstate 270" on the invitation. There are few exits on the interstate. Minutes count. True, you have a Common Interest of getting to the meeting on time, but at the moment your boss has a very different position, his choice of routes, and often a driver is reluctant to change course. How many married couples get into arguments over this very sort of conflict? Here, given the power imbalance, it seems the only safe bet is to say nothing. But saying nothing could lead to disaster too. So, what would you say?

You might be tempted to hint and hope, saying, "Hmmm, I wonder if we're on the right track . . ." Or you might sit in silence. Alternatively, you might be tempted to blurt out, "What are you doing? You're going the wrong way! We'll never get there!" But APSO gives you another choice, like this: "Sheila, I'm concerned we're about to get on the wrong route. I think I remember we're supposed to take I-270, and if we take the wrong turn we'll miss the meeting. We can't get GPS or Wi-Fi, so I suggest we stop for one minute at this gas station and ask for directions. What do you think?"

At the foundation of APSO and CRM is the idea that a team can succeed where a single leader might fail *if* the team feels safe contributing fully, and the leader feels safe that his or her authority will be honored. APSO and CRM make that teamwork possible. The power of that kind of teamwork in aviation became evident a few years after the Flight 173 disaster.

On July 19, 1989, another United Airlines plane, Flight 232, left Denver's Stapleton International Airport bound for Chicago with 296 souls on board. Shortly after takeoff, the plane suddenly suffered a catastrophic loss of most of its flight controls, an event so extraordinary that none of the pilots on board had ever seen anything like it. The crisis was a bit like what you'd face if you suddenly lost steering and brakes while driving a bus down a mountain road. Normally, such a loss in flight would have meant certain disaster, killing everyone on board. But somehow, the pilot and crew managed to guide the seemingly uncontrollable plane to Sioux Gateway Airport in Sioux City, Iowa. Though it crashed there, killing 112, another 184 people on board survived, an extraordinary achievement. The captain, Al Haynes, credited CRM with saving his life and many others that day:

> Up until 1980, we kind of worked on the concept that the captain was THE authority on the aircraft. What he said, goes. And we lost a few airplanes because of that. Sometimes the captain isn't as smart as we thought he was. And we would listen to him, and do what he said, and we wouldn't know what he's talking about. And we had 103 years of flying experience there in the cockpit [of Flight 232], trying to get that airplane on the ground, not one minute of which we had actually practiced [under those failure conditions], any one of us. So why would I know more about getting that airplane on the ground under those conditions than the other three? So, if I hadn't used [CRM], if we had not let everybody put their input in, it's a cinch we wouldn't have made it.[5]

By the way, in extreme emergencies, CRM teaches crews to basically shout about the danger even when they don't know what to do. But even then, CRM emphasizes the critical importance of respect, teaching crews to avoid saying things that will trigger the captain's defensiveness like "This is stupid!" and

"You're going to get us killed!" and instead using a phrase like "Red flag!" or "Wait—I have a problem with what we're doing!" That's right, even in a life-and-death situation, reframing is vital.

No script always works, and you *may* need to adapt APSO to the culture you're in. Still, CRM and the ideas in APSO have worked effectively in airlines and hospitals around the world, so it has a good chance of working for you.

Tool in Brief

APSO: Attention, Problem, Solution, OK?

Challenges

The APSO Challenge. The next time a senior colleague (or even a loved one) is about to do something you think is going to get them in moderate trouble, use APSO to respectfully, clearly call their attention to the problem and help them solve it.

The APSO Card. Put a tiny sticker on a car dashboard, a refrigerator, or a desk with the four words of APSO listed—"Attention, Problem, Solution, OK?"—so you can refer to it in a crisis. Put it in your phone too.

The Teach APSO Challenge. Share the APSO acronym with a colleague so he or she knows what you're doing the next time you use APSO, making it clear you'll use it as a way to show respect and help, sharing, if you like, how effective it's been in aviation, for EMTs, and in hospital culture. Invite your colleague to use it if they see you making a mistake.

CHAPTER 11

Use the Hostility-to-Harmony Hacks

Tool: Golden Minute

Tool: Common Interests Hack

Use these tools when you . . .

- anticipate a bad meeting with lots of interruptions
- or meanness
- find hostility is thwarting group collaboration
- find in-fighting, anger, jealousy, self-interest rule
- find your team is acting like a herd of chickens
- lack authority to tell others what to do.

Use these tools to . . .

- help a troubled group work together effectively
- start a constructive discussion.

What was it about the Allies' supreme commander in World War II that most worried the Nazis? If you had to guess, you might reasonably list things like strategic vision, boldness, poise in battle, personal charisma, cunning, and so on. But consider a secret Luftwaffe report about Dwight Eisenhower, the man who became head of joint forces, British and American. The report warned that Eisenhower's "strongest point is said to be an ability to adjust personalities to one another and smooth over opposing viewpoints."[1] Put another way, the thing that most worried the Germans about Eisenhower was that he could run a good meeting and help people in conflict to get along with each other. *Huh?*

No one ever carved a statue of a general sitting at the head of a conference table. Or a general getting two angry fellow officers to soften and shake hands. Yet the Nazis feared, more than anything about him, Eisenhower's ability to foster harmony. Let that sink in for a moment. Harmony.

Most of us think military leaders are all about barking orders. Yet virtually every military officer I've met has told me the same thing: military leadership is more about consensus building and negotiation. To the point: the U.S. Military Academy at West Point has an entire Program on Negotiation. Military leaders—and leaders generally—must negotiate. Why? Because contrary to popular belief, to be in leadership usually means being in a position of stress, adversity, and, yes, powerlessness. When you can't simply tell people what to do, you need to get them to agree.

One morning in January 1953, outgoing President Harry Truman was sitting in the Oval Office with a young aide named Richard Neustadt. Truman was in a reflective mood that day and chatted with Neustadt about the fact that Eisenhower would replace Truman as president in just a few days. Truman laughed at the thought. "He'll sit here," Truman said, "and say, 'Do this! Do that!' *And nothing will happen!* Poor Ike—it won't be a bit like the Army."[2] Neustadt was scandalized at the idea and respectfully pushed back, reminding Truman that as president, he was the most powerful man in the world, a man who could drop a nuclear bomb or start a war in Korea. But Truman wouldn't have it. "I sit here all day trying to persuade people to do things they ought to have sense enough to do without my having to persuade them. That," said Truman, "is all the powers of the President amounts to."

Neustadt could not believe it. So, after the administration ended, he became a political scientist at Columbia University and researched the point for several years. Finally, in 1960, he published his conclusion in what became a classic text in the field, *Presidential Power: The Politics of Leadership.* There, Neustadt concluded that Truman was right: in almost no case Neustadt could find did the president of the United States ever successfully just *announce* a decision and have it carried out. To be president, Neustadt found, required a great deal of negotiation and consensus building. Or, to put it another way, harmonizing. Like, you know, General Eisenhower did.[3]

If you've ever found yourself leading a group, you may have some idea what

Truman is talking about. You've probably found you have a *lot* of responsibility and not nearly enough authority, a problem we began to grapple with when we looked at Three Little Words, ❧ [Chapter 1]. You've discovered you can't just order people to do things the way you want and expect them to do it. You're not alone. *Most* leaders face the same conundrum. A classic study published in *Harvard Business Review* found managers regularly negotiate with colleagues and subordinates, as well as outsiders, and other studies have reached similar conclusions.[4] As Neustadt found, when leaders have to resort to commanding people, they are showing weakness.

Even if you are not a leader, you may have found that a group you're part of can easily fall into conflict, endangering whatever it is you hope to do together. At times like these, you may have thought to yourself, If only the leader would make everyone do their job. Secret: the leader may have tried and, like Truman, found it's easy to say but hard to do. What then? Ironically, as we'll see, *you* may have the ability to help turn discord into harmony, even with no authority at all.

Or perhaps your group doesn't have a leader; you're a team of equals, or a family grappling with a hard problem, or an informal gathering of parents dealing with a problem at school. Meetings seem interminable, hostile, dull, and the group is acting like a herd of toddlers. You may have thought, Without decisive leadership, this group is going nowhere. Yet a strong authority figure may not be what the group needs.

As we started to see when we looked at Three Little Words, ❧ [Chapter 1], and as Truman, Eisenhower, Neustadt, and *Harvard Business Review* suggest, authority *isn't* the sole key to leadership. Which means that even if you have no formal title whatsoever, here too, you may be able to help increase the harmony. We've already considered how one tool, Three Little Words, can help. But other negotiation tools can help too.

But what if you're not dealing with a group in need of leadership but are simply in a straight negotiation? Rest easy: these new tools are every bit as useful in two-party (and multiparty) talks where you're just a participant. In fact, many of my students have used them primarily that way. And one is so effective in direct talks that alumni rated it one of their very favorite negotiation tools.

So here, I want to introduce to you what I call Hostility-to-Harmony Hacks: two surprisingly simple but powerful ways to help whether you're trying to get a struggling group to work well together or you're trying to get hostile counterpart(s) to work *with* you, not against you.

The Golden Minute

To see how the first tool can help you help a group, consider this question: What *does* effective leadership look like? Often, it's something different from what we usually imagine.

Years ago, a former MBA student of mine I'll call Barry was part of a team that won a $10,000 prize in a national project competition involving twelve teams, including students from Harvard, Stanford, and the University of Texas. What made the difference happened in the first moments of the project. While all the other teams had just launched into the work when they got the assignment, Barry suggested the team take a moment and first agree on some simple discussion rules. Barry had no formal authority over the team, yet he believed that one suggestion, and his offer to help facilitate and help enforce the rules, probably won the day.

Ironically, Eisenhower's approach to leadership was similar to Barry's. When he first arrived at the Supreme Headquarters of the Allied Expeditionary Forces in London, Eisenhower made it a point to meet with everyone and make it clear he was open, honest, and approachable. He also brought a keen awareness, born of experience, that in-fighting could quickly stop a military organization in its tracks. That would be especially true in London, where Ike had to lead *two* armies, British and American, a task so challenging that few joint military campaigns had ever succeeded. Soon Ike discovered the leaders of the two armies didn't like each other. Backbiting and insults were rife among the officers, meetings were filled with posturing, and the two sides elbowed each other for resources. So, Ike soon instituted rules to deal with the conflicts. First, he warned the Americans that if anyone insulted someone in the British military, he'd be demoted and sent back to the States, perhaps even imprisoned. He also announced that at all meetings, everyone would be treated equally and respectfully and that there would be open discussion with no sucking up and no squashing subordinates who voiced a concern. Harmony began to replace hostility. Ike took a similar approach to field conflicts between generals like Patton and Montgomery. While it didn't always work, Ike's way seems to have helped carry the day—just as the Luftwaffe had feared. Here is one way to measure the achievement: no other general had successfully led a major joint campaign since the Duke of Wellington did it in the Napoleonic Wars 130 years earlier. [5]

Ike and Barry relied on something that can influence a group much like a rudder can influence a ship: they instituted discussion rules. Their experience illustrates a little-appreciated but powerful way to help turn the tide in a group by drawing on an insight from best negotiation practice: that civility and listening are keys to better talks. In fact, the thing they relied on is more than a secret for leaders; it's something you can use in any challenging group or one-on-one negotiation, even if you're one participant among equals. All it takes is a willingness at the start to suggest trying it.

Teams, a gathering of negotiators, and many other groups all benefit from that one suggestion. Even amicable groups often suffer from weak listening, fostering confusion, alienation, and low buy-in. ("What *was* that meeting about?" "Who knows. Let's get lunch.") Conflict can make it worse, turning confusion into anger, disengagement into alienation, weak buy-in into hostility. Meetings can become sullen or meaningless affairs where people nod their heads with their arms crossed, then walk out and ignore everything they agreed to. That's especially true if the meeting feels unfair—if some in the room dominate the conversation, others sit silent, and no one is listening when someone tries to speak.

But goodness often follows when people sense a meeting is fair and that everyone will be heard and respected. Studies find that when negotiators or participants feel the *process* is just, they tend to commit to whatever the group agrees to.[6] That may be true even if someone isn't crazy about the substantive results. Did you get that? Universal delight about the outcome may not be necessary if the *process* is satisfying.[7]

But well-led discussion doesn't just foster better engagement and buy-in. It produces better results too, and leaders in many fields are taking notice. For example, top design firms like IDEO insist on discussion rules when a design team begins a project. Similarly, construction companies and developers transformed their dysfunctional, litigation-strewn relationships into excellent ones where projects finished on time, under budget, and with few injuries. They did it by introducing a process called Construction Partnering that began with a set of discussion rules. Similarly remarkable processes that start with discussion ground rules have saved dysfunctional contract relationships, saving billions of dollars.[8]

What follows, then, can help you help a group a lot. Just be sure you don't usurp a leader's authority. When in doubt, get permission from your leader first. That said, you can give a group much of the power that a good process offers by using a tool I call the Golden Minute.

The Basics. The Golden Minute is the sixty seconds it takes at the start of a meeting to suggest a few simple discussion rules. Modeled after the discussion rules I trained to use as a mediator, these rules can seem trivial but can make a big difference. In brief, you say something like the following:

1. Before we start, let me suggest we take sixty seconds to talk about *how* we'll talk, so we're constructive and use our time well. OK?
2. Can we agree we'll listen to each other, won't interrupt each other, and won't multitask?
3. [*If there's tension*] Can we agree we'll speak to each other with respect?
4. [*If you wish*] Can someone take notes and occasionally summarize?
5. Can we all politely help each other keep these rules?

Because the Golden Minute is only sixty seconds long, there's a good chance people will be willing to take that time to talk about process, especially if you mention it will save time later. Otherwise, they may tend to say, "Can we just get on with it?" Because you start by inviting agreement on a small suggestion, something that takes sixty seconds, it's pretty easy to get acceptance, which is a small but valuable victory for you; winning a first yes improves the odds you'll get yeses on the other suggestions. Most people are willing to agree to listen to each other, and many are relieved at the suggestion. Committing to not multitask adds further reassurance people will pay attention. That's a big deal too. One study found that if you attend a class and surf the web, you might as well have come to class drunk. Worse, others sitting next to you might as well have joined you at the bar; their ability to listen to the class plummets about as much.[9]

No Interruption. The No Interruption rule can be a game-changer, especially when, later, someone says something provocative or challenging. Years ago, I mediated a dispute between two brothers and their wives. The two couples had long delighted in each other until the previous Thanksgiving, when one brother thought the other was coming on to his wife. Fireworks and slammed doors followed. For the next several months, the two couples avoided each other until one day, the two wives, each pregnant, ran into each other on the sidewalk, argued, and wound up shoving and wrestling. Police came, the judge referred the couples to my mediation center, and here we were. After we'd set some discussion ground rules, each spoke in turn until one wife began to speak tearfully about how heartbroken she felt that her new son would grow up never knowing his aunt and uncle. "Don't talk about that!" said her husband, trying to silence her. But then I had to remind him he'd agreed to the No Interruption rule, so she continued, and now for the first time, everyone, including her husband, heard her sorrow and pain. Soon after, the other wife began to weep, and when it was her turn, she expressed the same feelings. "Don't talk about that!" said her husband, trying to silence her. But once again, the No Interruption rule was invoked, so everyone heard things no one had known before. A short while later, the two couples were hugging each other. They left arm in arm, and I remained in the room, a little shaken but marveling at what had just happened.

The No Interruption rule is powerful enough that it can even help bring about a heavy-duty agreement in a place that often seems incapable of it: Congress. For example, in a meeting in Senator Susan Collins's office on January 19,

2018, talks among seventeen centrist senators to prevent a government shut-down were growing so fractious that the senators were constantly talking over each other. So, Collins used the Golden Minute: she took a Maasai talking stick she'd received as a gift and announced that only the one holding the stick could speak. Many lawmakers later gave Collins the credit for the breakthrough that emerged over the following two days of intense weekend talks, which led to the passage of a spending bill in the Senate by 81 to 18. Speaking later about the talking stick, Collins said, "It's very helpful in controlling the discussion, because as you can imagine, with that many senators in the room, they all want to talk at once. I know it shocks you to learn that."[10]

The No Interruption rule also prevents a phenomenon I call leapfrogging. There, the listener assumes he understands where the speaker is going, stops listening, misses the point, cuts the speaker off, and then boldly pushes back against the wrong point. Not surprisingly, leapfrogging infuriates the speaker, muddies the waters, intensifies conflict, and invites others to do the same. Sensing the only way to be heard is to shout, everyone starts speaking angrily, and the meeting spirals away. Meanwhile, the interruption can trigger a feeling of disrespect that kills the first speaker's ability to listen to the interrupter's point. For some businesses (and families), constant interruption is part of the culture, and often a source of stress. Some labor-management talks are such shouting matches that even good ideas get lost in the noise of the meeting. Many doctors today interrupt patients from almost the first moment of the visit. [11]

Civility. The Civility rule—speak to each other with respect—is particularly important if there's conflict and ill will in the room. At Allied headquarters, Ike made it a point to institute a Civility rule, precisely because trash talk kills collaboration. A Civility rule adds safety to a setting where people are afraid someone will humiliate them, insult them, or dismiss them. Without it, trash begets trash, often escalating the noise and crippling the listening. That's because even people seemingly indifferent to trash talk often feel the stab and react badly to it.

To the point, you may have wondered why legislators in parliaments and congresses use such super-respectful language when addressing each other: "the right honorable gentleman," "my distinguished colleague," "the honored senator." The reason is because it is so dangerously tempting to call someone you disagree with a horse's ass (or worse). In 1798, a fistfight broke out in one of the first sessions of the U.S. Congress.[12] In 1854, Senator Charles Sumner of Massachusetts called Senator Stephen A. Douglas of Illinois a "noise-some, squat, and nameless animal." Then, Sumner mocked Douglas's ally, Senator Andrew Butler of South Carolina, likening his support of slavery to hiring a prostitute. Soon, Butler's kinsman Congressman Preston Brooks came over to the floor of the old chamber of the Senate with a metal-topped cane and beat Sumner so badly that Sumner had to convalesce for two years and never fully recovered from the beating.[13] Fortunately, physical fights in congresses and parliaments are so rare that when one does happen, it becomes the stuff of TV news and history. Civility rules may be a key reason such incidents are so rare.[14] As hard experience illustrates, you most need a Civility rule when you sense people may not be civil without it.

Godzilla versus Civility. Introducing a Golden Minute, especially one that includes a Civility rule, can also be a helpful response when you face a Godzilla who's trying to intimidate you in a one-on-one negotiation by speaking aggressively, or interrupting, insulting, ignoring, or threatening you, and so forth. If you have reason to anticipate such behavior, you can take the Golden Minute at the start of the talks. After seeking to build Rapport and set a constructive tone, you can segue into it, perhaps like so:

"OK, Hank, before we start, let me take a minute and suggest one other thing. To help us make the best use of time and hear each other, let me suggest we listen to each other without interruption and let's each agree to speak respectfully. I know you want the conversation to be respectful, and I can commit to it myself. Does that sound good to you?"

Even if Hank objects on dubious grounds, saying, "Hey, *I'm* totally respectful; *you're* the one who's insulting and interrupting me!" you can use that: "I'm sorry you felt like I was being disrespectful and interrupting. Since it sounds like neither of us wants that, it should be easy for us both to commit to being respectful and not interrupting going forward. OK?"

Alternatively, if you find yourself getting attacked and didn't deploy the Golden Minute earlier, you can stop the proceedings and introduce it before you go further with the substantive talks. Put another way, you can negotiate *how* to negotiate, in midstream if necessary, perhaps like so:

"OK, Hank, time out. Before we go further, let's figure out how we want this conversation to go. We'll hear each other better and discover more satisfying deal terms if we're actually hearing each other and speaking respectfully. I can commit to that. What do you say? Should we try that?"

Notice you want to be strong and kind as you convey these points. You never want to propose discussion rules in a Golden Minute as if you're cowed and afraid or angry and judgmental. The more detached your affect, the more likely your Godzilla will read the suggestion as a sign of strength. You may want to prepare to say something like this in a roleplay with a friend playing your Godzilla. The Golden Minute is not your only possible response to intimidation tactics, but it can help.

Note-taking and Summarizing. Asking someone else to serve as note-taker and summarizer can help assure the team is tracking. It's hard to absorb a lot of detail from several voices; summarizing gives everyone another chance to hear and crystallize where things stand. Often, that one task is a revelation.

When I was a junior corporate lawyer, I would accompany a renowned senior associate named Bryan to meetings. While everyone else there was talking, Bryan would just sit there, seemingly doing nothing. What does this guy get paid for? I wondered. He doesn't even talk. Then, after about a half hour, Bryan would say, "Let me see if I've got where we are right now. On issue one, we've agreed that we can live with *W*. On issue two, we've agreed we want to do *X*. On issue three, we've decided we need more information, and we haven't tackled issues four, five, six, and seven yet. Am I getting that right?" Silence. Then everyone would nod. Until Bryan had spoken, I (and probably most others) hadn't even realized we had agreed on two issues and had no clear sense of where we were on the others. Bryan's one utterance had likely saved us an hour of needless discussion.

Enforcing the rules. The Golden Minute lets you play a pivotal role as a discussion leader at minimal cost and risk by giving you a tool to win support for discussion rules. But by design, it doesn't require you to formally lead the discussion that follows: to *facilitate* the subsequent talks. That's because good facilitation takes a suite of skills, and while much of this book, in effect, equips you with many of these skills, it would take more than we can cover here to fully do justice to the task.

But there's a problem: If, say, Katy keeps breaking a discussion rule the group has agreed to, what happens? If no one intervenes, Katy's violations can spur others to follow suit until the discussion becomes a loud free-for-all. But if you take sole responsibility for enforcing the rules without the group's prior approval, you may seem like a scold or worse: "Who made you the head of this meeting?" That's the reason to add the question at the end of the Golden Minute, "Can we all politely help each other keep these rules?" That way, you can be one of several who help remind Katy about her promises, easing your burden and recruiting the group's influence. (If you expect or experience fighting over the rules, you may want to nominate someone other than yourself to politely enforce them: "I wonder if someone would care to be the one to help us keep the rules? Perhaps Mohammad?" In extreme cases, you may also want to call for a break and then privately ask another participant to help enforce the rules.)

But there is another Hostility-to-Harmony Hack that can help you turn a battle into a chorus. It's a tool so valuable that over 150 alumni of my course voted it one of the three most popular concepts they learned there.

The Common Interests Hack

Sonja faced a distressing incident at work in a meeting about her department's staffing. The pressure was growing for people to work longer hours or, worse, fire subordinates. Things quickly grew tense and heated; a feeling of scarcity and fear filled the room, moving colleagues to snipe at each other, until everyone became so myopic and blind that it felt as if the lights had gone out. But when Sonja spoke two sentences, it was as if the lights went back on; quickly, her colleagues began to soften their tone, turn back toward the task at hand, and, to her surprise, collaborate. So, what was it Sonja said? While I can't quote her exact words, I can share the gist:

"Look, we're not enemies here—we're on the same side. If we work together, we can handle staffing fairly and save our best people; we'll all be better off that way than if the CEO decides on his own whom to fire." What was the secret to her effectiveness? She appealed to a Common Interest.

A Common Interest is a shared goal you and others can achieve by working together; it's an interest everyone shares that you can all realize by cooperating. Put another way, it's a destination everyone wants to reach that you can get to by collaborating. It's a powerful way to unify people. How powerful?

There is a theory that much of the unity of a group, a tribe, or a nation depends on its ability to identify common goals and common enemies.[15] True, at its worst, a Common Interest can foster group hatred. But, at its best, it can foster an inexplicable ability to achieve the seemingly unachievable. At many of the earliest large human settlements, we find evidence of monuments, walls, and other massive building projects. While they often had a function, their larger purpose seemed to be to unify a group around a shared aspiration or a common threat. And, as the study of prejudice itself demonstrates, you can harness a common goal to help unite people from different groups who otherwise even hate each other.[16]

But focusing on Common Interests can do still more. In November 1960, John Kennedy won the presidency by less than two-tenths of 1 percent of the popular vote,[17] and many suspected he hadn't really won it at all. If you were in his place, what would you say to a divided and skeptical nation in your inaugural address to help the nation unite behind your leadership? Kennedy's answer was to appeal to Common Interests. Here's what he said:

> Now the trumpet summons us again—not as a call to bear arms, though arms we need—not as a call to battle, though embattled we are—but a call to bear the burden of a long twilight struggle, year in and year out, "rejoicing in hope, patient in tribulation"—a struggle against the common enemies of man: tyranny, poverty, disease and war itself. Can we forge against these enemies a grand and global alliance, North and South, East and West, that can assure a more fruitful life for all mankind? Will you join in that historic effort? . . . And so, my fellow Americans: ask not what your country can do for you—ask what you can do

for your country. My fellow citizens of the world: ask not what America will do for you, but what together we can do for the freedom of man.

Kennedy's approval ratings hit 72 percent the week of his inauguration, one of the highest for any elected modern president, and stayed near that number for much of his presidency. After his death, many communities carved words from that portion of the speech into buildings to honor his memory. And fifty years later, cabinet secretaries and senators say that speech helped inspire them to serve in government.[18]

Kennedy wasn't alone. Listen to many of the most influential and memorable speeches of the twentieth and twenty-first centuries, and you'll find leaders appealing to Common Interests to unite a divided people. For example, in his "Finest Hour" speech during the Battle of Britain, Winston Churchill sought to unite his quarrelsome country and an ambivalent America against Hitler. He did it by appealing to Common Interests: "If we can stand up to him . . . the life of the world may move forward into broad, sunlit uplands. But if we fail, the whole world, including the United States, including all that we have known and cared for, will sink into the abyss of a new Dark Age made more sinister, and perhaps more protracted, by the lights of perverted science. . . ."[19] Lyndon Johnson made an appeal similar to Kennedy's in his speech to Congress for the Voting Rights Act of 1965: "These are the enemies: poverty, ignorance, disease. They are the enemies and not our fellow man." Martin Luther King's "I Have a Dream" speech concludes with a Common Interest appeal to the day when "all of God's children, black men, and white men, Jews and Gentiles, Protestants and Catholics, will be able to join hands and sing in the words of the old Negro spiritual: *Free at last! Free at last! Thank God Almighty, we are free at last!*" In 1996, Nelson Mandela gave a speech saying South Africa sought to learn the truth about the past, not for vengeance but so that the whole country, regardless of race, could "move forward together." And in the nineteenth century, we see a similar appeal in Abraham Lincoln's Gettysburg Address, where he ends with a call for his fellow citizens to be devoted to a great shared cause: "that government of the people, by the people, for the people shall not perish from the earth."

Expert negotiators are just as fond of appeals to Common Interests. One study found that excellent negotiators think and talk about Common Interests at least twice as often as mediocre negotiators do.[20] Why? Why do so many people in so many ages and lands appeal to them, especially when the stakes are high?

Common Interests can turn wariness into trust, adversaries into partners, and competitors into collaborators, precisely because they show listeners that they aren't enemies and that they have a better chance of getting what they need by pulling together.

But how do you deploy a Common Interest effectively? That's where the Common Interests Hack comes in:

1. You start by saying something that shifts the focus toward the common good, like:

   "Look, we're not enemies here; we're on the same side."
2. Then you add a sentence that begins:

   "If we work together, we can . . ."
3. You finish it by naming a specific shared concern that's

- we-focused (not self-serving),
- compelling (not trivial), and
- specific (not vague).

Or, more memorably, We, Wow, What Exactly.

For example,

"We can survive and defeat the British army."

"We can stave off bankruptcy and save our best people."

"We can avoid a ruined vacation like we had last year and have one we all love."

Each of these examples completes the sentence well and identifies specific, compelling goals we all want. As in ending tyranny, poverty, disease, and war itself. As in saving the world from an abyss of Nazism so that it can move forward into broad sunlit uplands. As in government of, by, and for the people. Each says, "We, Wow, What Exactly."

In contrast, "We both want me to be happy" is self-centered. "We'll save $1 on parking fees" is not compelling. "We all want to agree" is vague.

So, imagine a divorcing couple with the usual issues to work out, including alimony, child support, the sale of the house, a recent ugly scene in a restaurant, and money worries. What might one spouse say to the other using "We're not enemies here . . . " plus We, Wow, What Exactly to turn the tide from hostility and fighting to cooperation? Here's one possibility:

"Look, I know we've had our differences, but we're not enemies here; we're on the same side. We both love the kids and want the best for them; I know you do, and I do. If we work together, we can reduce legal expenses and get a better price for the house, so we have more money for their education. And we can communicate in ways that minimize the emotional pain they're feeling and avoid scenes that hurt everyone's reputation."

Similarly, a young married couple fighting over money might shift from Hostility-to-Harmony with the help of the same hack:

"Look, we're not enemies here; we're on the same side. If we cut some spending now, we can save enough to pay off our loans and have enough to buy our dream house sooner."

One more example: count how many Common Interests one partner utters in the following reply to another after a long fruitless argument about profit sharing:

"Look, we're not enemies here; we're on the same side. If we keep fighting over nickels and dimes, we're going to miss the deadline for getting the prototype done in time for the convention, the competition will get all the buzz, media, and contracts, and they'll eat our lunch. So, let's come up with a fair deal quickly—I know you want to be fair, and so do I—so we can get the prototype done in time, get to the convention, get the buzz, the media, and the sales, and beat the competition."

Put Common Interests in I FORESAW IT. One way to bake the benefit of Common Interests into your planning is to include them as a separate category under Interests. They're so powerful they deserve a separate sublist. While specifics often depend on the Facts, here are several Common Interests worth having in mind when you create an I FORESAW IT for a business negotiation:

Common Interests
- Reduce shared costs
- Legally reduce taxes and share the savings
- Resolve the matter quickly
- Mutually satisfying long-term relationship
- Fairness (Most find this seemingly vague Common Interest so compelling it's useful.)[21]

Combining Hostility-to-Harmony Hacks

Consensus builders often use these two hacks—Common Interests and the Golden Minute—to help turn hostility into harmony, and you can too. After you've helped set discussion ground rules, let each talk in turn without interruption, shared your own views, and let the notetaker recap the discussion, you can make a few observations to encourage the group by highlighting Common Interests you've noticed people unconsciously mention. For example, "It sounds like we all want the mall to be up and running soon so we can get the jump on the other mall across town, we all want heavy foot traffic in the mall starting opening day, and we all want our stores to be up and running, so the mall creates a good first impression. Does that sound right?" Doing that can help group members collaborate and become more open to creative ideas.

The Adult Children's Christmas Story

How can the Hostility-to-Harmony Hacks work in combination in a real-life setting where you have no authority and face a vexing conflict?

Fighting had become a holiday tradition for Nguyen and her two brothers.

Every November, they would bitterly disagree about what to give their parents, who would pay what, and how much each would do. Eager to prevent another round of aggravation as the new holiday season began, Nguyen decided to take another tack for their annual gift-giving conversation. First, she suggested a meeting at a vacationing friend's house instead of the usual phone calls. This change helped a lot, allowing the siblings to talk face-to-face while they prepared snacks in the kitchen over a glass of wine. Nguyen found that from the beginning, their conversation had a more collaborative tone than it had in the past.

To start the conversation, Nguyen took the Golden Minute to suggest a simple discussion ground rule: Each of them, in turn, would make a case without interruption. Only after would they discuss solutions. This approach worked well because it helped each of them to listen to the others. In the past, they had interrupted and argued with each other from the start. Nguyen also planned to go last so she could then summarize their comments. After each had spoken, she briefly recapped everyone's points and pointed out a critical Common Interest: they all felt the most important thing was to find a present their parents would like. She also noted two other Common Interests: equal participation and shared cost.

At this point, there was a visible shift from arguing to collaborating. Nguyen turned to her brothers, confirmed that they both agreed, and asked them what they thought they should do next. After talking some more, they decided the best way to select a gift would be to have a designated sibling identify two choices of equal value, then let each sibling vote so a majority would decide. Each year a different sibling would propose the two choices. They also agreed they would support the choice the siblings made. Everyone was pleased. For the first time, their conversation had gone well. There wasn't even a hint of the old animosity they'd endured in the past.

Nguyen's conclusion? By setting discussion ground rules, recapping, and pointing out their Common Interests, she'd helped the family focus on what they all cared about instead of their separate opinions.

Challenges

The Golden Minute Challenge. In your next difficult conversation or meeting, ask to take sixty seconds to work out some brief discussion ground rules to help make the conversation more comfortable and useful. Then suggest a No Interruption/No Multitasking rule, a Civility rule, and, if you like, ask someone to take notes and periodically summarize. Then ask everyone to help enforce the rules.

The Look, We're on the Same Side Here! Common Interests Challenge. The next time you find a group or a negotiation is reaching an impasse, use this phrase: "Look, we're not enemies here; we're on the same side. If we work together, we can . . ." and then introduce at least one Common Interest that's we-focused, compelling, and specific (We, Wow, What Exactly).

The I FORESAW IT Common Interests List Challenge. Before your next significant negotiation or meeting, list several Common Interests in the Interests section of your I FORESAW IT plan.

PART III

Decide

No Other Offers?
Find Wisdom:
Notional BATNA

Test an Offer:
**Measures of Success
Dashboard**

Spot Time Bombs:
WIN LOSE

The *New York Times* once published a puzzling story titled "Martha Stewart Fails to Reach New Kmart Deal."[1] Poor Martha, you might have thought, glancing at the headline: she failed. A shame, really, since, after all, the whole point of business and negotiation is to get to yes. Only if you'd read the full article would you have learned that Kmart had been ruining Martha Stewart's brand and that she was about to enter a new deal with Home Depot. By the logic of that headline, we might expect a similar article titled "Passenger Fails to Stay on Sinking Ship."

What does it mean to get a good offer? How do you know when to say yes? Especially when you feel powerless, it can feel like the correct answer is just to say yes. After all, as the *Times* article illustrates, we swim in cultures where yes is success, and no is failure, and you want to be a success, don't you? On top of that, pressure can make you want to get the talks over with, especially since, as we've seen, negotiation is literally "not leisure." And you get a dandy feeling of completion when you agree.

And it's just hard to say no to someone. Social scientist Stanley Milgram once commissioned his students to go up to people on subways and ask them for their seats. Sixty-eight percent of subway riders gave up their seats without objection.[2] In New York City. And in negotiation too, we often buy in, confident we've gotten a good deal, no matter the terms. You need a better way to decide.

Anyone can get to yes. My eleven-year-old can do it: "Just sign here, dear." The critical question is how to get to *wise* yes or *wise* no—and know it. As many businesses go bankrupt entering bad deals as those that enter too few. Many employees settle for unjust compensation, many retail "sales events" aren't, and most mergers fail. Entrepreneurs, employees, customers, and CEOs often celebrate bad deals. And many negotiation courses inadvertently teach students that they can always find a good yes. One of the most widely used negotiation simulation publishers once told me that of over two hundred simulations they offer, "no deal" was the correct result in exactly one of them. One. Which means many students have been systematically trained to believe that there's always a good yes just waiting for them to discover. Alas, that's not true.

So, this final part of the book will first equip you with tools that help you keep your eyes on the prize and decide accordingly. Then it will help you cope when you feel you have *no* choices, by using an innovative tool that's grounded both in time-tested business experience and decision science. Then it will pull many of the tools from the book together to show how you can use several tools to win wise yeses that solve even existential problems.

CHAPTER 12

Decide with Three Birds in the Bush

THE TOOL: NOTIONAL BATNA

Use this tool when you . . .
- have one bad choice, and must decide soon
- you have no clear BATNA.

Use this tool to . . .
- decide wisely between a bad choice and a possible future choice.

In the 1730s, the young Ben Franklin founded a newspaper called *The Pennsylvania Gazette*. It didn't go well. Franklin realized that if things didn't turn around, he would soon go out of business with no clear future. Then one day, a customer offered Franklin a good sum of money *if* Franklin would publish a certain article. There was just one problem: Franklin realized the piece was dishonest and slanderous.

Franklin felt great pressure to publish the piece. But then he looked at the question in an unorthodox way, a way that arguably violates one of the most celebrated negotiation principles. That way completely changed his thinking, and he turned down the offer.[1] Though it took awhile, Franklin's newspaper eventually became the most successful in America. His printing and other businesses grew so prosperous that economists consider Ben Franklin the wealthiest American of his era.

A fundamental principle of negotiation is that it's important to be ready to walk away from a final offer if it's worse than your Best Alternative to a Negotiated Agreement (BATNA). As we saw when we first explored I FORESAW IT, ✈ [Chapter 2], BATNA is the best thing you can do without your counterpart if you and the other negotiator can't agree. So, for example, if you're negotiating with a supplier, your other choices besides doing a deal with that supplier might include buying from another supplier, making the parts yourself, using a substitute, or suing for price fixing, and the best of these other choices is, by definition, your BATNA. Your BATNA is what you'll choose instead of a weak final offer.

But what if you have no BATNA at all? What if you have a single offer but no other choices? What if, like Ben Franklin, you feel like your counterpart's final offer is an offer you can't refuse?

Typically, those of us who teach negotiation recommend that you should do research, get creative, and so develop a better, nonobvious BATNA. Often that is good advice. For example, a grocer whose last butcher left the meat department in lousy shape might find the only good candidate wants a salary that the grocer cannot pay. The grocer might find novel Alternatives to Agreement: renting the space to an outside meat seller, or outsourcing the department entirely. One of these choices might work well, putting the grocer in a better bargaining position with the candidate. Thus, my earlier advice about I FORESAW IT, ✈ [Chapter 2], to develop at least *five* possible Alternatives to Agreement. Simple enough.

But what if you realize that none of the Alternatives to Agreement you can deploy right now would work? Or what if you see no other choices at the moment, and you feel you're at your counterpart's mercy? In theory, you should accept *anything* since your best Alternative would seem to be nothing. But should you take *anything* your counterpart offers? Should you hire a butcher for $1,000,000 a year? Accept a job for a dollar a year? Take a loan at 50 percent interest? Sell a house for a penny? Do business with a slanderer?

Notional BATNA ➖

Here I want to introduce you to the idea of instead identifying and using your Notional BATNA to help you decide what to do. It's a tool I've developed to fill a gap in the negotiation literature.[2] To use a Notional BATNA, you predict what other choice you'll likely get pretty soon, adjust its value to reflect your risk tolerance, and then compare it with an offer you have now. It's your *adjusted future* best Alternative. Notional BATNA builds on the old saying "A bird in the hand is worth two in the bush"; it invites you to consider whether the offer of one bird is worth taking if, say, you can reasonably hope to soon find *three* birds.[3]

Here's an example. Imagine you have a final job offer for $55,000. Assume salary is the deciding issue, and your first research tells you the offer is quite low. Alas, you have no other offers right now, you're under pressure to replenish savings in the next few months, and every cent counts. You have to answer in just a couple of days, and you think you have no choice but to accept it. What to do?

1. Guesstimate the value of your future choice(s). Imagine you do further research and find there's a good chance you'll get another offer for more in a manageable three months. Specifically, imagine you:

> read reliable surveys and job postings, and consult with people who
>> know about the current market[4] and
> look at historical data, such as talking to friends who faced similar
>> choices in the past.[5]

Typically, research like that reveals a range of guesstimates about how much you might be offered elsewhere. Here, imagine the range of prices in this market is fairly broad, and guesstimates range from $100,000 to $40,000. Taking the average gives you a base Notional BATNA of $70,000.* Though we're not done yet, a number like that suggests you might want to refuse the current offer and either press for more from the offering firm, ask to revisit the possi-

---

* If, however, your research suggests one of these numbers is an outlier and most of your prospects skew toward one part of the range, you may want to guesstimate using a weighted average. One way to do that is to throw out the extreme high and low prospects. For example, if you've seen guesstimates of offers for $100,000, $80,000, $76,000, and $40,000, you might take the average of $80,000 and $76,000: $78,000. Another is to list each of the several prospects and take the average: $74,000.

bility in three months, or walk away. Doing such work can give you a baseline guesstimate of your near-term prospects.

2. Test your heart. But life and the human heart can be funky. Some of us are more comfortable with risk, others less. So, to adjust for risk (in)tolerance, you may want to test your heart.

One way to do that is to visualize, in turn, your hopes and fears and see how you react.

First, imagine how you'll feel if, a couple of months after you accepted the offer, you got a belated offer elsewhere for $100,000, an offer you now can't accept, an offer your research said was quite possible? What would your situation have been like if you'd gotten that much? Could you live with that missed opportunity, or would you be haunted by regret?

Then, imagine how you'll feel if you turn down the offer and don't get another offer for, say, nine months and only then find a $40,000 offer. Could you live with that story? What would your finances and your life look like? What does it feel like as you close your eyes and picture it?

The idea isn't to get cocky or freak out; it's to try on a couple of alternative futures. You may at first fear the worst-case scenario, only to discover the worst is OK, strengthening your resolve to walk away. Or you may find it's dreadful, strengthening your decision to take the sure thing. And vice versa: you may at first feel like taking the sure thing until you discover you'd be crushed to find you let a later, better offer get away. There's no right answer, it's just about testing your heart, which will be living with your decision too.

Once you visualize these futures, how do you feel? More risk-tolerant than before? If so, you may want to raise your Notional BATNA somewhat, say, to ~$80,000. Conversely, if you feel more risk *in*tolerant than before, you may want to lower your Notional BATNA somewhat, say, to ~$60,000.

Ben Franklin tested his heart as he weighed whether to publish that slanderous article. To do that, he did an experiment to see if he could live on the poor wages he guessed he might make after the business died. He ate bread, drank water, and slept on the floor of his room. To his surprise, he found he was quite content living that way. So, even though he had no other prospects to save his newspaper, he turned down the offer to publish the article.

3. Check with a wise opposite. But before you decide, it's wise to make sure you've gotten counsel from an experienced adviser you trust who has your opposite risk tolerance. That is, if you're an optimist, talk to a wise pessimist. If you're a pessimist, talk to a wise optimist. (Hint: many lawyers and parents tend to be conservative about risk; many entrepreneurs and investors tend to be more tolerant of risk.) If you've already had such a conversation, great. If, instead, you've only spoken to people like yourself, do find your opposite. Doing so can temper your feelings, giving you valuable perspective.

Consider the celebrated investors Warren Buffett and Charlie Munger, chair and vice-chair of the highly successful Berkshire Hathaway. Buffett is a celebrity, widely known for his good cheer, sense of humor, and avuncular, positive outlook. Munger, far less well known, has a reputation for being a curmudgeon, an exceptionally rational man who is particularly alert for cognitive bias and tends to be more of a pessimist. Munger puts each business decision through the wringer, testing it rigorously. Buffett recounts many cases where he and his team were poised to approve a large acquisition until, sometimes at the last minute, Munger would veto the deal because it failed one of his tests. This pattern prompted Buffett to affectionately refer to Munger as "the Abominable No-man."[6] Yet, together, the two men have prospered in ways few others ever have.[7]

Your adviser is not there to decide for you, and no adviser should ever become your scapegoat if things turn out poorly; the point is to let others test your conclusions. As the saying goes, "With many counselors comes wisdom." Another reason it's wise to check with someone unlike yourself is that doing so can partly help you guard against the temptation to use any decision tool as a basis for rationalizing your natural tendencies.

So, in our example, let's imagine you're extremely risk-averse, so much so that you're leaning toward assigning a Notional BATNA of just $50,000. Your counterpart's $55,000 offer looks good by comparison. But say your wise adviser tells you your worries are exaggerated; it's quite unlikely you'll do so badly. Her advice tempers your fear. So, instead of a $50,000 Notional BATNA, you raise your Notional BATNA to ~$60,000. That result suggests you still have some reason to negotiate for more than you otherwise might have and that there's a case for walking away if you can't do substantially better. Or imagine you're risk-tolerant enough that you're leaning toward a Notional BATNA of $60,000. That number makes your counterpart's $55,000 offer look a bit weak by comparison. But now, imagine your wise adviser tells you your hopes are exaggerated; it's quite unlikely you'll do so well. His advice tempers your hope. So, instead of a ~$60,000 Notional BATNA, you lower it to ~$55,000. That number suggests it may be wise to accept your counterpart's offer, or negotiate with great caution.[*]

In short, you've developed a Notional BATNA that represents (1) your learning, (2) your heart, and (3) a mix of temperaments. Developing your Notional BATNA can save you from accepting an unjust offer out of false desperation, or rejecting a decent offer out of false hope.

A Simple Way to Remember the Notional BATNA Process Using *The Wizard of Oz*

Here's a simple way to remember how to think through your Notional BATNA. In the movie *The Wizard of Oz,* Dorothy befriends three characters: the Scarecrow, who wants a brain, the Tin Man, who wants a heart, and the Cowardly Lion, who wants courage. Each eventually finds he has what he longs for. Like the Scarecrow, you first use your brain to guesstimate the future. Like the Tin Man, you use your heart to gauge your risk tolerance. And like the Cowardly Lion, you use your courage to challenge your assessment with someone wise and temperamentally different.

The Widespread Practice of Adjusting Under Uncertainty

Notional BATNA is a cousin of several other practices decision makers routinely use in a fast-changing and uncertain world. For example, investors make

---

[*] Notice if your decision strongly affects someone else—a spouse, a company, a business partner— then you'll also want to talk about the choice with them until you're in agreement, a task that involves, yep, negotiation.

most financial decisions by adjusting; they first convert projected future costs and benefits into present value, giving them a baseline valuation. Then they adjust to account for risk, using one of several different well-established methods to decide. Some methods favor optimism,[8] some pessimism,[9] some an average;[10] some try to minimize the regret the decision makers might feel later.[11] The process we've sketched out for determining your Notional BATNA draws on the wisdom of several of these methods.

Similarly, most businesses make decisions based on pro forma projections of future revenues and costs, adjusted for the possibility the projections may be wrong.

Separately, many tech companies and electronics manufacturers plan, design, and even build on the expectation microchips will become more powerful by the time the product is ready, based on their reasonable, evidence-based projection. Betting on better, future microchips is somewhat like betting on one's Notional BATNA.[12]

Most negotiation students say BATNA is one of the most powerful tools they learn in basic negotiation training, yet one of the most frequent questions students ask is what to do when they have no BATNA. In an uncertain world where you need guidance in the face of it, Notional BATNA can help fill a critical gap.

Not every Notional BATNA is better. Your Notional BATNA isn't necessarily better than your apparent BATNA. If you are a hostage, your BATNA is a shot to the head. Your Notional BATNA could be even worse; trying to escape like a Hollywood action hero strongly raises the chance of not only getting yourself killed but getting other hostages killed too. Similarly, one study found that most plaintiffs and many defendants do better settling for what the other side offers than taking their chances in court.[13]

Notional BATNA may work best not as an exact numerical value but as an impressionistic way to see the choice in a clearer light by combining mind, heart, and wisdom. There is art as much as science to it.

Comparing packages. Often your decision isn't merely about a single number like, say, price, but a bundle of things (e.g., in talks for the sale of computer parts—price, financing, closing date, guarantee, etc.). One way to use Notional BATNA with a package offer is to first consider another package: the opportunity you reasonably hope to find elsewhere within a reasonable amount of time. Then you test that notional package with your heart and a wise adviser. Imagine it holds up well. Then you compare the result to the offer you're considering. To return to our computer parts example, imagine you have received an offer from the buyer with:

> little cash up front (your number one priority)
> low price (priority number two)
> burdensome guarantee (priority number three)
> late closing date (priority number four)
> mediocre delivery terms (number five).

Your adjusted Notional BATNA—a sale in three months to another buyer—would give you

> most cash up front (your number one priority)
> good price (priority number two)
> bearable guarantee (priority number three)
> mediocre closing date (priority number four)
> mediocre delivery terms (number five).

Here then, your Notional BATNA is more attractive. If so, you may have reason to negotiate for more, postpone further talks, or walk away.

Using Notional BATNA with Other Tools

Once you've determined your Notional BATNA, include it in your I FORE-SAW IT plan under Alternatives to Agreement. When you create a TTT grid, you can use your Notional BATNA to define your Walkaway targets and your Least Acceptable Offer. And when you roleplay, you can practice negotiating with it in mind. Since it's usually unwise to tell the other negotiator your BATNA, it's also unwise to mention your Notional BATNA. As you roleplay, practice instead negotiating from whatever position of strength your Notional BATNA suggests you have and see what your gut and your teammate tell you. Did it sound compelling? Did you feel highly anxious, or comfortable?

Notional BATNA and moves away from the table can complement each other. Each is a nonobvious way to gauge and gain strength at the table, and each can strengthen the other. If, for example, your Notional BATNA is weak, see what happens if you develop it with Who I FORESAW, not to the point where you have a clear BATNA but to the point where you have a more plausible Notional BATNA.

For example, in our case, if you're uneasy about your chances of finding another job for $60,000, consider using Who I FORESAW to develop it so you see a real prospect.

Conversely, suppose you're making moves away from the table. In that case, you may be able to talk to a Godzilla figure before you're confident you have every pivotal deal in place if your Notional BATNA looks reasonably strong. Recall the story, ⚅⚅ [Chapter 6], of Hannah's talks with Bening about a warehouse. While it may be best for Hannah to have a deal with Skyward lined up before she sees Bening again, she may want to treat Skyward as a Notional BATNA and go back to Bening now if time is pretty short, she has good, well-researched reasons to think Skyward will make a strong offer fairly soon, and she's tested the prospect with her heart and a wise adviser.*

Warning Label: *Use as Directed*

Notional BATNA is not about bluffing and praying; it's not an excuse for talking big and secretly hoping against hope that things work out. Instead, it's a measured way to weigh your future prospects when you have none in hand at the moment. Its purpose is to help you better guesstimate your value than a simplistic use of BATNA alone would produce. So, if you're prone to ignoring risks, selling

---

* And, if she has them, partners or a board of directors.

others on your dreams, or kidding yourself, don't use it; it may just lead you and others astray. But if you're prone to caving in when a bit of thought would have revealed you're selling yourself short, it may be a valuable tool.

Beyond Notional BATNA: Work the Rest of I FORESAW IT

Finally, what if your best efforts reveal that neither your BATNA nor your Notional BATNA is at all good? Then, as we noted when we explored Three Little Words, ⚭ [Chapter 1], often the best thing you can do is work the rest of your I FORESAW IT plan harder. That means understanding Interests and Facts even more deeply. It means developing even better Options that make both you and your counterpart better off than the counterpart's lousy offer can. And it means reaching out that much more to others Who can be influential, working your TTT grid more rigorously, and so on. Or seek instead to limit or *avoid* negotiation for now, which may itself require negotiation. Or, use other tools from this book as well.

That phrase "other tools" brings us to a critical point: when you combine several of your tools, you may well be able to do more than you think, even in tougher situations than we've explored here. We'll see how later with 📊 [Chapter 14].

But before we do, we need to ask one other question first: How do you *know* an offer is good?

Tool in Brief

Notional BATNA: The adjusted value of a likely future Alternative to Agreement.

Challenges

The Notional BATNA Challenge. Do this the next time you face a negotiation where the other side makes the only offer you have, and there's evidence that the offer is weak and, perhaps, unfair. First, research and develop your possible current Alternatives to Agreement, things you could unilaterally do *now*, listing at least five, identifying the best as your potential BATNA. Then, separately, (1) learn what you reasonably can hope to get elsewhere in a reasonable amount of time. Then guesstimate the value of that plausible alternative offer. (2) Adjust it to reflect your risk tolerance; if you feel nervous imagining what life will be like if that prospect doesn't pan out, discount the value substantially. If you feel bad imagining what life will be like if you take the definite offer and pretty soon after get a better offer, raise the value substantially. (3) Finally, if you haven't yet, talk about the alternative offer with at least one other person you respect, preferably someone with a different temperament: if you tend to be pessimistic, seek an optimist, and vice versa. Adjust your valuation of the envisioned offer accordingly: if the conversation makes you feel more comfortable, don't discount so much; if it makes you more worried, discount more. This is your Notional BATNA. Then compare your counterpart's offer to your BATNA and your Notional BATNA. If the counterpart's offer is weak by comparison, press for more, postpone further discussion, or seriously consider walking away and either taking your BATNA or pursuing your Notional BATNA.

CHAPTER 13

Use a Yes/No Instrument Panel

Tool: Measures of Success Dashboard

Tool: WIN LOSE

Use these tools when you . . .
- don't know whether to accept an offer
- feel pressure to say yes
- fear deadlock=failure
- fear yes will leave you remorseful
- feel confused about when to say yes.

Use these tools to . . .
- measurably test whether an offer is good
- spot hidden traps
- decide with confidence when to say yes, no, or not yet.

In 2011, a twenty-two-year-old recording artist named Kreayshawn found herself with $300 to her name. But then the impossible happened: she received a $1 million record offer from Sony records. She received the offer because earlier that year, she had released a music video on YouTube called "Gucci Gucci" that had generated almost three million views in the first three weeks. She promptly accepted Sony's offer and soon had hundreds of thousands of dollars in her bank account.

In 1993, a nineteen-year-old singer-songwriter named Jewel Kilcher found herself homeless and living in her car in Southern California. But then the impossible happened: she too received a $1 million record offer, this one from Atlantic Records. She received the offer because she had gained a mushrooming following of devoted fans and because a radio broadcast of her demo tape on a top L.A. station had produced a powerful listener response. But then she did something very odd. She turned down Atlantic's offer.

Imagine being that age and getting a $1 million offer . . . when you're homeless. Would you—or anyone in their right mind—say no to life-changing money like that? Clearly, one of these two artists wasn't afraid of success and simply chose to live her best life. The other was, well, crazy.

But in 2014, Kreayshawn tweeted that she had earned $0.01 on her first album for Sony. Then, in July 2020, she tweeted: "Don't buy 'Gucci Gucci' or stream it. I get 0$ and I'm in debt to Sony for [$]800K. . . ."[1]

Jewel Kilcher never suffered a fate like that. Instead, she became a multimillionaire. Better known as Jewel, she did something few recording artists ever do in the cutthroat music business: she made a lot of money and kept it.[2] How? And how *did* Kreayshawn wind up bankrupt? Part of that answer: Jewel did her homework and knew how to recognize a lousy offer; Kreayshawn didn't.

What Kreayshawn didn't understand was that Sony's $1 million offer had a string attached to it. Sony wasn't just giving her the money; it was *lending* it to her in the form of something her contract called recoupable expenses. The idea was that Kreayshawn had to pay to produce her albums and then pay all the costs of touring to promote them. She would get royalties *if* the albums' revenues were more than $1 million. When the first album bombed, she earned $0.01, and owed Sony every part of the $1 million advance she'd spent.

But Jewel had spotted a similar trap in Atlantic's offer. How? She'd gone to the library, gotten a book about the record business, and learned about recoupable expenses, back-end money, royalties, advances, unit sales, and other recording industry terms of art. She added to her knowledge by getting the advice of an industry veteran, who later became her manager. Then Jewel asked herself what she really wanted and realized a large advance and the pressure to sell huge numbers of records would rob her of her happiness. Her Interest, she realized, was staying in a place of contentment she'd found by producing music she believed in—and getting a large royalty on the back end if her album sold.

In other words, she took little risk up front and asked for a big return later. If her first album had bombed, she would have owed nothing.

Fortunately, it didn't. Instead, Jewel's first album, *Pieces of You,* became one of the top-selling debut albums of all time, going platinum twelve times.

Kreayshawn's and Jewel's stories illustrate a critical yet little-known point about negotiating: even when you find yourself in a seemingly desperate position, often no is the correct answer.

It often seems as if the goal of negotiation is to reach an agreement. Heck, one of the most famous negotiation books is *Getting to Yes.* We celebrate dealmakers, delight in bargains, and hold elaborate signing ceremonies complete with a crush of reporters. Sometimes there are even fireworks. Museums have lots of paintings of people signing treaties and constitutions. Salespeople and CEOs alike often get compensated based on the number of deals they close.

But many, perhaps most, deals are bad. Consider Barry Nalebuff, a seasoned entrepreneur turned Yale business professor who became a multimillionaire founding Honest Tea. He warns students *not* to be an entrepreneur. Why? Because, he notes, you can get dozens of deal terms right, one or two wrong, and lose the company. He recalls he came *this close* to losing his company at least a couple of times when he nearly agreed to a ruinous deal term.[3] Studies find that most new firms that win impressive-looking investment deals in the first eighteen months have an extremely high failure rate; the deals themselves often contribute to their downfall.[4]

It's not just entrepreneurs who face such traps. Studies routinely find that 70 percent or more of all mergers fail to produce the benefits CEOs promise they'll achieve,[5] a fact the stock market appreciates so well that it typically reduces the stock price of at least one party on news of a merger. Separately, in the aftermath of the 2008 financial crisis, it became evident that millions of mortgages and countless Wall Street deals based on them were ruinous, but few questioned them.

And in desperate moments, it's even easier to believe too much in dealmaking. Then a deal—any deal—can seem like a life preserver, but often it's an anvil. Loan sharks and payday loan firms have long preyed on such desperation, pauperizing their clients.

It's quite easy to fall into a decision trap I call Deal Euphoria–the widespread psychological tendency to defend and even celebrate a demonstrably bad deal. Each semester, my students simulate talks for a major business transaction. Secret: I've designed the simulation so no good deal is possible. Yet inevitably, some students, and sometimes all of them, enter a deal, report they're well satisfied, and make a strong case for it in debriefing. They're shocked when they find their boards are displeased and want them fired.

Whole industries prey on Deal Euphoria. Tourists traps in Times Square and other retailers permanently run "50 percent off" sales and "going out of business" sales because many consumers falsely believe a concession is the same thing as a bargain.[6] Other industries rely on high-pressure tactics that bamboozle customers into paying far too much.

We routinely confuse yes with success and no with failure. Google the phrase "talks fail" and you will find over one billion hits. Articles like these contribute to the widespread Fear of Deadlock, a side effect of our success culture.

And, alas, as I noted, a satisfying deal is possible in virtually every published negotiation simulation instructors use. But in real life, that lesson can lead to disastrous results.

So here, I want to introduce you to a tool that can help you discern the difference between a bad offer and a good one, especially when you're under pressure and feel like you've got to say yes: the Measures of Success Dashboard.

The Measures of Success Dashboard

The dashboard gives you three simple tests to protect you from the Fear of Deadlock and Deal Euphoria. In brief, it asks three questions:

1. *The collaborative test.* How well does the offer satisfy your (and their) Interests now and later?
2. *The competitive test.* How does it compare to your best and worst Targets?
3. *The relational test.* Is it fair, and is the relationship sound?

Let's see how it works. To help us do that, let's use a simple case and see if we can use the dashboard to help us decide whether to accept an offer. So, recall the computer parts case we used when we explored the TTT grid, 🗋 [Chapter 4], for which we created a TTT grid as you prepared to sell parts to a buyer. Let's also use the grid as a quick reminder of what we're hoping for.

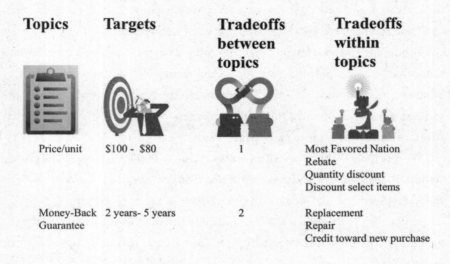

Topics	Targets	Tradeoffs between topics	Tradeoffs within topics
Price/unit	$100 - $80	1	Most Favored Nation Rebate Quantity discount Discount select items
Money-Back Guarantee	2 years- 5 years	2	Replacement Repair Credit toward new purchase

Now, imagine the buyer initially made this offer:

$75/unit + 6-year money-back guarantee.

Imagine too the buyer has made concessions and is now making this offer:

$90/unit + 4-year money-back guarantee with a right to modify as they see fit the computer parts you guarantee.

You feel a great sense of satisfaction that the buyer has conceded so much, and you're sorely tempted to take the deal. But is it a good offer? Should you accept it?

The collaborative test: How well does the offer satisfy your (and their) Interests now and later? Here we test to see how well the offer serves each side's Interests.

-Your Interests. This test first means keeping your eyes on the prize by focusing on your concerns. If a deal doesn't satisfy your key Interests, you must seriously consider walking away. It's surprisingly easy to know the price of everything and the value of nothing—to assume that getting a big number, or a creative term, is a win. Often, it isn't. In our example, imagine these are the Interests:

You (Seller)

Increased profit margins

Improved cash flow

Reduce inventory on slow-moving parts

Buyer

Quality control in more competitive industry

Cut servicing costs

Costs no higher than competition

Say your previous research shows the buyer's offer only improves profits and cash flow somewhat. That suggests a yellow warning light: the offer only somewhat serves your key Interests.

Time bombs-

This first test also asks how well the offer serves Interests *later on*—that is, it asks you to check for time bombs. A time bomb is anything in a deal that's fine now, but that could foreseeably cripple vital Interests days, weeks, months, or years later. Of course, you can't spot every time bomb. And past a point, fretting about them becomes neurotic. But several kinds are predictable and well-worth defusing, and if you're not watching out for them, you're playing with fire:

- *Overlooked likely future events.* What if sales are lower than you expect? Costs are higher? A key person leaves? You run out of cash? Jewel spotted a severe time bomb in her "$1 million offer" from Atlantic Records: if her album bombed, a not unlikely scenario, she'd have to pay all the money back. In the computer parts case, what if the buyer modifies parts badly and then demands a money-back guarantee? Since you would have no control over what the buyer does with the parts, the offer in effect creates potentially serious uncontrollable risk for you, which could destroy your profits and cash flow and thus the economic advantages of the deal. If you hadn't looked for a time bomb like this, you might have thought the offer was OK. It's not. Red light.

- *Perverse incentives.* Some deals reward bad behavior. Cost-plus pricing gives a supplier little incentive to control costs. Pegging a CEO's compensation to sales growth incentivizes her to buy up bad companies with considerable revenue. Rewarding a dealmaker when the parties sign the contract encourages him to not care about time bombs. Giving a dealer a bonus if she sells a set number of cars each month encourages her to sell at a loss to meet her quota if she's behind near the end of the month. In our computer case, your offer incentivizes the buyer to experiment with computer part modifications at no risk. That makes the red light redder.

- *One-sided deal.* Even if a deal is otherwise attractive to you, if it's too much in your favor, it may breed resentment and poor performance. As I and my fellow negotiation experts know, resentful counterparts are uncooperative, more inclined to underperform, and may even look for revenge, which is why it's wise to consider the other's Interests in the collaborative test too. Here it doesn't look like either of you is getting a very one-sided deal.

- *Bad financials.* A deal may look appealing at first, but sometimes, after crunching the numbers, you discover the future is awful. A finance student once went to buy a car only to have the dealer insist a lease would be cheaper. Embarrassed at how little he understood, he asked for the lease details and spent the evening reviewing them with a calculator and a finance textbook. The next day he asked the dealer if his calculations were correct that leasing would cost him exactly twice as much as buying would. "Uh, yep," the dealer admitted. Skilled business negotiators master the numbers, projecting how an offer will affect vital signs like cash flow, taxes, costs, etc., and testing financial claims. Failing to do so can lead to ruin. When Greek negotiators told diplomats from the European Union they should admit Greece to the EU because its financials had rebounded, the EU diplomats took the Greeks at their word. Unfortunately, they didn't check the numbers to confirm Greece's surprising change of fortune. Only after Greece gained admission did the EU discover Greece had misrepresented its situation and was in financial trouble. Now, the

EU had to guarantee massive Greek debt, which almost collapsed the EU.[7] In our case, projecting the possible future costs of the parts modification clause might reveal serious potential losses await you, making the red light still brighter.

- *Dangerous legal terms.* You are probably in trouble if the other says, "You name the price; I'll write the contract." Many counterparts do something similar, sending you a "standard" contract, often in PDF format, to discourage revision. It's tempting to jump to the few provisions you're excited about and let your eyes glaze over the rest, but contract terms can contain a host of time bombs. Here, gentle reader, I'll share a humble shout-out to business lawyers, whose job it is, among other things, to spot these very time bombs and help you figure out how to negotiate them out. A classic example of a term you might not even realize is dangerous but a good lawyer will: many Hollywood contracts promised artists a percentage of net profits, profits after various expenses. Unbeknownst to them, the contracts' definitions of "net profits" and "expenses" were such that even a blockbuster movie like *Coming to America*, which grossed over $288 million, produced no "net profit."[8]

- *Bad fit.* If a couple marries and only belatedly discovers one wants children and the other doesn't, the marriage is probably a bad idea. Bad fit can easily happen in business too, as when an investor is eager to make a lot of money soon and has little to offer but a check, while the entrepreneur wants to grow slowly and needs industry connections to help the firm grow. So, it's wise to ask what the other side's expectations are. In our case, bad fit doesn't seem to be a problem—unless the buyer's desire to modify parts is a warning it sees you as a different supplier than you are.

WIN LOSE. 🐭 I've simplified the task of spotting time bombs by creating a tool within a tool, a mnemonic to help you catch many of these sorts of traps in an offer by doing the very things I've suggested. It's called WIN LOSE:

What if: this, that, or the other thing happens?

Incentives: Are there perverse incentives here?

Numbers: What do the financials look like now and later?

Lawyer: What does your attorney say about the legal terms?

Other Side's Expectations: Are they in sync with yours?

The Other's Interests. It may seem like a waste of energy to ask whether the offer serves your counterpart's Interests; after all, isn't it the *other* side's job to worry about their own Interests? Yet if the deal clearly ill serves your counterpart, chances are you'll pay a business and karmic price for it. Conversely, if the deal also serves the other well too, magic can happen.

For example, when FedEx and Dell found ways to reset their bad relationship, both sides thrived as collaboration blossomed; when each was unhappy, each took that unhappiness out on the other, which led to a downward spiral.[9] Similarly, as we saw earlier, when Egypt and Israel reset their bad relationship, peace lasted for decades; when each was wary of the other, war was a constant threat.

One way to help make sure your counterpart is happy with a deal you're about to enter is to invite a Second Look meeting, where you say, "OK, before we sign off, let's take one more look to see if there's a way to make you happier without hurting me." Regardless, you can test the offer against the other's Interests as you've come to understand it. For example, when a publisher offered Joe a princely advance for a book he'd proposed to write, Joe reviewed the publisher's Interests and asked his agent, "How do *they* make money here?" If the answer was that the publisher had badly overbid, Joe knew it could hurt both of them; the publisher would lose money and Joe might have trouble selling a second book. Only when Joe was sure the publisher had a good chance to prosper did he consider the offer might be wise for him to accept.

Even when it's a onetime deal, it's wise to test it for the other's Interests. That's the advice of top sports agent Bob Woolf, who warned that "if someone feels you held them up, they're going to take it out on your business—or on you.... Your good reputation is incredibly important. If it really is a one-time deal then I wouldn't leave as much, but I still wouldn't try for the last dollar."[10] As we've seen, a reputation for greediness can kill your ability to negotiate even if you're a seasoned professional. And counterintuitively, when you ask if the offer might be hurting the other side, you sometimes discover strong reasons why your ideas are better for *both* of you.

Here, the computer parts buyer's offer would, at first glance, *seem* to serve the buyer's Interests well. But is this really the best offer for the buyer? There may well be other Options that help the buyer control costs and quality better. For example, your firm may be equipped to customize parts more quickly, cheaply, and precisely than the buyer can, so it may be better for both to work out a deal for you to customize parts for a reasonable fee. Yellow light.

So already our dashboard is flashing a mix of red, yellow, and green lights, strongly suggesting this offer is not OK and needs revision. But even if we fix the problems we've spotted, is it good in other respects?

The Competitive Test: How Does the Offer Compare to Your Best and Worst Targets?

Here we test to see how much of the total value of the deal you will claim through this offer. If the other's offer creates a great deal of value but then claims almost all of it, you'd probably be wise to reject it. Kai's boss offered him an "exciting" promotion with a better title, office, status, and travel and entertainment budget, but when he belatedly found he was killing himself for a salary far lower than his peers were getting, he realized the boss had treated him unfairly. As he later said, he so wished he'd known about this second test before he'd accepted the offer.

To deploy the competitive test, you compare each part of the offer to the range you've set for that topic in your TTT grid. How close does a given term come to your Best Target for that issue? Is it close to your Walkaway? Or worse than your Walkaway? Are the terms addressing your favorite topics close to your Best Targets? That's especially important, given their value to you. Since, as we've seen, tradeoffs are a wise part of negotiation, it's OK to do well on your favorites and not so well on your least favorites. Kai would have been happy to get a mediocre office upgrade if he'd gotten a rich salary increase. But if you're doing badly on most of your favorite Topics (as Kai did), that's a problem; your dashboard's yellow warning light will start flashing. In our computer parts case, the offer is mediocre; the proposed price and the proposed duration of the guarantee are each in the middle of your ranges. A better deal would give you a higher price (perhaps for a longer guarantee). So, on this test the yellow light is flashing.[*]

---

[*] Even if you've decided to compromise, satisfice, or be generous (as we discussed in Chapter 7), it's still wise to use the competitive test to see if you're going beyond your limits.

The Relational Test: Is It Fair, and Are the Relationships Sound?

Here, you ask two related questions: First, how reasonable is the offer according to benchmarks? Second, are there warning signs that the relationships may be unhealthy?

-Independent Criteria. The easiest way to test the fairness of an offer is to check it against Independent Criteria, benchmarks that tell you what's reasonable in this market or this sort of conflict. If you've done an I FORESAW IT plan, you already have this information. If not, you'll want to find it before you accept. Often, Independent Criteria report a range of reasonable terms. For example, if you're shopping for a new car in the U.S., TrueCar is one of several websites that report reasonable prices for the car you want. Typically, TrueCar reports a range for the same car (and suggests a Best Target). Ideally, benchmarking will confirm that the offer is giving you fair and favorable terms on your key Topics (when you're seeking an ambitious result). Here in the computer parts case, let's assume a respected industry journal reports prices range from $100 to $75, suggesting $90 is a fairly reasonable offer, though hardly a generous one. That might justify a light green light.

-Relationship quality. This test is the most subjective, but in some ways the most important. The idea is to ask questions like this: How well do you trust the other party? Is there good rapport? Commitment? Has someone here broken an ethical norm, or crossed a boundary? If the other party is an organization, is it harmonious or dysfunctional? How about yours? If the answers are ambiguous, or worse, take heed: you may be entering into a deal that you'll regret later. True, if it's a onetime deal for a small matter like the purchase of a used bicycle, then relational quality *may* matter less in some ways—you may never see this person again—but in other ways it may matter more; what if this is a hustler selling stolen or damaged bikes out of the back of a truck?

What about talks with an adversary or a violent enemy? Doesn't this test rule out a deal with someone like that? Not necessarily. As several statesmen have put it, you make peace with your enemies, not your friends.[11] And we've seen case after case of deals between enemies that lasted for decades. If you have reason to be wary but you still want to make peace, it becomes all the more important to understand the relational dangers clearly *and* add mutually satisfying terms to improve the odds that the deal, and you, will survive.

In our computer parts case, let's assume you're dealing with a well-established and harmonious company and that competitors have dealt with it successfully for years. Let's assume too you've made no ethical compromises, your counterpart has a strong reputation in the industry, its credit rating is good, and talks have been civil and constructive. While the buyer isn't being generous at all, nothing about its manner or requests or history signals relational danger, so here our dashboard is flashing a green light.

In short, here's how the computer parts buyer's offer looks on your Measures of Success Dashboard:

How well does the offer satisfy your (and their) Interests now and later?

Yellow (your Interests now)

Red (your Interests later: time bombs)

Yellow (their Interests)

How does it compare to your Best and Worst Targets?

Yellow

Is it fair and are the relationships sound?

Light green (fairness)

Green (relational quality)

Your dashboard is telling you this offer is not good: it's mediocre in some ways, plainly bad in others. And it suggests there may be a deal you can work out that's better for *both* of you—and that it may also be wise to press for more, at least on your favorite Topic.

But what if your only current BATNA is to accept an offer with a worse counterpart? Identify your Notional BATNA, as we discussed earlier, ⬤ [Chapter 12].

If you've created sample offers with your TTT grid, you can quickly glance at them and suggest one as a counteroffer. Regardless, you can glance at your grid and suggest a counteroffer on the fly, using a mix of creative Options and cushioning, especially for your favorites. If time permits, you can make moves away from the table to change the dynamics at the table. Regardless, if you face a final offer, you can compare it to your Measures of Success Dashboard and your Least Acceptable Offer before you decide to say yes or no.

Saying no to a deal is not easy. Years ago, my wife and I fell in love with an apartment we wanted to buy so much that we took to calling it the White House. The price was attractive and the place itself was beautiful. One problem: the building had come close to bankruptcy two years earlier, and two independent financial advisers who reviewed the financials warned us to run away from it. We spent weeks trying to decide what to do, and finally turned it down. Given the risks (and our situation), it was a wise decision, as the Measures of Success Dashboard arguably confirmed, but walking away was agonizing. The dashboard can't save us from the inevitable pain of decision. But it can point us toward wisdom.

Your goal as a negotiator is *not* to get to yes but to demonstrably get to *wise* yes or *wise* no.

You can't always spot good offers and bad offers, but having the Measures of Success Dashboard in front of you can often help you steer from danger toward opportunity, often saving you. Over time, that advantage can make the difference between drowning and thriving.

Tools in Brief

Measures of Success Dashboard: Is the deal wise Collaboratively? Competitively? Relationally?

WIN LOSE: What if? Incentives? Numbers? Lawyers? Other Side's Expectations?

Challenges

Measures of Success Dashboard Challenge. Before your next major purchase or contract, or the next time you see a big transaction announced in the news, see what happens if you test the offer by using the three Measures of Success, asking if the offer gives you collaborative success ("Interests? Time bombs?"), competitive success ("Best Targets? BATNA?"), and relational success ("Fairness? Relational quality?").

Variation: to get more objective clarity about an offer you're considering, ask a teammate or a Red Team to vet it closely, using the Measures of Success to help it spot problems.

WIN LOSE Challenge. When you next consider an offer in a significant negotiation, test for time bombs by deploying the WIN LOSE mnemonic, asking, "What if?" "Incentives?" "Numbers?" "Lawyers?" and "Other Side's Expectations?" See if you can spot at least one serious time bomb worth defusing.

Measures of Success Postmortem Challenge. Take a deal you (or your team) negotiated awhile back and use the Measures of Success Dashboard to assess it. Any surprises? If you discover the deal was better than you expected, what lessons does *that* reveal? Which tools deploy principles that helped here? How can you repeat a success like that, and are there people on the team who can mentor others, using the deal as an example? On the other hand, if you discover a deal you thought was great wasn't, what lessons does that reveal? Which tools might help you (and the team) do better next time? Are there people on your team who can mentor others using the deal as a cautionary example?

CHAPTER 14

Putting It Together to Roar Out of Recession

Task: Help save a firm that's struggling in a bad economy, when you're the leader and even when you're not.

Tools: Three Little Words, I FORESAW IT, TTT grid, APSO, Win Warmly Recipe Card, Common Interests, Who I FORESAW, Measures of Success, etc.

Carry out this task with these tools when you . . .
- face serious economic reversal, recession, or inflation
- are under serious pressure to cut costs
- would like the firm to invest for growth but fears block it.

Carry out this task with these tools to . . .
- survive and thrive
- cut costs
- increase investment *and*
- enhance business relationships with wary counterparts.

Can your negotiation tool kit help you save the day even in tough times? Can it help you save your job? Your firm?

For example, what do you do if a recession hits, endangering your business? Your first impulse might well be to raise prices and cut costs. That's precisely what many companies understandably do in tough times, often quite quickly, often indiscriminately. Yet an excellent *Harvard Business Review* study of 4,700 firms found that strategy doesn't usually help firms survive or thrive. Neither does the opposite approach: investing in the business, spending more on research, hiring, or acquisitions. So, what does work? The study found that a third strategy allowed 9 percent of studied firms to "roar out of recession," surviving bad times and emerging stronger than their competitors when better times arrived. What was the strategy? *Do both*—cut costs *and* invest. Easy say, hard do. Advice like that can sound like a Steve Martin comedy bit: "Yes, you can be a *millionaire* and *never* pay taxes! How? Simple. First, get a million dollars. Then..." Oddly, the study didn't say *how* to cut costs and invest simultaneously. So, if you want to roar out of recession, what should you do? Surprisingly, the answer may hinge on negotiation.

Consider something that happened to Noble Lithium, a $700 million U.S. mineral exploration firm. A few years ago, I trained Noble's managers and executives to use Three Little Words, I FORESAW IT, and the TTT grid. A year later, I called my contact there, Isaiah, to see how the training had served them. "Fantastic," he said. Really? How so? "Well, when you were here, we were coming out of a recession, and inflation was kicking in—supplier prices were soaring. But using what we learned helped us cut our operating costs by thirty-eight percent, and we used the savings to invest in new ventures." Thirty-eight percent? "How much is that in dollars?" I asked. Isaiah calculated for a moment. "One hundred million." Stunned silence. "Would you repeat that, please?" Isaiah said, "One hundred million." Pause. Then I said, "You know, I take tips."

Almost as stunning as the numbers: Isaiah reported that Noble's vendors had come to *love* them. Nothing Noble Lithium did bled its suppliers; it actually helped several of them.

How do you do something like that? How can tools we've explored help Noble Lithium and you roar out of recession? And do it in a way that makes other firms *love* you?

More broadly, how can you negotiate recession, inflation, and other tough economic times? That is, what tools can help you negotiate looming havoc and scarcity? If, for example, your firm loses a key customer and sales plummet, what can help you get through the crisis? And how can you help save the day, and your job, when you are not the leader?

Here, we'll face into this seemingly impossible task by drawing together several of the tools and seeing how you can use them to help your firm win against the odds. We'll use this challenge as an example of how your new tool kit can empower you to serve in remarkable ways, even in tough times.

Hard Data and Soft Skills

Noble's story so gobsmacked me that I had to learn more, so I asked its chief operating officer Todd how the company had done so much in so little time in the face of harsh economic conditions. Todd had led the effort to deploy the training, and he'd spearheaded efforts to cope with the tough economy in fresh ways. He said that if he had to sum up the answer in a phrase, it would be Hard Data + Soft Skills.

Noble had, historically, encouraged its team, especially its purchasing agents, to haggle with vendors for lower prices. Most other companies do too. As a result, most vendor-supplier relations are strained and competitive; often, suppliers feel harried by their customers. Also, like many other companies, Noble assumed that price control was much the same thing as cost control; Noble had only a sketchy awareness of the hidden costs in its supply chain. And Noble did something else too that's all too common: it tended to treat each supply negotiation as an isolated event. That is, it ignored how, say, a raw material supplier's late delivery deadline would delay a second supplier who needed that material, resulting in rush fees. Instead, Noble focused on each link but ignored the chain.

Todd decided to take a different approach. Gathering a cross-functional team, he told team members they wouldn't just fight with vendors or focus naively on price. Nor would they each work in separate silos, oblivious to what each other was negotiating. Instead, he first asked his team to create a dashboard so everyone could see how one contract's terms affected another. He also asked the team to review every existing supply contract to identify and quantify every cost, see which were unnecessary, and then prepare to negotiate to eliminate them. For example, they discovered one large supplier charged a fee for storing minerals. Noble could readily store the minerals itself, an easy source of savings. This mastery of the terms, numbers, and the dashboard—that is, the Facts—was central to what Todd meant by "hard data."

Most important, though, he asked his team to treat suppliers not as adversaries but as potential partners. That's where the Three Little Words, I FORE-SAW IT, and the TTT grid most applied. The idea was to intentionally look for creative ways Noble and a given supplier could help each other with creative trades. Indeed, Noble noted in its requests for proposals that it hoped to take a more collaborative approach, an unusual thing to do that some experts refer to as a request for partnership. Used to the old combative style, not every supplier was able or willing to try a collaborative approach. But several accepted Noble's negotiators' invitations.

Noble's team members soon discovered that several recession-wearied suppliers badly needed cash (a critical Interest). Noble, by comparison, had pretty good amounts of cash on hand and good credit too. So, Noble negotiators proposed an unusual arrangement (Options): have Noble finance, at low rates, equipment the suppliers needed to perform their contracts with Noble. Several suppliers jumped at the offer, gladly offering large price cuts in return.

Noble invested substantially in its operations with the savings it realized from its innovative supply deals, further strengthening its position when peers were struggling just to cover costs. Its negotiation strategy let it cut costs and increase investment, the key to roaring out of recession.

So how do you use your negotiator's tool kit to turn recession into opportunity? The basic idea is to first use our first three tools to (a) gain a deep understanding of costs and then (b) negotiate collaboratively with a supplier or customer to cut costs and create value. Then you can use some of the gains to fund investment. Just doing that can work well if you're a leader like Todd and you can tell your team how to manage. But what if you aren't? As we'll see, adding other tools we've explored can help. Let's first explore the basic strategy Todd used, then build on it to find ways to help when you're not the COO.

The Basic Strategy: Three Preparation Tools

The first task begins with simply using the Three Little Words: Interests, Facts, Options. Like Noble, you master hard data (that is, Facts) by closely studying and analyzing your existing contracts and practices to deeply understand your expenses. Indeed, as supply chain experts note, it's surprising how even large companies have a weak understanding of their total costs, let alone their suppliers'. "I'm always surprised when a big corporation doesn't know this," says Bonnie Keith, a procurement expert who served as Chief Supply Chain Officer for five renowned organizations, leading procurement for divisions of Pepsi and other Fortune 500 firms. For example, what hidden costs do delays impose? What storage costs is the firm paying for supplies that arrive too early? To what extent is it paying suppliers to complete an unnecessarily complex request for proposal? (Sometimes it can cost a supplier $250,000 on spec, a cost it often bakes into its bid.) And can these costs be creatively negotiated away? Deeply exploring contracts, interviewing line staff, studying expense statements, and analyzing the data can all reveal valuable surprises. The fact that many firms *don't* know these sorts of hidden costs can be a competitive advantage to you.

Meanwhile, you focus on your soft skills, first by considering your Interests and your prospective counterparts' too. Hidden costs often reveal hidden Interests; the high cost of capital some suppliers faced to fulfill orders from Noble implied they had strong Interests in getting help with capital and cash flow. Then you can explore creative Options (such as lending a supplier capital at low cost and supplier discounts).

The next step is to work through the full I FORESAW IT plan and the TTT grid. As you do, more possibilities and insights emerge: ethical traps, other key players, benchmarks, surprising trades, wise ranges, savvy offers, and more. In some cases, your work will point you toward a simple but creative onetime transaction; in others, a virtual partnership, or something in between. The idea is to tailor the solution to the needs and the numbers.

If you have teammates create and post TTT grids to an internal website and then add updates as deals progress and close, you can create an online dashboard. As Todd's story illustrates, a dashboard can help everyone see how each isolated negotiation affects the others. For example, say Sally's part of the dashboard reports she's negotiating for a key widget to arrive in ten to fourteen days. If Mohammad needs that widget in five to seven days or to avoid paying late fees to a client he's negotiating with, Sally and Mohammad know they need to fix the problem, saving money and revenue.

"I'm a huge advocate of hard data and soft skills," says Keith, who has led both procurement and manufacturing for firms in several industries. "Yet many don't know how to use them." That inability may have something to do with the fact that only 9 percent of studied companies roar out of recession.

So, a key way for a firm struggling with recession to survive and thrive is to look beyond mere price; to seek instead an arrangement that gives it lower overall cost (or greater value) and serves the supplier or customer well. Negotiating deals like that helped Noble thrive in tough times. In fact, Noble did so well in just twelve months that a few months later, another firm bought it for a 35 percent premium, one of the highest in the industry, which made the founders multimillionaires.

Help for Small Businesses

You don't have to be a public company to use the Three Little Words (and other preparation tools) to roar out of recession; a small business owner can use it too. During one recession, I was delighted to see that local store owners in northern Manhattan found several creative ways to renegotiate with their landlords, often saving their businesses. For example, many small businesses pay a substantial amount for common area upkeep, even though store owners with idle staff can have their people pitch in to keep the area clean. By learning the Facts—studying the lease, reviewing the expenses, and then exploring Interests and Options—some shopkeepers work out with their landlords creative ways to save. That includes temporarily shifting common area cleaning responsibilities to the store owner, trading a rent discount now for profit sharing later, getting amortized deals on build-outs, and so on. These and other arrangements can help the store owner cut costs and, in some cases, invest in ways that improve the well-being of the store and the building in the long run.

Saving Billions, Helping Suppliers

Using the Three Little Words and other preparation tools to roar out of recession or inflation can also save a firm billions. One example involves a firm that, admittedly, is hardly small or weak. But since even the largest firms (like General Motors) can face bankruptcy in the face of a serious recession, its story has relevance for us. While there's nuance to the story, it's worth knowing about.

In 2012, Procter & Gamble faced a downturn. Concerned about its cash flow, a cross-functional team of P&G managers used hard data to see where they could do better. Looking closely at accounts payable (Facts), they realized they were accepting from suppliers payment terms that were considerably worse than P&G's competitors enjoyed. An easy solution would have been to simply demand longer payment terms to gain savings at suppliers' expense. But then P&G took a more creative approach, thinking about the suppliers' Interests and Options, which might make the change attractive to them too. One Interest suppliers had, especially in a downturn, was improved cash flow and financial health. Was there a way to better both P&G's and theirs? That seemed unlikely. Suppliers and corporate customers almost always see cash as a fixed pie: the sooner I pay you, the worse my cash flow. But by in effect using the Three Little Words and elements of I FORESAW IT (like Who), P&G came up with another solution. Realizing a supply contract with P&G gave a supplier better creditworthiness, P&G arranged with its banks to help suppliers finance their contracts at a lower cost than the suppliers could alone, a method called supply chain finance, or SCF. That idea meant suppliers could receive payment sooner than ever before, netting slightly *more* money than before. This arrangement offered suppliers slightly better cash flow and also better financial health in several ways: it gave them greater flexibility, a healthier balance sheet, better access to capital, timely notice of invoice approval for better cash flow management, and more reliable payment by P&G. And by requiring longer payment terms in return, the arrangement seriously benefited P&G's cash flow. By 2015, P&G reported hundreds of its suppliers had accepted its plan. P&G realized ~$1 billion in increased cash flow by 2015 and $5 billion by 2019. And with increased cash flow, a firm can more easily invest in its future.[1]

(One nuance: some have warned small suppliers can suffer if big customers pressure them to extend payment terms, and have asked if SCF does so. Though not entirely clear, there is evidence P&G took a fairly transparent approach and that some of its suppliers liked its SCF program. More broadly, there is solid evidence a well-run SCF program can help suppliers. Which means the sound use of hard data + soft skills can also address suppliers' needs well. And rightly so. Conversely, misusing hard data + soft skills to take advantage of counterparts could justly trigger blowback, from suppliers themselves and government.)[2]

Basic negotiation preparation tools can also save a business facing a catastrophic revenue loss. In 2012, DHL, a courier service, faced an existential crisis when Intel, a top customer, announced it would exit a core business and so cut 50 percent of DHL's business. Yet within two years, DHL had managed to *increase* margins by 14 percent, and the DHL managers who had dealt with Intel received a CEO Award. How?

In effect, DHL and Intel together used Three Little Words, using it more as a joint process than as a unilateral preparation tool. Taking an unusually collaborative approach, the companies first discussed their Interests and studied the Facts about DHL's costs and performance. That work revealed surprising possibilities for savings. In the process, they decided they wanted to negotiate a new agreement that shifted their dealings toward something closer to a partnership. So, they developed over forty Options, then culled them. One set of Options they agreed to incentivized DHL to deeply review its costs with the help of Facts, discover big hidden redundancies, cut them, and use some of the savings to improve service. Also, though Intel had a strong reputation for micromanaging vendors, it agreed instead to focus on "what not how," giving DHL vital latitude to decide how best to improve service, as long as it met clear, measurable goals. These changes helped DHL improve its service so well that Intel saved more than it expected. So, as they'd agreed, Intel rewarded DHL with a large bonus and a contract extension. And Intel went further, making a slightly more modest 45 percent spending cut and recommending DHL to other customers. Those rewards, together with DHL's leaner approach and improved service, helped it roar out of something worse than a recession, thriving where other firms would have collapsed. In the process, DHL pulled off a classic example of cutting costs *and* investing.

In the supply chain world, there's a term of art for the kind of collaborative work DHL, P&G, and Noble Lithium used: strategic procurement. Even though the term has been around for twenty-five years, few business people understand it. Yet it can be a key to roaring out of recession. One of many reasons is because surviving recession depends on knowing what you buy and how you buy it and turning Facts into financial strength, things strategic procurement fosters. The process depends on being well prepared for talks with the help of data and analysis about costs, then negotiating collaboratively from one end of the supply chain to the other. Many businesses that have embraced it have fostered excellent relationships with suppliers and, at the same time, increased their profits by tens of millions of dollars or more, often in tough times. After studying 105 firms, McKinsey reported that "companies with advanced supplier-collaboration capabilities tend to outperform their peers . . . by 2X in growth and other metrics."[3] Often, the downturn itself is the catalyst for a firm embracing strategic procurement, which can transform it. In that sense, crisis can be a good thing.

When You're a Subordinate: Helping Your Firm Roar with Other Tools

Like some of the other stories I've noted here, Noble Lithium's story hinged on the work of one of its leaders. That's noteworthy. As a consultant and trainer, I've learned that if a firm's *leader* appreciates the value of negotiation training, the training helps the firm thrive; if its leader doesn't, the training usually doesn't. But that raises a problem: What if you're *not* the leader, and the firm faces stiff pressure from a tough economy? Must you be a passenger on a sinking ship? Is there nothing you can do to help?

In this section, we'll look at ways you can use other tools we've explored to help save the day in respectful, deferential ways that honor your leader's authority. In all that follows, I recommend thoughtfulness and care, which may be especially important in times of trouble. Understand that action here involves some risk. That said, one immediate source of encouragement is the DHL story. There, mid-level managers thoughtfully took the lead, convincing their leader to support their efforts. Another is Diego's story we saw when we explored I FORESAW IT, ✈ [Chapter 2]; there, a mid-level manager first used one of our tools to help his distressed boss find hope, which moved her to support Diego's efforts to save their firm. So, when you're not the leader, your task may be to very thoughtfully negotiate in more than one direction, including negotiating respectfully with one or more bosses to do the things that can help the firm roar out of recession, inflation, or other economic trouble.

DHL's story began when two supply chain managers, Todd Shire and Doug Whaley, realized they needed to negotiate a breakthrough relationship with Intel. They'd demonstrated their ability to do it on a small scale with an early pilot collaboration between the two firms. But as they considered a full-blown collaboration, they realized they lacked full support from their leaders. Winning enough support was no small challenge: while some leaders were interested, others were quite skeptical. So Todd and Doug practiced a form of moving away from the table: they recruited champions to help them win support for a second, bigger collaboration. They recruited support from several participating DHL colleagues from different departments, including more senior DHL managers John Hayes and Ruud de Groot. John and Ruud's support, in turn, helped win the support of still higher-ranking DHL manager Andrew Allan, who particularly trusted Ruud. (The new pilot collaboration also appealed to Andrew's Interest in innovation.) With DHL on board, the DHL team was able to convince Intel to try a second, bigger pilot by appealing to their Interest in shifting to more collaborative relationships with suppliers. That groundwork laid the foundation for Intel and DHL's excellent collaboration.[4]

(Notice they worked as a team. Having trustworthy teammate(s) can help you vet ideas, avoid traps, and navigate rough political waters more thoughtfully.)

In effect, Todd and Doug combined Who I FORESAW with Three Little Words. They identified champions Who had similar Interests and Who could Respond as advocates for them to senior management. And they (and their advocates) used Three Little Words to offer Facts (their first pilot's success) and addressed key Interests (their leader's concern for innovation) to win support for a new negotiation approach.

But these are just a couple of the tools you can draw on to win that kind of support. Another is to treat the economic crisis as an occasion for using APSO 𝍁𝍁 [Chapter 10], and for using other tool(s) we explored such as If We Agree/If We Disagree 🖐🖐 [Chapter 9] and You're Right 🐎🐎 [Chapter 9]. For example, recall the crisis Rachael faced in Chapter 1 where a recession was prompting her boss Wanchee to threaten layoffs and massive budget cuts. Imagine Wanchee is so anxious that she wants Rachael to deliver a budget in twenty-four hours. Imagine too that Rachael needs an extra week to work things out with her team, and also wants to convince her boss to negotiate collaboratively with key suppliers (and invest some of the savings) to help their firm roar out of recession. How might Rachael have done it?

To win a week's reprieve, she might have first used APSO: "Wanchee [**A**], if we press the team to deliver the budget in twenty-four hours, the team may be so distressed it will create a turf battle that leads to impasse, we'll miss that deadline, the CEO will be unhappy when we update him, and the department will be needlessly gutted [**P**]. Since the team members know me and I've won consensus from them before, I recommend you give me one week to help us work out ways to cut costs more thoughtfully so we cut fat and keep muscle [**S**]. What do you think? [**O**]."

Once Rachael delivers the team consensus she promised, how might she win Wanchee's support for taking a strategic, collaborative approach with key suppliers? One way might be to use You're Right and If We Agree/If We Disagree: "Wanchee, you're right to be concerned about spending and budget cutting as we deal with recession. So, I thought you might be interested in an approach I've learned about that can help us cut costs *and* improve our competitive advantage. It's worked for firms in a bunch of different industries. It's an approach to negotiations with suppliers that's less adversarial and more collaborative, an approach that can help us make key suppliers happy and our CEO *very* happy. I'd be glad to tell you more about it. If we use it, it can help you seriously cut costs without sacrificing service, *and* give the CEO money to invest in R and D, *and* actually build better relationships with suppliers. If we don't, I'm concerned we'll face worse budget cuts that could cripple the department, and we'll miss a chance to get ahead of the competition."

But now imagine Wanchee is intrigued but skeptical that her fellow department heads would support that approach, doubtful they'll back a cross-functional negotiation team. Perhaps they'll simply doubt you can ever collaborate with suppliers. Perhaps they'll worry a collaborative approach will signal weakness. Perhaps they'll say they and their subordinates can't be bothered to help when they face their own troubles. Or perhaps they'll fear Wanchee doesn't have their best Interests at heart and see her as a competitor. Rejection for any of these reasons could leave Wanchee feeling she's damaged her political standing.

One good response might be to use the Common Interests Hack, perhaps too with You're Right (again) and Three Little Words: "You're right, Wanchee—if other department heads oppose a collaborative approach, it might leave you out on a limb. That's a reasonable thing for you to be concerned about. So it might help to share with them that we're not enemies here, we're on the same side. If we work together on a collaborative approach, we have a seriously better chance of avoiding painful across-the-board cuts and layoffs we all want to avoid, and we have a seriously better chance to get a leg up on the competition." You could suggest she augment the point with an appeal to Facts and Options: "You might add there are lots of cases where firms have done just that, which has helped them roar out of recession. And you can offer a couple of choices: a full-blown commitment to a collaborative approach, or a pilot project where we try it with a cross-functional team in a few supply talks and see how the approach compares." *

---

* She might also suggest Wanchee recruit one or more champions, peer(s) Who'll likely support the approach and Who can help Wanchee win over other peers, much the way Todd and Doug recruited Ruud to help win over Andrew. Here though we're assuming Wanchee faces several potential internal opponents. So, finding peer(s) to act as champion(s) raises the idea of forming an internal coalition,

Notice that Rachael could discover and organize these ideas by first using the I FORESAW IT mnemonic to help her think through the conversation with Wanchee. Doing that would have helped her spot Wanchee's Interests she could appeal to, Facts about collaborative negotiation she could assemble, Options to offer her, persuasion tools like APSO she could use to build Rapport, and other tools to help her Respond to likely Reactions—tools like You're Right, and If We Agree/Disagree. She could use Empathy to spot Wanchee's fears better, could spot Ethical (and perhaps political) traps to avoid, spot key players Who they need to think about, and more. In that way, the mnemonic can help her (and you) organize and deploy the tools more intentionally.

As we saw with Diego, still another approach is to walk your boss(es) through I FORESAW IT itself as they grapple with how to deal with a difficult client or supplier or other third party in the face of severe economic weather. Doing that can win you a mandate in the form of a TTT grid. The grid, in turn, can help you create and claim wealth well, especially if you also use the Win Warmly Recipe Card.

Negotiating for Support and Overcoming a "Junkyard Dog"

As Bonnie Keith notes, it's common when you're seeking ways to wisely cut costs and collaborate that someone on your side (or the counterpart's side) understandably throws up obstacles as a way to protect his turf. It's so common she has a term of art for it: a Junkyard Dog. Keith has found that if the rest of your team and the other side's team see the roadblock, and the opportunity that cost-cutting and collaboration create, they'll press the Junkyard Dog to stand aside. This point means you may need to negotiate with your teammates and the counterpart's team to win the support it takes to do that.

---

which is a politically complex task. We've seen several instances of negotiators successfully building coalitions, such as Diego in Chapter 2 and Hannah in Chapter 6. But forming an internal coalition takes still greater care, because it can trigger more blowback. Proceed with caution. That said, we consider one way to thoughtfully form a coalition in the last part of this chapter.

Not that negotiations like these are easy even in good times. But in tough times, fear can intensify turf battles and myopia. And finding allies that isolate a Junkyard Dog can trigger blowback, especially if you're not thinking deeply about ways to mollify and respect him. So before setting out to win support, it may be a very good idea to do an I FORESAW IT about the matter (perhaps with a loyal teammate), with your Junkyard Dog very much in mind, in part to help Empathize with him, spot Ethical dilemmas, anticipate tough Reactions, and consider Options that might dampen hard feelings. Yet, as Keith and other supply chain experts note, tough times can also create a strong motivation for change, something you can harness. And you can use most of the tools in this book to help you do that, winning support from leaders and counterparts and perhaps even taming your own Junkyard Dog. Indeed, Rachael's story in Chapter 1, copilots and nurses' stories in Chapter 9, and DHL's story here are just a few of the case studies we've seen where one person convinced resistant leaders or colleagues to make crucial changes in times of crisis. When you're not sure what to do but you sense inaction would do more harm than good, consider making a little bet first: test the waters, suggest a pilot project, or do a simpler, low-stakes demonstration like DHL's Todd and Doug did. Doing that can harness the wisdom we've previously learned from Sir Francis Bacon: "In all negotiations of difficulty, one may not hope to sow and reap at once, but must prepare business, and so ripen it by degrees."

So how do you help your firm roar out of recession? By using tools like Three Little Words, I FORESAW IT, and TTT, negotiating collaboratively with key suppliers and customers (among others), and using some of the savings to invest. But how do you do that if you're *not* the leader? By winning your leader(s)' support using other tools. There's no single right way to do that. But that's actually good news: there may be several ways to win, and preparing an I FORESAW IT plan can help you tailor your approach to your leader(s), and help you pick the right tools for the task.

Roar Out of Inflation

Many of the same insights can also help you roar out of inflation—survive and thrive when your suppliers' prices rise, especially if you combine these insights with your TTT grid. Many firms facing inflation understandably respond by fighting suppliers and passing increases on to customers. But a more collaborative approach may help you (and your suppliers and customers) do better. To the point, consider an AT Kearney survey of 304 company supply chain managers, about half of whom worked for midsize companies, half larger companies. The study found that "most respondents (67 percent) report focusing on supplier relationship management to help identify approaches to jointly mitigate cost inflation."[5] The study also found that while 53 percent recognize the importance of cross-functional collaboration, "almost half report either no communication or only ad-hoc communication with finance and other stakeholders." These findings suggest a collaborative approach that relies on our tools and that's grounded in cross-functional teamwork may give you a competitive advantage.

So, imagine you are part of your firm's cross-functional procurement team and that a key supplier is insisting on an immediate double-digit price increase on its entire line of supplies due to inflation. Knowing your costs will be valuable but not sufficient. Since the supplier demands more because of its costs, it's at least as important to master them, starting by studying the bill of materials and other details of past supplier bills. If you don't have this information, you can go to your supplier and signal a willingness to collaborate, asking for a cost breakdown as a precondition to considering a price hike, noting you want to understand the supplier's situation better. Then, instead of merely haggling, your team can develop several potential Options and together create a TTT grid. Then, in the talks, you can explore the price increase as just one part of a more holistic discussion. Here's an example of such a TTT grid. (I've included more Options than usual to give you a richer sense of what's possible.)[6]

Topics	Targets	Tradeoffs Between Topics	Tradeoffs Within Topics
Price increase	0% – 5%	1	Surcharge on specific, volatile costs Replacements (e.g., plastic not steel) Price indexing Price indexing with collar Sunset clause (i.e., Increase price for just 6 months) Quantity discount Discount select items Price increase only on low-volume items Price cuts on other, stable inputs Clawbacks on commodity dips Longer payment terms Specific future date for price increase
Future cost breakdowns	Full to partial	4	Agreed-upon data source to support audits Receipts for surcharged costs More-detailed future bills of materials
Sourcing support	Long run Short run	3	Loan to back LR commodity purchase Help purchasing futures: price-forward coverage Help with warehousing Help with sourcing Buy early and save Commodity swap support/hedge LR contract Shorter payment terms

Improved efficiencies	15%–51% savings	2	Automated ordering option Better payment terms Consignment Cost savings on logistics Cost savings on fulfillment Cost savings on warehousing/inventory

Beyond a single supplier negotiation, it will help too to create an online dashboard so your team can track how terms in one inflation-adjusted contract affect terms in another. For example, if you can negotiate with a landlord for more space to inexpensively warehouse material, you can ask a supplier seeking a price increase next month to deliver more material sooner at the current price.

Depending on the terms you work out, you may even be able to create joint savings. If so, you can apply some of the savings to research and development—and so roar out of inflation.

Challenges

The Roar Out of Recession Challenge. The next time your organization faces a downturn, seek to cut costs *and* increase research and development spending. Do it by suggesting your team work together to systematically negotiate cost cuts with key counterparts such as suppliers or customers, and then invest some of the savings. That means (1) first work together with your team to master the facts and numbers and perhaps create a dashboard so everyone can track deals. Then (2) alone and together use Three Little Words, I FORESAW IT, and the TTT grid to discover mutually satisfying, nonobvious deals with suppliers or customers. Then (3) negotiate to use some of the savings for research and development.

The I FORESAW IT Win Over Your Leader Challenge. The next time you need to convince leader(s) to support a negotiation strategy you believe can strongly help the firm weather hard times, use the I FORESAW IT mnemonic (perhaps with a trusted teammate) to help you think through how best to approach them, asking as you go, "What negotiation tools in my tool kit can help me here?" Then use the tools and the strategy the mnemonic suggests to guide you.

CHAPTER 15

True Confession—I'm Powerless. You?

On January 15, 2009, US Airways flight 1549 hit a flock of geese moments after departing from LaGuardia Airport in New York. You've probably heard of it; the flight, which landed safely on a nearby river, became known as the Miracle on the Hudson and became the subject of a movie directed by Clint Eastwood starring Tom Hanks as Sully Sullenberger, the captain of the flight. How did Sullenberger and his crew cope when they had just a few minutes to respond before the plane crashed?

Though his courage and poise that day deserved great praise, Sullenberger strongly resisted the idea that he was some sort of lone hero. What saved them, he said, was their readiness to use checklists, trained listening, and other tools that together helped them manage the cognitive load, focus on what most needed attention, and work as a team. Sullenberger was speaking of Crew Resource Management, some of which we saw in Chapter 10: a suite of tools designed to help pilots and crews manage crises. Tools made the difference.

You and I will probably never have to land a plane on a river. But we've faced and will face stress, adversity, and powerlessness at critical moments of conflict and negotiation, and there the tools we've explored can help save us.

But the tools are more than just ways to manage crises. They're ways to practice something that sounds good but seems as impossible as landing a plane on water: to be strong and kind. That is, to be caring *and* powerful. It's that almost paradoxical quality that Martin Luther King, Jr. was talking about when he made a rather shocking observation about love itself—and power: "Power without love is reckless and abusive, and love without power is sentimental and anemic. Power at its best is love implementing the demands of justice, and justice at its best is power correcting everything that stands against love."[1]

You don't have to be MLK to put power and love together, and you don't have to wonder now about how to do it. It takes tools—tools designed to help you do both. That's what this book is about.

I Am Powerless. You?

A confession: as I've worked on this book, I've wondered often how readers might use it. After all, in a sense, it's all about power. Equip someone with a lever, and he might use it to free a family trapped in an overturned car . . . or he might use it to destroy an ambulance. Arm someone, and she might guard a battered women's shelter . . . or kill an adversary. So, someone could read this book and use the tools in reckless, abusive, or selfish ways. And I've cringed at that thought.

I've also wondered if my frequent references to kindness, generosity, and respect would sound trivial at best, sentimental and naive at worst. "Give us the power, and drop all this nicey-nice stuff."

So, I've come to realize *I'm* powerless. Just as inventors, founders, and teachers are ultimately powerless to know how others will use their work, so am I. Oh, the irony.

Just one thing: by design, the tools in this book bend toward mixing seeming opposites, power and kindness, and they may not work the way I've promised if you use them for mere power alone. BS or mistreat someone, and they'll probably sense it, no matter how you use a tool.*

But I wouldn't have written this book if I'd thought most of my readers would receive it cynically. Many years of teaching students have shown me that people can and do remarkable things with this stuff, things that foster surprising reconciliation, harmony, prosperity, and even forgiveness. There's a

---

* Kindness or compassion are so important that an otherwise powerful tool may be ineffective without them. To the point: Dr. William Miller pioneered an outstanding therapeutic tool called motivational interviewing (MI) that has saved countless lives of people trapped in alcoholism, drug addiction, and other dysfunctions. But Miller was chagrined to find that many practitioners were using MI mechanically without summoning much compassion for their patients. The compassion gap, he found, muted or negated MI's effectiveness. So, for both MI and any of our tools, we might say the same thing: whenever you put it to use, bring your humanity too.

Hebrew word for it when goodness like that prevails: *shalom,* the full flowering of human potential. It's the thing we crave, even though we often doubt we can have it. But we can.

In the early 1980s, GM's Fremont, California, assembly plant was a conflict-ridden nightmare most known for drugs, sabotage, terrible labor-management relations, and, not surprisingly, awful cars. But by the late 1980s, through the intentional use of humane strategies and tools, it was a harmonious and prosperous showcase that repeatedly won national awards for quality.[2] The plant's story showed that working relationships can heal and transform, giving us a practical glimpse of what *shalom* looks like.

Most of the stories in this book too are examples of *shalom* made real. They're cases where fear, intimidation, despair, and frustration gave way to shared gladness, whether it's about an eleven-year-old boy and his father, or a pilot and copilot, a bereaved fiancé and his would-have-been father-in-law, or DHL and Intel. It's a pleasant byproduct that often, shared gladness can spin off millions or even billions of dollars in wealth (and that it's possible to share it favorably and fairly). But that's just a small part of the story. In every sphere, there is more hope than we first think. When we see a sea of troubles in life, a tide of ugliness, it can feel as if we are *all* powerless to do anything to turn it around. We aren't. You aren't. *Shalom* is something you can help bring into being. Now you have the tools to do it.

Seven Ways to Keep and Hone the Tools

How can you take the tools you've learned and turn them into lastingly useful instruments?

Here are seven ways to keep and hone them so they serve you for a lifetime:

1. ***Download templates from Professorfreeman.com to your electronic furniture and Google Docs.*** If you get summaries and templates of the tools onto your laptop, your smartphone, and your tablet, you don't have to memorize them; you can simply summon them when you need them. Having them literally at your fingertips can help you deploy them in the moment. Also upload these tools to Google Docs so teammates can see a tool and contribute to it. You can find summaries, templates, and more at Professorfreeman.com.

2. ***Print out the 15 Tools one-pager and keep it near your desk.*** That is, print out a one-page summary of the tools. Having simple reminders of the tools near your workplace can help remind you to deploy them. Find them at Professorfreeman.com.

3. ***Practice (take the challenges).*** Try taking just one of the challenges for just one of the tools for a few minutes and see what you find, treating it as an experiment or a little bet. Try it on a fairly low-stakes matter. If a friend or colleague is reading the book too, try collaborating on putting a tool to use. For example, take twenty minutes and create a TTT grid, alone or with a colleague's help, and see what happens when you use it at a meeting. Tell

someone how it went, what went well, not so well, and what you'd do next time. Then try another challenge, and another. Try using more than one tool for an important negotiation and see how your experience compares to working without them.

4. ***Roleplay.*** Practice using a tool as you roleplay with an ally. For example, bring a TTT grid to the practice session. Or intentionally use tools from Part II (Meet) such as the *Exactly!* Challenge and the Hostility-to-Harmony Hacks. Ask your ally to give you specific feedback about how you're using the tool and how you can do it better. Don't worry if the first efforts are funky; rehearsing is what top performers do in all fields, from astronautics to sports to entertainment, precisely because it helps build muscle memory and work the kinks out before the big event.

5. ***Watch and talk to excellent negotiators.*** Reach out to someone you know who's renowned for being a fine negotiator and ask if you can watch or interview to see how your mentor does it. Watch and listen for signs your mentor is in effect using ideas that one or more of the tools crystallize. For example, your mentor may tell you she never just names a price; she first listens and explores the other's needs—ideas you've seen in Three Little Words, the *Exactly!* Challenge, and the Winning Warmly Recipe Card, among other tools. It's not essential to ask or share about the tools to grow your understanding of them, though it may be helpful to ask a question or two about an idea you've learned through a given tool. (For example, "What helps you listen better?") That said, you may find your mentor does things that *don't* fit neatly into one of the tools. For example, she might say, "I never cushion or concede." Try to identify her "zone of truth"; it may be her approach is wise in the rarified situation she specializes in with specific counterparts. It's OK to provisionally adjust your mental map accordingly. Or it may be she means something else.

6. ***Do postmortems.*** Air travel is safer now thanks to lessons the airline industry learned from crash investigations. Similarly, you

can improve your skills by chatting with an ally about a completed negotiation, asking, "How'd we do? What helped? What hurt? What should we do differently next time?" and seeing how tool(s) might help you do better. For example, "Wow, we made a costly mistake letting that buyer modify parts and letting them get refunds if the parts don't work. Maybe next time we should take twenty-four hours to have a colleague use the Measures of Success Dashboard before we agree to a novel deal." If you found your tool use didn't work as well as you might have hoped, talk about it. Was there confusion about how to deploy it? Was its novelty an issue, suggesting practice might help? Tools can take a bit of time to master like an app or a new skill, but it's well worth it.

7. ***Teach someone else a tool.*** Each semester, I ask my students to teach an outsider to negotiate using a simple tool like Three Little Words or the *Exactly!* Challenge. Roughly 70 percent of the time, my students' students (or my "grandstudents," as I call them) do well, often measurably, and they're often surprised how confident they felt. Of course, you, gentle reader, like my students, can do better because you're more steeped in negotiation skills now, but even a forty-to-fifty-minute training session is enough for most to outperform their expectations and their experience. Helping others is a great thing in itself. Another reason to do it: one of the best ways to learn is to teach. When you know a friend is counting on you, it naturally tends to focus your thinking. And as Nobel laureate Richard Feynman noted, if you find you can't explain something to a novice, it's a good sign you don't understand it fully, which can inspire you to review and up your game.

8. ***EXTRA: Coach your organization.*** The last and perhaps most valuable way is to help your team, your department, or your organization learn tools so they become a basic capability. Having a team that knows tools like I FORESAW IT and roleplaying is the difference between one person knowing how to play a musical instrument and an entire orchestra knowing how. Throughout

the book we've seen examples of groups putting tools to use and reaping benefits, often worth millions of dollars. And of course, your leadership won't only help you help others master tools; it can make you a hero as the team gains and uses valuable skills.

The rest is in your hands, dear reader. Go make me proud.

The 15 Tools Summarized— Plus More We Also Explored

(in order of appearance)

Three Little Words: Interests, Facts, Options.

I FORESAW IT: Interests, Factual and financial research, Options, Rapport, Reactions, and Responses, Setting and Scheduling, Alternatives to agreement, Who, Independent criteria, Topics, Targets, and Tradeoffs.

Topics, Targets, and Tradeoffs: A four-column grid capturing the agenda, ranges, priorities, and best creative Options, together with sample packages.

Roleplay: You and a teammate each prepare, then roleplay, review, resume.

Who I FORESAW: To deal more effectively with a Godzilla, identify key players by asking "Who?" as you review most parts of I FORESAW IT, then schedule a series of moves away from the table to obtain more valuable things to trade, more independence, and more leverage.

Targeted Negotiation: Find ideal counterparties by starting with a large pool of candidates and culling them using Who I FORESAW.

Win Warmly Recipe Card: (1) Cushion your first offer. (2) Especially cushion your favorite Topic(s). (3) Signal a willingness to be creative with (4) a thoughtful preface and perhaps (5) a thoughtful offer.

5 Percent Rule of Thumb: Moderate ambition slightly by setting as your Best Target a number that's 5 percent worse than the best outcome research shows you could get.

Exactly! **Challenge:** Actively listening or affect labeling so well the other says, "Exactly!"

Reframe: Say it in a way that's hard on the problem, soft on the person.

If We Agree/If We Disagree: Show how yes is good for your counterpart, no is bad.

You're Right: Affirm the other is right to care about Interest(s) prompting a no, then show how yes can serve Interest(s) well.

Positive No Sandwich: Say no by first truthfully sharing your Interest(s), then declining because of your Interest(s), then inviting a yes that serves the other's Interest(s) and yours.

APSO: Attention, Problem, Solution, OK?

Golden Minute: Time at the start of a conversation to suggest discussion rules, e.g., no interrupting + civility + notetaker/summarizer + help enforcing these rules.

Common Interests Hack: Appeal to shared goals that are specific, compelling, and not self-serving: We, Wow, What Exactly.

Notional BATNA: The discounted value of a likely future Alternative to Agreement.

Measures of Success Dashboard: Is the deal wise collaboratively? Competitively? Relationally?

WIN LOSE: What if? Incentives? Numbers? Lawyers? Other Side's Expectations?

Negotiator's Tool Kit to Roar Out of Recession: Master the Facts, then use Three Little Words, I FORESAW IT, the TTT grid, and other tools to negotiate cost cuts then invest some of the savings to help you grow.

I FORESAW IT Template

(Visit Professorfreeman.com for a Word version of this form.)

Interests (that is, the underlying concerns and needs; the reasons why someone wants something)

(Mine)

_____

_____

_____

_____ . . .

(Throughout this form, " . . . " means "feel free to list more ideas")

(Other Person's ["OP's"]*

_____

_____

_____

_____ . . .

(Common: shared needs you and OP can satisfy together; "If we work together, we can . . .")

_____

_____

_____

_____ . . .

Factual and Financial Research: (Note useful questions you need to answer, and then note the answers you learn through your Research; attach materials you've gotten, and spreadsheets you've created.)

---

* Appeal to the OP's Interests to show why your proposal is good for him/her.

Options: (For each topic, list at least six qualitatively different Options. (Each Option is a separate possible tradeable.) Each should satisfy at least one Interest someone has (e.g., one Option for your interest in providing more for your family is "ear-end bonus"). Don't create whole packages; that comes later under *T*.)

_____	_____	_____
_____	_____	_____
_____	_____	_____
_____	_____	_____
_____	_____	_____

Rapport, Reactions and Responses: (List things you want to say to set the right tone. Also list things you fear the OP will say. For each, write how you'll respond. No need to write a dialogue—just note several separate interactions: "If he says this, I'll say that." *Advanced technique:* roleplay with a teammate.)

Constructive points to help build Rapport:

-
-
-

If OP says: "_____"
I can say: "_____"

If OP says: "_____"
I can say: "_____"

Empathy and Ethics:

(First speak in OP's internal voice about how matter seems: "I think . . . I feel . . .")

Ethical dilemmas: (Then list ethical problems you each face, e.g., "What if they press me to decide before I've gotten everyone's OK?" "Can I go behind the landlord's back and take over the lease without her approval?")

Setting and Scheduling: (Note when and where you'll negotiate. *Advanced technique:* note discussion rules you'd like to use. *Advanced technique:* sequence who you'll talk to when.)

Alternatives to Agreement (That is, things you will do if you don't agree with the other side, and vice versa. Thus, this part is quite different from Options.): List several you *each* have, based on brainstorming and research. Include your Best Alternative to a Negotiated Agreement (BATNA) and your Worst (WATNA).*

(Mine)   (OP's)

_____   _____

_____   _____

_____(BATNA)   _____

_____   _____(BATNA?)

_____(WATNA)   _____(WATNA?)

_____...   _____...

Who (List those who can influence the negotiation, besides you and the other negotiator. *Advanced technique:* List each key player in each side's

---

* Appeal to the OP's Alternatives to Agreement (see below) to show why saying no will hurt him.

organization, as well as allies who can strengthen your side's bargaining strength. List each player's Interests in the Interests section.

_____

_____

_____

_____

_____...

Independent Criteria: List information you've learned that can serve as fair standards you and the OP will both trust, e.g., respected publication, experts, pricing websites, salary surveys, widely accepted market practices, rulebook, credible third party. Attach materials you've acquired if any.

Topics, Targets, and Tradeoffs

Topics	Targets	Tradeoffs b/w Topics	Tradeoffs w/i topics
(That is, what matters will you discuss in the negotiation?)	(That is, first, what is the most you can realistically hope for for a given Topic, and second, what is the least you will accept for that Topic? (Check Factual Research and Alternatives))	(That is, rank Topics from dearest to least important)	(That is, list 2 to 4 favorite Options that would satisfy your interest in that Topic)

_____   ____-____   ___   _____
                                       _____
                                       _____
                                       _____

_____   ____-____   ___   _____
                                       _____
                                       _____
                                       _____

_____   ____-____   ___   _____
                                       _____
                                       _____
                                       _____

_____   ____-____   ___   _____
                                       _____
                                       _____
                                       _____

Now, Construct Offers Using Your Topics, Targets, and Tradeoffs

Opening Offer: Before you write something here, jot down on a scrap paper the best possible deal you can realistically imagine by listing the upper Target for each Topic. (These are your Best Targets.) Then add to it a reasonable cushion so you can make concessions. Especially cushion your favorite topics. Write down that cushioned proposal here.

Least Acceptable Offer: Write down here the worst possible deal you will accept by stating the best deal you have elsewhere, or, if you have no such alternative offer, by listing the lower Target for each Topic. Later, compare any tentative deal to this one to make sure you're not accepting a bad one.

Creative Proposal(s): Write down here at least one other possible deal. You might describe a deal that gives you lots of your favorite Topic and less of your least favorite Topic; or a deal that uses creative Options (i.e., Tradeoffs w/i Topic) to satisfy your interest in a Topic at low cost to the Other Person. Have such deal(s) ready in case an impasse arises during the talks.

Finally, Test Your Offers:

1. Do the offers satisfy the Interests you've listed and are there any time bombs in it?
2. Which of your offers give you the chance to achieve the best Targets you've set for your favorite Topics?
3. Are the offers at least as good as your best Alternative to negotiated agreement?
4. Do the Independent Criteria you listed confirm these offers are fair and are there any Ethical traps?
5. How will the OP React to your offers and how will you Respond?

Acknowledgments

Depending on how you look at it, this book has been three years or several decades in the making. I've become indebted to many people along the way, and it's my pleasure to thank most of them here. If you enjoy this book, give them most of the credit; blame me for any shortcomings.

My wonderful wife, Cary, has borne with this project—and borne witness to it—for years. I'm grateful to her for a thousand things, including how dearly she sends me out into the world in strength. I'm glad, too, for her patience, her kind and helpful feedback, and her encouragement. I love her dearly.

My daughters, Hannah and Rachael, inspired this book. I wrote every page with them in mind and with them in my heart. I am so grateful for them.

Nick Amphlett, my editor at HarperCollins, believed in me and this book from the start. He's been a cheerful, gracious, and thoughtful editor throughout and he's managed to achieve a remarkable balance: he's given me full freedom to create, even as he's offered excellent suggestions and just the right number of constraints to keep me focused and on track. The book is so much better thanks to him. Everyone told me to expect writing a book like this to be painful. It never happened. In fact, it's been a pleasure. My theory is because I had such an excellent editor in my corner.

Esmond Harmsworth, my agent at Aevitas Creative Management, has believed in me for years and decades. This book would not exist without him. He amazed me with the way he devoted himself to developing the project, spending months honing the proposal with me. And as a student of negotiation, I bow to him for his excellent negotiating; he has represented me beautifully at every step. Another key reason this book has been such a pleasure for me to produce has been because of his wit, his encouragement, his guidance, and his masterful understanding of the publishing world. May every author have the great good fortune to have an agent like him in their corner.

Will Murphy, my freelance editor, worked with me on this project before anyone else did. He has been in my corner on this and previous projects, and I am grateful to him for all of it. Here, he took the lump of clay I brought him and helped me shape it and reshape till it was ready to share with others. He is an excellent editor and a dear person. I get a warm feeling whenever I think of him. It's been a privilege working with him.

My mother, Gina, and father, John, deserve pages of praise for their love and support all my life. On my mantel is a photo of my mother reading to me when I was four; she helped instill a love of books and learning. So too did my father, a great reader himself, who has cheered me on throughout this project. Both of them have lovingly encouraged me as I've developed my writing. I am so grateful for them.

My sister, Carol, has been one of my sweetest and kindest cheerleaders for as long as I can remember. She has always been in my corner, overly praising my material and making me feel much more accomplished than I have the right to feel. Her birth is one of my very first memories, and she has been a gift to me ever since.

Charles Barker and Gary Lausch, two of my dear brothers-in-law, have long been my faithful and generous readers, dear encouragements, and, far more important, models to me. So too have been my dear sisters-in-law, **Kate Barker and Ann Lausch**.

Jeff Barefoot, also my dear brother-in-law, has also been a kind encouragement of my work (and a brilliant model of hospitality too).

My cousin Elizabeth Lesser has been generous with her help and encouragement for a long time. A celebrated best-selling author herself, she is a model to me. I count myself fortunate to call one of my dear cuzzes.

Steve Blader and Melissa Schilling of NYU Stern School of Business have each helped me along the way with wise advice and encouragement, both in my teaching and in my writing. I am fortunate to be able to work under their leadership.

Ken Davis, a dear friend and fellow professor and writer, has encouraged and counseled me, commiserated with me, celebrated with me, and always delighted me from the sheer pleasure of his company throughout this and earlier projects. I'm a better writer and person for knowing him.

Stanley Fuchs of Fordham Graduate School of Business gave me my start as a business school professor and allowed me to teach my first negotiation course many years ago. He gave me a chance when he had reason not to, and I will always be grateful to him for it. This book would not be possible without his kind support. May he rest in peace.

David Rogers of NYU Stern School of Business gave me my start there teaching negotiation and conflict management. Few professional days I've had were as delightful or consequential as the day he gave me a chance there. This book would not have happened without him. I'll always be grateful for him. May he rest in peace.

John Donaldson of Columbia Business School gave me my start there teaching negotiation and conflict management. He too had reason not to, yet he gave me more than one chance and so opened a wonderful door. This book is better for the chance he gave me, and I will always be indebted to him.

Andrea Bartoli did the same for me at Columbia's School of International and Public Affairs, welcoming me to that dear school and encouraging me long after. I'm grateful to him.

My students have inspired me for decades. They've given me the inspiration to create most of the tools in this book. They've also given me the ability to test the tools in countless real-life situations. And they've given me still more valuable feedback from our delicious discussions and their always fascinating survey responses. It has always been my great pleasure to serve them. To each of them I repeat my concluding words: Thank you for being my student. Go make me proud.

Jeanne Brett, a doyen of the field of conflict management and negotiation, was one of the first people to welcome me to it. When I first visited her, she lavished me with materials, wise counsel, encouragement, and referrals. And she's been an ongoing mentor and help ever since, patiently responding to me whenever I've needed advice. Now, whenever someone expresses interest in teaching our subject, I try to pay forward the kindness she's shown me, though I never seem to do it as well. This book is better for my having known her.

Jim Kuhn, my dear friend and the founder of the negotiation program at CBS, was a great mentor to me for many years. He was as kind and generous as he was accomplished, and he was very accomplished indeed. I'm so grateful to have known him. I honor him and miss him. May he rest in peace.

Lela Love and Josh Stulberg first taught me to mediate. In the process, they helped spark a lifelong love of negotiation and conflict management. It was their excellent training that led me to first explore the idea of teaching conflict management myself. Many years later, I still draw on their training in my own teaching— and in this book too.

Ann Bartel did more to teach me how to teach negotiation and conflict management than anyone else. She graciously agreed to let me sit at her feet and learn from her for an entire semester at Columbia Business School, as she taught the subject to graduate students, then sponsored my first course at Columbia. Even when I faced adversity, she encouraged and supported me, which led me to build a career at Columbia and beyond. Decades later, I'm honored and delighted to co-teach with her each semester. Much of this book reflects insights I learned from her.

Josh Weiss, my fellow author and student of negotiation and conflict management, has advised me more than once about writing and publishing, giving me valuable ideas and insights each time. He also kindly let me vet my work on Notional BATNA with him, and offered me valuable feedback and encouragement that helped me move forward with confidence. I appreciate it.

Gaurav Mittal has been unceasingly and remarkably generous from the moment we first worked together on a training and for years after. I've been thrilled by his kindness in frequently guest lecturing my students about the TTT grid, and thrilled to be able to interview and quote him about the TTT grid for this book. To have the support of a world-class business leader like Gaurav is one of the delights of my work.

Bob Louden, Jack Cambria, and Dr. Jeff Thompson, all former key figures in the New York Police Department Hostage Negotiation Team (HNT), have been my mentors, teachers, guests, and models for a long time now. I still quote them to my students. Several insights in this book I've drawn from their wisdom.

Cynthia Franklin, my dear colleague at NYU Stern, was unceasingly generous with her time and effort connecting me with helpful interview candidates. I learned from them and I'm once again indebted to her.

Ellie Shackleton repeatedly served as my faithful and helpful researcher. She often discovered gems that markedly enriched the book, never more so than the oustanding research she did to help me learn key principles of decision science that inform the chapter on Notional BATNA. I would gladly recommend her to anyone.

Joe Bartel has been a friend, peer, adviser, guest lecturer, and collaborator for many years. I'm grateful for his letting me interview him for this book, and for all the kindness and friendship he's shown me. He is a gentleman and a scholar.

David Juran, my NYU Stern colleague, patiently let me talk out the ideas that form the basis for Notional BATNA, giving me vital feedback and encouragement.

Sheena S. Iyengar, my Columbia colleague, gave me valuable feedback early in my work developing Notional BATNA; her insight as a world-renowned expert on choice helped me shape the idea so it was more grounded and clear-eyed about the risks one faces making decisions based on projections. I'm grateful for her time and wise counsel.

Bob Bontempo, my dear Columbia colleague, has been a mentor and friend for decades. My interview with him enriched this book; so too have many of the other things he's taught me about our subject over the years, through conversation, brilliant materials he's created, and simply watching him in action.

Neil Rosini, my attorney, has helped me at several important points in this project. As one who teaches law students to care about clients' interests, I can say with confidence that Neil is excellent. More than a mere business lawyer, he is a true counsellor who understands his client's needs and serves them well.

Toby Rice gave me a rich and valuable interview about his and his team's extraordinary success using our training to help negotiate collaboratively with suppliers. He is a model leader and I am proud to know him.

Rita McGrath, my esteemed Columbia colleague, was perhaps my most patient correspondent. She was unceasingly gracious. She has taught me much both in conversation and in her written work and lectures, and I'm indebted to her in several ways for her time and wisdom.

Richard Andrews was gracious to take time to share with me his insight as a leader of a highly successful business book series. As a newcomer to the field, I'm grateful for his generosity.

Manny Cacciatore was a kind and generous early reader of this book, offering thoughtful feedback that touched me dearly.

Franz Wohlgezogen, co-author of the excellent HBR article, "Roaring Out of

Recession, " is a kind and talented scholar who, years ago, generously agreed to explore with me ways negotiation can help firms thrive through hard times. Though our collaboration didn't produce an article, our conversations, joint interviews, and correspondence inspired me to develop tool-based answers for the book. I'm grateful to have had the privilege to work with such a gentleman and scholar.

Kate Vitaksek has been a mentor, teacher, and friend for several years now. Her work on the Vested Way in the supply chain field has long inspired me. Her generous encouragement and her referrals to other experts in the field have enriched this book. They've also enriched my understanding of the remarkable things teams can accomplish with the right collaborative structure.

Liz Elting was uncommonly generous to share her wisdom, insight, and experience with me in a welcome and inspiring interview. Her remarkable success founding and leading TransPerfect and her unique perspective enriched my thinking about what students and readers can do when they feel empowered—especially women—and enhanced my eagerness to nurture that hope in them. I know Liz nurtures that hope for many through her philanthropy and her example. I'm indebted to her.

Bonnie Keith was generous and kind to let me interview her about strategic procurement and supply chain negotiating generally. Our conversation was fascinating and she very much enriched the penultimate chapter of this book.

Endnotes

Introduction

1 https://www.edutopia.org/blog/scaffolding-lessons-six-strategies-rebecca-alber.

https://www.niu.edu/citl/resources/guides/instructional-guide/instructional-scaffolding-to-improve-learning.shtml.

https://psycnet.apa.org/record/1997-08246-000. "Scaffolding student learning: Instructional approaches and issues."

https://www.diva-portal.org/smash/record.jsf?pid=diva2%3A1163190&dswid=-3339 "Scaffolding—a style of instruction that provides students with the intellectual support to function at the cutting edge of their individual development. Scaffolding allows students to perform tasks that would be slightly beyond their ability without that assistance and guidance from the teacher. Rather than simply transmitting knowledge, teachers enter into conversational dialogues with students, helping them construct knowledge and understand and develop their thinking processes on instructional tasks."

https://link.springer.com/article/10.1007/s12564-016-9426-9. Self-regulated learning scaffolds in computer-based learning environments generally produced a significantly positive effect on academic performance (ES = 0.438). It is also suggested that both domain-general and domain-specific scaffolds can support the entire process of self-regulated learning since they demonstrated substantial effects on academic performance.

https://link.springer.com/article/10.1007/s10648-010-9127-6. "Scaffolding in Teacher–Student Interaction: A Decade of Research": "Results suggest that scaffolding is effective."

https://www.igi-global.com/article/multiple-scaffolds-used-to-support-self-regulated-learning-in-elementary-mathematics-classrooms/287533. "Multiple Scaffolds Used to Support Self-Regulated Learning in Elementary Mathematics Classrooms":

1) The self-regulated learning model supported by multiple scaffolding performs better than the traditional teaching models in learning mathematics. And it is also superior to the traditional narrative of only teaching materials provided by the digital learning platform. 2) The learning performance of high achievement students is higher in Experimental Group 1 compared to all the other groups. 3) Students in Experimental Group 1 have more confidence in themselves as compared to those of Experimental Group 2 with regards to these five aspects including self-regulated learning/planning, self-monitoring, evaluation, reflection, and effort.

https://ieeexplore.ieee.org/document/6327625. "The Design and Effect of a Scaffolded Concept Mapping Strategy on Learning Performance in an Undergraduate Database Course": "Students who used the strategy had better learning achievements than those who only experienced traditional lectures. Moreover, the implementation of the strategy received positive student feedback."

https://www.tandfonline.com/doi/abs/10.1207/S15326942DN2101_2. "The role of early parenting in children's development of executive processes": "*Developmental Neuropsychology* recorded verbal scaffolding between mothers and their 3- and 4-year-old children as they played together. Then, when the children were six years old, they underwent several measures of executive function, such as working memory and goal-directed play. The study found that the children's working memory and language skills at six years of age were related to the amount of verbal scaffolding provided by mothers at age three. In particular, scaffolding was most effective when mothers provided explicit conceptual links during play. Therefore, the results of this study not only suggest that verbal scaffolding aids children's cognitive development, but that the quality of the scaffolding is also important for learning and development."

https://en.wikipedia.org/wiki/Instructional_scaffolding#Applications.

Part I: Get Ready

1. There is evidence the original quote was, "Everybody has plans until they get hit for the first time," https://www.newspapers.com/image/?clipping_id=57527486, but when asked about the more famous version, Tyson has embraced it as his words and has even tweeted it: https://twitter.com/miketyson/status/1052665864401633299?lang=en.

2. https://theblast.com/112540/mike-tyson-says-losing-to-buster-douglas-was-best-day-of-his-lif/.

Chapter 1: Use Three Little Words to Find Hope

1. As we'll see in Chapter 2, it's also wise to jot down one other kind of Interest: Common Interests. But let's keep things simple for now.

2. Woolf, Bob, *Friendly Persuasion: My Life as a Negotiator*. New York: Putnam, 1990.

3. "There is not an agent in baseball more prepared for contract negotiations. His research team is deep and his data bases have the most volume of information, statistics, history and details of any agency that I negotiated with or against." "Negotiating with Scott Boras," ESPN, by Jim Bowden, 2011, https://www.espn.com/blog/the-gms-office/insider/post/_/id/238. "He needed more and better information to stay a step ahead in an increasingly crowded field, so in the late 1980s he created a new division and staffed it with statisticians and economists." "Boras Calls All the Shots for His Clients," ESPN, by Matthew Cole, 2007, https://www.espn.com/mlb/news/story?id=3039348.

4. "25 Ways to Raise the Stakes in Your Script Writing You Need to Know," Blog: Scriptfirm, Gideon's Screenwriting Tips: Now You're a Screenwriter, March 17, 2017: "Screenwriters are taught to raise the stakes for their characters to create excitement, tension, intrigue and anxiety." https://gideonsway.wordpress.com/2017/03/07/25-ways-to-raise-the-stakes-in-your-script-writing-you-need-to-use/.

5. Rackham, N. and Carlisle, J. (1978), "The Effective Negotiator — Part I: The Behaviour of Successful Negotiators," *Journal of European Industrial Training*, Vol. 2, No. 6, pp. 6–11. https://doi.org/10.1108/eb002297.

6. Rackham's 1978 study is, admittedly, pretty old now, and he only surveyed negotiators in England. So, take it with a grain of salt. But most everything I've seen in my work in negotiation

supports Rackham's findings that developing several options per topic is a powerful and valuable thing to do.

7 https://www.sciencediplomacy.org/perspective/2012/water-diplomacy. For a related example of a peace accord between the same nations over water, see, "Israel and Jordan Sign Draft of Wide-Ranging Peace Treaty," *New York Times,* October 18, 1994. https://www.nytimes.com/1994/10/18/world/israel-and-jordan-sign-draft-of-wide-ranging-peace-treaty.html.

8 See Roger Fisher, William Ury, and Bruce Patton, *Getting to YES* (revised edition). New York: Penguin, 2011, pp. 43–44.

9 Technically Carter also won his for his later work through the Carter Center. But the Nobel committee also honored his work at Camp David. https://www.nobelprize.org/prizes/peace/2002/press-release/.

10 Henry Mintzberg, "The Manager's Job: Folklore and Fact," *Harvard Business Review,* March–April 1980. See also Rosemary Stewart ed., 2020, *Managerial Work.* Philadelphia: Routledge (extensive discussion of negotiation by managers) and Linda A. Hill, 2008, *"Exercising Influence Without Authority: How New Managers Can Build Power and Influence."* Cambridge MA, Harvard Business Review Press.

11 See Hill, *Exercising Influence Without Authority,* for more on this idea.

12 See https://blog.hubspot.com/sales/6-popular-sales-methodologies-summarized, https://mailshake.com/blog/sales-methodologies/, https://www.forbes.com/sites/georgedeeb/2017/03/01/the-top-3-selling-techniques-which-is-best-for-your-business/?sh=660221574f56.

13 https://www.richardson.com/sales-resources/defining-consultative-sales/.

14 https://www.homequestionsanswered.com/do-eskimos-buy-refrigerators.htm; https://www.irishtimes.com/news/inuit-need-funds-to-buy-freezers-to-store-game-1.788830.

15 "Who would ever have believed that a commodity item, like chicken, could become a branded, premium-priced product? Perdue Farms was a very successful breeder and reseller of chicken, and it could have easily continued on this path — a path that involved little risk but steady and manageable growth prospects. Observing the technological advances in automated chicken raising that evolved in the 1960s, Franklin Perdue (CEO from 1953 to 1988) saw an opportunity to transform his family's company. Bucking a family tradition of avoiding debt, Perdue borrowed $500,000 and set about to fundamentally change his operation from a chicken farmer and reseller to a fully automated chicken raising and retail operation . . . Perdue saw a vision for what his company could become and took the risks to achieve that vision. Perdue did what others considered impossible. He branded a product that was historically thought to be a low-end, unmarketable commodity." https://hbr.org/2007/11/beyond-vision-the-ability-and.

"There's no better example [of the idea that there's no such thing as a commodity] than Perdue Farms. Frank Perdue has built a three-quarter-billion-dollar chicken business . . ." Thomas J. Peters and Nancy K. Austin, *Passion for Excellence: The Leadership Difference,* New York: Random House, 1985.

"Perdue, Franklin Parsons ('Frank')." The Scribner Encyclopedia of American Lives. Encyclopedia.com. November 15, 2022. https://www.encyclopedia.com/humanities/encyclopedias-almanacs-transcripts-and-maps/perdue-franklin-parsons-frank.

Chapter 2: Build a Swiss Army Knife for Adversity

1   See Rackham and Carlisle, "The Effective Negotiator — Part I," pp. 6–11.

2   Carroll, Jim, "A Love Supreme: The Spiritual Journey of John Coltrane," jimcarrollsblog.com, December 15, 2020, https://www.jimcarrollsblog.com/blog/2020/12/16/a-love-supreme -the-spiritual-journey-of-john-coltrane. "Coltrane practiced obsessively, 25 hours a day. While on tour, a fellow hotel guest complained about the noise. Coltrane simply removed the saxophone from his mouth and carried on playing in silence. He would practice a single note for hours on end and fall asleep with the horn at his side." Hendrix: Mostly legendary accounts tell of Hendrix playing constantly and even sleeping with his guitar: see, e.g., "How Much to Practice," Studybass, https://www.studybass.com/lessons/practicing/how-much-to-practice/. "Jimi Hendrix never put his guitar down. He even took it with him when he went to the bathroom!"

3   Valley, Kathleen, Interview with Regina Fazio Marcusa, "The Electronic Negotiator," *Harvard Business Review,* January–February 2000. "We found that more than 50% of e-mail negotiations end in impasse; only 19% end that way in face-to-face negotiations." See also Winkler, Claudia, "INSIGHT: Improving Virtual Negotiation Skills in Cross-Cultural Interactions," Bloomberg Law, June 16, 2020, https://news.bloomberglaw.com/environment-and-energy/insight -improving-virtual-negotiation-skills-in-cross-cultural-interactions.

Kurtzberg, Dunn-Jensen, and Matsibekker (2005) pulled from both social exchange (Blau, 1964) and social identity (Ashforth and Mael, 1989) theories by manipulating familiarity and similarity in a four-person virtual negotiation. First and foremost, they found that many negotiations reached an impasse, highlighting the difficulty of virtual negotiations in general.

4   Reginald Hudlin, dir. *The Black Godfather,* Boardwalk Pictures and Makemake, 2019 https:// www.netflix.com/watch/80173387.

5   I wish I was always as effective negotiating a travel crisis as Myra was. But though my average is very good, I freely confess that sometimes I'm not. One holiday, my family and I reached the airport only to find our bargain airline was running so late that morning that the airport had bounced our flight from its gate. So, at the last minute, the airline simply canceled the flight, leaving us stranded. I immediately did what Myra did, working the I FORESAW IT as hard as I could. But gentle reader, nothing I learned, brainstormed, asked, or said to the desk clerk, or anyone else, made any difference; the airline simply refused to do anything to help, and it took me some doing even to get a refund. Whereever you were that day, it's possible you heard my head exploding with frustration. So, we quickly developed a Plan B and found a way to our destination without the airline's help.

Did I fail? Not exactly. If I had simply gone up to the desk clerk and made angry demands (as others usually do to no effect), I would always wonder if my approach had been the problem. But because I'd quickly done my homework, I was probably as ready as one could be in that situation. I've since learned that airline is notorious for this very kind of service and that there was probably no winning with it that day. Using I FORESAW IT gave me reassurance that I'd explored the possibilities fully.

Myra's and my experience illustrate one way to use the I FORESAW IT under pressure: simply work it as fully as you can in the time available. But there are several other ways to use it even when you can't do it all by yourself.

Chapter 3: Get More Help Than You Expected

1 See Matt Taibi, *The Divide: American Injustice in the Age of the Wealth Gap.* New York: Random House (2014), especially Chapter 7 (Little Frauds).

2 Hopkins, Michael S. "How to Negotiate Practically Anything: Interview with an attorney who has an unconventional negotiating manner: kind, honest, fair," *Inc. Magazine,* February 1, 1989, https://www.inc.com/magazine/19890201/5526.html.

Chapter 4: Get a Glance-and-Go Play Sheet

1 "Coaches Use Laminated Game Outlines for Any Situation," October 27, 2006. https://www.nytimes.com/2006/10/27/sports/football/coaches-use-laminated-game-outlines-for-any-situation.html.

2 "His arm is bent awkwardly—perhaps, he has speculated, because he was glancing at the checklist on his wrist." TIME 100 Photographs: The Most Influential Images of All Time, 2018, cited in "Buzz Aldrin Tweets Story Behind Iconic Photo on Moon," *Men's Health,* July 21, 2017, https://www.menshealth.com/trending-news/a19527021/buzz-aldrin-story-iconic-moon-photo/#:~:text=%E2%80%9CHis%20arm%20is%20bent%20awkwardly,%2C%20it%20did%20everything%20right.%E2%80%9D.

3 "Training and Learning: One-Pagers." https://www.masterclass.com/classes/chris-hadfield-teaches-space-exploration/chapters/training-and-learning-one-pagers.

4 Most illustrations by Akindo. Usage rights purchased through iStock and directly from Akindo at akindostudio@gmail.com.

    iStock URL: https://www.istockphoto.com/search/2/image?mediatype=illustration&phrase=akindo&servicecontext=srp-searchbar-top. Illustration under "Topics" is a generic image from an unidentified source.

5 Roy Lewicki, "Pacific Oil (A)" in *Negotiation: Readings, Exercises and Cases* (7th Revised Edition), 2021, New York: McGraw Hill, p. 609.

6 https://www.express.co.uk/life-style/life/844721/the-beatles-lost-millions-manager-brian-epstein-blunders.

7 See Peter Brown and Steven Gaines, *The Love You Make: An Insider's Story of the Beatles,* 1983, New York: New American Library.

8 A term we explored in Chapter 3. We'll enrich your chances of having a good BATNA in Chapters 6 and 8.

9 You might wonder if it's a good idea to assign point values to each increase in a given topic instead of just ranking them numerically: "OK, $100 is worth 100 points, $90 is worth 80 points, $80 is worth 60 points . . . A two-year guarantee costs me 20 points, three years costs me 30 points . . ." Economists love this idea, and if you can do it, great, by all means do. The thing is, I find students have a hard time doing that, and so do I, even though I have an economics degree.

10 Alas, while I remember the survey and share my memory of it each semester, it appears it may no longer be available online and my efforts to find a copy have not succeeded, so I must ask you to trust my recollection.

11   Readers of *Consumer Reports* know well what that means. Tens of thousands of them have
     reported in surveys that they've effectively gotten, on average, 35 percent discounts on published
     hotel room rates. How? They collectively report almost two dozen options they've learned to ask
     about, including AAA member discounts, weekend rates, free breakfast, "run of the house" rates,
     multi-night discounts, AARP discounts, student discounts, and so on. Not that you should ask
     any hotel representative about twenty-four options, but asking about a few can be reasonable and
     wise. https://www.consumerreports.org/cro/news/2011/01/how-to-get-a-great-hotel-rate
     /index.htm; https://www.today.com/news/score-cheaper-hotel-room-wbna19072166; https://
     www.wral.com/news/local/story/1088875/.

12   G. Richard Shell, *Bargaining for Advantage: Negotiation Strategies for Reasonable People*, New
     York: Penguin, 2006, citing Pruitt and Lewis, "Development of Integrative Solutions in Bilateral
     Negotiation"; Elizabeth A. Mannix, Leigh Thompson, and Max H. Bazerman, "Negotiation in
     Small Groups," *Journal of Applied Psychology*, Vol 74, No. 3 (1989), pp. 508–517; Gary A. Yukl,
     Michael P. Malone, Bert Hayslip, and Thomas A. Pamin, "The Effects of Time Pressure and Issue
     Settlement Order on Integrative Bargaining," *Sociometry*, Vol 39, No. 3 (1976), pp. 277–281.

13   Notice packaging doesn't mean allowing the other side to confuse you, hiding costs and traps in a
     "simple, all-in-deal," a common practice used by car dealers. *Consumer Reports* explains in a warning
     to car buyers: "By starting with your monthly payment as the focus, the salesperson can lump the
     whole process together: the price for the new vehicle, the trade-in, and financing, if appropriate. This
     gives him too much latitude to sow confusion. Instead, insist on negotiating one thing at a time.
     Your first priority is to settle on the lowest price you can get on the new vehicle. Only after you've
     locked that in should you begin to discuss a trade-in or financing." Or do talk about a package but
     break out each part of it so it's clear what each term costs." https://www.consumerreports.org/car
     -pricing-negotiation/how-to-negotiate-a-new-car-price-effectively-a8596856299/.

14   "Top holiday destinations with markets to haggle in," *Good Housekeeping*, September 11, 2014,
     https://www.goodhousekeeping.com/uk/consumer-advice/money/a544570/top-holiday
     -destinations-with-markets-haggle-tips/.

15   Finkelstein, Lawrence S. "Remembering Ralph Bunche," *World Policy Journal*, Fall 2003, p. 70,
     https://www.jstor.org/stable/40209877.

16   Northcraft, Gregory B. and Neale, Margaret A. "Experts, Amateurs, and Real Estate: An
     Anchoring-and-Adjustment Perspective on Property Pricing Decisions," *Organizational Behavior
     and Human Decision Processes* 39, pp. 84–97 (1987); see also, Shell, *Bargaining for Advantage:
     Negotiation Strategies for Reasonable People*, New York: Penguin, 2006, p. 159.

17   Bontempo, Robert, Interview by Seth Freeman, Zoom, July 14, 2022.

18   Miller, Sterling. "Ten Things: Creating a Good Contract Playbook," Sterling Miller, July 17, 2018,
     https://sterlingmiller2014.wordpress.com/2018/07/17/ten-things-creating-a-good-contract
     -playbook/.

Chapter 5: Rehearse Your Dance with Godzilla

1   "Khrushchev and Kennedy: Vienna Summit 1961," 35:20-25, YouTube excerpt from David
     Reynolds, Vienna 1961, Russell Barnes, dir, BBC Four 2008, https://www.youtube.com
     /watch?v=G2KhwFbIdUc&t=2439s.

2   https://www.history.com/news/kennedy-krushchev-vienna-summit-meeting-1961.

3   Ken T. Trotman, Arnold M. Wright and Sally Wright, "Auditor Negotiations: An Examination of the Efficacy of Intervention Methods," *The Accounting Review* Vol. 80, No. 1 (Jan. 2005), pp. 349–367.

4   "The Effects of Mental Practice on Motor Skill Performance: Critical Evaluation and Meta-Analysis," https://journals.sagepub.com/doi/abs/10.2190/X9BA-KJ68-07ANQMJ8?casa _token=eUwPcfaMsnsAAAAA:rQ3cy_ADVh9sKoHwd6qRPH40rXSBqwZApe4u8BkiwG wL5pSyZMSjY5wXhgUHqn_RjpBL7BHAY4Oz; Quinn, Elizabeth, "How Imagery and Visualization Can Improve Athletic Performance," Verywellfit, July 4, 2021, https://www .verywellfit.com/visualization-techniques-for-athletes-3119438; Erica Warren, "Teaching Visualization Can Improve Academic Achievement for Students at Any Age," Minds in Bloom, https://minds-in-bloom.com/teaching-visualization-can-improve/.

5   Hannah Jewel, "How do presidential candidates prepare for debates? | Hannah Explains," YouTube, 2019, https://www.youtube.com/watch?v=F_h8u1LJd2s.

6   Wikipedia, 2022. War Gaming. Last modified May 4, 2021. Wikipedia, https://en.wikipedia.org /wiki/Military_wargaming.

7   Federal Aviation Administration, "FAA Issues New Flight Simulator Regulations," April 14, 2016, https://www.faa.gov/newsroom/faa-issues-new-flight-simulator regulations#:~:text=The%20 FAA%20now%20allows%20up,FAA%2Dapproved%20aviation%20training%20device.

8   Schoemaker, P., "Why You Need to Play War Games," *Inc.* February 28, 2013, https://www.inc .com/paul-schoemaker/why-you-need-to-play-war-games.html.

9   Andrew Glass, "JFK and Khrushchev meet in Vienna, June 3, 1961," Politico, June 2, 20117, https:// www.politico.com/story/2017/06/02/jfk-and-khrushchev-meet-in-vienna-june-3-1961-238979.

    Becky Little, "JFK Was Completely Unprepared for His Summit with Khruschev," History.com, July 18, 2018, https://www.history.com/news/kennedy-krushchev-vienna-summit-meeting-1961.

10 Jeff is a now research scientist at the Molecular Imaging and Neuropathology Division at Columbia University Medical Center/New York State Psychiatric Institute.

11 See V. B. Van Hasselt and Romano, S. J., "Role-playing: A vital tool in crisis negotiation skills training," *FBI Law Enforcement Bulletin*, 73, 12–21, 2004.

    V. B. Van Hasselt, Baker, M. T., Romano, S. J., Sellers, A. H., Noesner, G. W., and Smith, S.,"Development and validation of a role-play test for assessing crisis (hostage) negotiation skills," *Criminal Justice and Behavior*, 32, 345–361, 2005.

    V. B. Van Hasselt, Baker, M. T., Romano, S. J., Schlessinger, K. M., Zucker, M., Dragone, R., and Perera, A. L., "Crisis (hostage) negotiation training: A preliminary evaluation of program efficacy," *Criminal Justice and Behavior,* 33, 56–69, 2006.

12 Errol Morris, director, *The Fog of War: Eleven Lessons from the Life of Robert S. McNamara,* 2003. 107 minutes, see "Lesson #1: Empathize with your Enemy."

13 Chernow, Ron, *Alexander Hamilton,* New York: Penguin, 2005.

Chapter 6: Trade Up and Up—Or Drill Down and Down

1   https://www.sage.exchange/post/of-negotiating.

2   See Livingston, Jessica, *Founders at Work: Stories of Startups Early Days,* New York: Apress, 2008;

Lax, David and Sebenius, James, *3-D Negotiating: Powerful Tools to Change the Game in Your Most Important Deals*, Boston, MA, Harvard Business School Press, 2006. Based on Sebenius, James and Fortgang, Ron, "Steve Perlman and Web TV (A)" and "Steve Perlman and Web TV (B)," Harvard Business School Press, Boston, MA, April 19, 1999.

3   See Caro, Robert, *The Passage of Power: The Years of Lyndon Johnson IV*, New York: Vintage 2013.

4   See, e.g., Shell and Moussa, *The Art of Woo*, New York: Penguin, 2008; Yates, Douglas, *The Politics of Management: Exploring the Inner Workings of Public and Private Organizations*, San Francisco: Jossey-Bass Business & Management Series, 1985; and Jay, Antony, *Management and Macciavelli: A Prescription for Success in Your Business*, Hoboken: Prentice Hall, 1996.

5   Robert Freeland, *The Struggle for Control of the Modern Corporation: Organizational Change at General Motors, 1924–1970*, Cambridge (2000), p. 59; David Conwill, "Copper cooled calamity: The 1923 Chevrolet Series C," 2016, https://www.hemmings.com/stories/2016/04/20/copper -cooled-calamity-the-1923-chevrolet-series-c; "History Lesson: The Copper-Cooled Chevrolet Was GM's First Major Disaster,"https://www.motortrend.com/vehicle-genres/copper-cooled -chevrolet-gm-first-major-disaster/.

6   Max D. Liston, Transcript of an Interview Conducted by David C. Brock and Gerald E. Gallwas in Irvine, California, and Fullerton, California, on 19 February, 2002 and 22 January, 2003 (PDF). Philadelphia, PA: Chemical Heritage Foundation (cited in Wikipedia).

7   Freeland, p. 59.

8   See, e.g., Shell and Moussa, *The Art of Woo*, New York: Penguin, 2008; Yates, *The Politics of Management*, Jossey-Bass; Michael Watkins, *Shaping the Game: The New Leader's Guide to Effective Negotiating*, Harvard Business Review Press (2006).

9   Targeted Negotiating is somewhat different from developing your BATNA on the eve of talks with a counterpart. First, most BATNA development usually involves just a handful of choices, some of which aren't even deals; they're pressure, like suing or calling the police. Targeted Negotiating in contrast often starts with dozens, hundreds, or even thousands of possible counterparts. Second, Targeted Negotiating involves culling, while BATNA development usually involves shopping or brainstorming. Last, since Targeted Negotiating usually reveals several prospects, each can serve as a possible additional negotiation you can do as well. Developing and using a BATNA, in contrast, usually forecloses a deal with the counterpart.

10   Interview with Professor Kate Vitasek, January 28, 2022.

11   Webb, Amy, *Data, a Love Story: How I Cracked the Online Dating Code to Meet My Match*, New York: Plume, 2013.

Chapter 7: Win Warmly

1   Shonk, Katie, "Claiming Value in Negotiations: Do Extreme Requests Backfire?," Program on Negotiation, Harvard Law School Daily Blog, February 11, 2019, https://www.pon.harvard.edu /daily/dealmaking-daily/claiming-value-in-negotiation-do-extreme-requests-backfire/, citing Wong, R.S. and Howard, S. (2018), "Think Twice Before Using Door-in-the-Face Tactics in Repeated Negotiation: Effects on negotiated outcomes, trust and perceived ethical behaviour," *International Journal of Conflict Management*, Vol. 29 No. 2, pp. 167–188. https://doi.org/10.1108 /IJCMA-05-2017-0043.

2   Hopkins, Michael, "How to Negotiate Practically Anything," *Inc. Magazine,* February 1, 1989, https://www.inc.com/magazine/19890201/5526.html.

3   I've borrowed and tweaked a term coined by Harvard negotiation professor Robert Mnookin. See Mnookin, Robert, *Good for You, Great for Me: Finding the Trading Zone and Winning at Win-Win Negotiation.* New York: PublicAffairs, 2014.

4   For example, imagine an industry journal says prices range as high as $105. For reasons we'll discuss below, you've set a slightly lower Best Target of $100. When you make your first offer, you might say, "My offer is $105. As you can see, this industry journal reports products like ours sell for up to $105."

5   If there are some topics you don't cushion, then for them it's often wise to ask instead for your Best Targets. But in some cases, it may make sense to include a soft offer.

6   "The target price that you calculated allowed for a reasonable dealer profit . . . Reassure the salesperson that your offer includes a fair profit." Linkov, Jon, "How to Negotiate a New-Car Price Effectively," *Consumer Reports,* updated July 26, 2021, https://www.consumerreports.org/car-pricing-negotiation/how-to-negotiate-a-new-car-price-effectively-a8596856299/.

7   Martin Luther King, Jr., "I Have a Dream" speech (Washington, D.C., August 28, 1963).

8   Adam Grant, *Give and Take: Why Helping Others Drives Our Success,* New York: Penguin, 2013.

Chapter 8: Become a Godzilla Whisperer

1   Muska, John, and Clements, Ron, *Moana,* Pixar, 2016. 107 minutes.

2   Marshall Rosenberg, *Non-Violent Communication: A Language of Life: Life-Changing Tools for Healthy Relationships,* pp. 502–18, Encinitas, CA: PuddleDancer Press, 2015; Alan Seid, story about Marshall Rosenberg in a Palestinian refugee camp, https://www.youtube.com/watch?v=SjIHSo8sALE.

3   "Is My Boss Really Listening to Me? The Impact of Perceived Supervisor Listening on Emotional Exhaustion, Turnover Intention, and Organizational Citizenship Behavior," *Journal of Business Ethics,* Vol. 130, pp. 509–24 (2015), https://link.springer.com/article/10.1007/s10551-014-2242-4.

4   "Army leadership doctrine recognizes the importance of listening to those we lead to make better plans and decisions. . . . Active listening helps communicate reception of the subordinate's message verbally and nonverbally... To capture the message fully, leaders listen to what is said and observe the subordinate's manners. Active listening is an essential component to the leadership competency of 'communicates.'" Cummings, Joel P., "Active Listening: the Leader's Rosetta Stone," Benning.Army.Mil, https://www.benning.army.mil/armor/EArmor/content/issues/2012/NOV_DEC/Cummings.html.

   See also Wikipedia's entry on Active Listening ("Active listening is used in a wide variety of situations, including public interest advocacy, community organizing, tutoring, medical workers talking to patients, HIV counseling, helping suicidal persons, management,") https://en.wikipedia.org/wiki/Active_listening - cite_note-Mineyama_et_al_2007-32 counseling, https://en.wikipedia.org/wiki/Active_listening - cite_note-Levitt_2001-2 and https://en.wikipedia.org/wiki/Active_listening - cite_note-33 settings. In groups it may aid in reaching consensus. It may also be used in casual conversation or small talk to build understanding, though this can be interpreted as condescending.

5   Douglas Noll, *De-Escalate: How to Calm an Angry Person in 90 Seconds or Less* (2017).

Chapter 9: Speak Softly, Solve Strongly

1 Rackham and Carlisle, pp. 6–11.

2 Disclaimer: They usually backfire. But not always. I know a few people who specialize in using irritators, and a couple of them have won success. True, sometimes their role is that of the one-and-done closer who prompts the other side to say, "And we'll never have to talk with Sid again, will we?" But for every successful Sid, there are probably fifty people who are scratching their heads, going, "Why do we keep losing deals? It's probably you, Brad; it's definitely not me."

3 Rackham and Carlisle, pp. 6–11.

4 William R. Miller, "Motivational Interviewing and Quantum Change, with William R. Miller," YouTube, September 24, 2014, https://www.youtube.com/watch?v=2yvuem-QYCo.

5 Mohammadreza, Bahrani and Rita, Krishnan, "Effectiveness of Yoga therapy in change the brain waves of ADHD children," *Asian Journal of Development Matters*, 2011, Volume 5, Issue 3, p 41, https://indianjournals.com/ijor.aspx?target=ijor:ajdm&volume=5&issue=3&article=007. Curiously too, singing can also improve mood and tranquility, as I find when I'm driving or skiing or executing another task that has a bit of danger to it (though I don't recommend singing during negotiation). See Grape, Christina, et al., "Does singing promote well-being?: An empirical study of professional and amateur singers during a singing lesson," *Integrative Physiological & Behavioral Science*, January 2002, https://link.springer.com/article/10.1007/BF02734261.

6 Kühberger, Anton. "The influence of framing on risky decisions: A meta-analysis." *Organizational behavior and human decision processes* 75, no. 1 (1998): 23–55 ("Results show that the overall framing effect between conditions is of small to moderate size"), https://www.sciencedirect.com/science/article/abs/pii/S0749597898927819. See also, Williams, Gary and Miller, Robert, "Change the Way You Persuade," *Harvard Business Review*, May 2002 (explores how to appeal to each of five decision-making styles, some of which are cautious and some of which are excited by new ideas), https://hbr.org/2002/05/change-the-way-you-persuade.

Chapter 10: Correct a Boss with a Four-Letter Word

1 https://www.tailstrike.com/281278 (pdf).

2 https://en.wikipedia.org/wiki/United_Airlines_Flight_173#In_popular_culture.

3 See Gerard I. Nierenberg, *Art of Negotiating*, Pocket Books (1968).

4 Gordon, Suzanne, Mendenhall, Patrick, and O'Connor, Bonnie Blair, *Beyond the Checklist: What Else Health Care Can Learn from Aviation Teamwork and Safety*, Ithaca, ILR Press, 2012.

5 Capt. Al Haynes (May 24, 1991). "The Crash of United Flight 232." Archived from the original on October 26, 2013. Retrieved June 4, 2013. Presentation to NASA Dryden Flight Research Facility staff.

Chapter 11: Use the Hostility-to-Harmony Hacks

1 Yates, Douglas, *The Politics of Management*, Jossey-Bass, 1985, p. 169.

2 Quoting from Ambrose, Stephen E., *Supreme Commander: The War Years of General Dwight D. Eisenhower*, p. 324, New York: Anchor, 2012.

3   Neustadt, Richard, *Presidential Power and the Modern Presidents: The Politics of Leadership from Roosevelt to Reagan*, New York: The Free Press: 1991.

"The Decide, Announce, Defend (DAD) method is not suitable in complex situations where implementation involves a lot of people who are not in an obvious command structure, but can choose whether to cooperate. In some cases, such as traffic congestion, water supply, domestic energy use, waste reduction, renewable generation, and flood risk management, the DAD approach is guaranteed to generate resistance to even the best ideas. Resistance eats up time and resources because it needs a response. The time spent overcoming resistance and defending the solutions against opponents often delays implementation and can lead to the plans being abandoned. Engaging the public avoids DAD becoming DADA, or 'Decide—Announce-Defend-Abandon.'" European Union's Action Plan on Science in Society, "Method: Decide, Announce, Defend (DAD)," https://participedia.net/method/4831.

4   Mintzberg, Henry, "The Manager's Job: Folklore and Fact," *Harvard Business Review*, March–April 1980. See also Stewart, Rosemary ed., *Managerial Work*, London: Routledge 1998 (extensive discussion of negotiation by managers).

5   Yates, Douglas, *The Politics of Management*, Jossey-Bass, 1985, p. 170–77.

6   "Negotiation research suggests that when the parties perceive a high level of procedural justice (i.e. both parties are actively involved in the bargaining process that generates the outcomes specified in the contract and see the process as fair), they are more committed to enacting that agreement." E. C. Tomlinson and Lewicki, R. J., "The negotiation of contractual agreements," *Journal of Strategic Contracting*, 2015.

7   See Lind, Allen and Tyler, Tom, *The Social Psychology of Procedural Justice*, New York: Plenum Press, 1988.

8   See, for example, the Vested partnership method discussed in Vitasek, Kate, Crawford, Jacqui, Nyden, Jeanette, and Kawamoto, Katherine, *The Vested Outsourcing Manual: A Guide for Creating Successful Business and Outsourcing Agreements*, New York: Palgrave MacMillan 2011, and at the Vested website: https://www.vestedway.com/.

9   "Laptop Multitasking Hinders Classroom Learning for Both Users and Nearby Peers," *Computers & Education*, Vol. 62, March 2013, pp. 24–31. https://www.sciencedirect.com/science/article/pii/S0360131512002254.

10   "How Do You Get 25 Lawmakers to Get Along? A Talking Stick," *Wall Street Journal*, January 22, 2018, https://www.wsj.com/livecoverage/shutdown/card/UjoCRLQI0ZpS05JeqsUH.

11   Studies find doctors on average interrupt patients within twenty-three seconds after the patient starts describing symptoms. Yet if a doctor waits ninety seconds, patients report dramatically higher satisfaction. And if the doctor practices active listening too, patients with mild or even serious illness can on average heal more than 20 percent faster. See Trzeciak, Stephen, and Mazzarelli, Anthony, *Compassionomics: The Revolutionary Scientific Evidence That Caring Makes a Difference*, Studer Group, 2019.

12   "Roger Griswold Starts a Brawl in Congress: Today in History: February 15," Kim Sheridan, Connecticuthistory.org, https://connecticuthistory.org/roger-griswold-starts-a-brawl-in-congress-today-in-history/.

13   See Williamjames Hull Hoffer, *The Caning of Charles Sumner: Honor, Idealism, and the Origins of the Civil War*, Baltimore: Johns Hopkins University Press, 2010.

14 To the point, consider this observation by Vermont Senator Ralph Sanders, who introduced the resolution censuring Senator Joe McCarthy, on the virtues of the tradition of Senatorial Courtesy: "In my twelve years of Senate service there was no case of a resort to physical violence or to a threat thereof. In the House, which lacks some of the traditions of the Senate, physical encounters occasionally, though rarely, occur." Flanders, Ralph, *Senator from Vermont,* Boston: Little, Brown and Company, 1961 as quoted in United States Senate—Idea of the Senate|Senatorial Courtesy and Discipline, https://www.senate.gov/about/origins-foundations/idea-of-the-senate/1961Flanders.htm.

15 Brooks, James, Ena Onishi, Isabelle R. Clark, Manuel Bohn, and Shinya Yamamoto. "Uniting against a common enemy: Perceived outgroup threat elicits ingroup cohesion in chimpanzees." *PloS One* 16, no. 2 (2021): e0246869. https://www.ncbi.nlm.nih.gov/pmc/articles/PMC7904213/ citing Hamilton, W. D., "Innate social aptitudes of man: An approach from evolutionary genetics." In: Fox, R.(ed.), *ASA studies 4: Biosocial anthropology.* (1975). See also, Choi, Jung-Kyoo, and Samuel Bowles. "The coevolution of parochial altruism and war." *Science* 318, no. 5850 (2007) 636–40. See also Radford, Andrew N., Bonaventura Majolo, and Filippo Aureli. "Within-group behavioural consequences of between-group conflict: A prospective review." *Proceedings of the Royal Society B: Biological Sciences* 283, no. 1843 (2016): 20161567.

16 Allport, Gordon W. *The nature of prejudice*, Addison-Wesley. Reading (1954).

17 John F. Kennedy Presidential Library and Museum, 1960 Presidential Election results (34,226,731 (49.7%) v. 34,108,157 (49.5%)), https://www.jfklibrary.org/learn/about-jfk/life-of-john-f-kennedy/fast-facts-john-f-kennedy/1960-presidential-election-results.

18 "'Ask Not . . .': JFK's Words Still Inspire 50 Years Later," NPR, January 11, 2011, https://www.npr.org/2011/01/18/133018777/jfks-inaugural-speech-still-inspires-50-years-later.

19 https://www.goodreads.com/quotes/938848-what-general-weygand-called-the-battle-of-france-is-over.

20 Rackham and Carlisle, pp. 6–11.

21 Warning: it's easy and dangerous to list counterfeit Common Interests, ones that sound like Common Interests but aren't. Many Competing Interests do so, even though each is an invitation to a fight. For example,

> "Shift costs" [onto each other?]
>
> "Profit" [at the other's expense?]
>
> "Avoid blame" [by shifting it onto each other?]
>
> "Reduce risk" [by shifting it onto the other?]

Another counterfeit is a Parallel Interest, something each wants but that each could get without the other's help. Merely talking about one of these things without clarifying could prompt your counterpart to feel cynical. For example:

> "Higher profits"
>
> "Better cash flow"
>
> "Less time spent handling chores"

You can sometimes turn a counterfeit into a Common Interest if you add something that emphasizes it's a common goal:

"Higher *shared* profits"

"Improve *both of our firms'* cash flows"

"Less time *for each of us* spent handling chores"

"Shift costs *from both of us*"

"*Mutual* profit"

"Shift blame *[to a guilty third party]*"

Part III: Decide

1 https://www.nytimes.com/2009/10/17/business/17martha.html.

2 Luo, Michael, "Excuse Me. Can I Have Your Seat?" *New York Times,* September 14, 2004. https://www.nytimes.com/2004/09/14/nyregion/excuse-me-may-i-have-your-seat.html.

Chapter 12: Decide with Three Birds in the Bush

1 Bloom, Harold and Hayes, Kevin, *Benjamin Franklin,* InfoBase Publishing 2008.

2 I'm indebted to several experts with whom I discussed the idea, including Professors David Juran, Josh Weiss, and Sheena S. Iyengar.

3 Notional BATNA is not the same as the Most Likely Alternative to a Negotiated Agreement (MLATNA), a term most used by mediators in litigation settlement talks. There, mediators try to advise litigants what they'll most likely get at trial if they don't settle (e.g., "You're suing for $1,000,000, but if you turn down their $500,000 offer, you'll most likely get $300,000 at trial."). That's a useful question, but, as we'll see, it's incomplete because it doesn't consider your risk tolerance, which Notional BATNA does consider. Risk tolerance matters because the most likely outcome is not necessarily what you'll wind up with; if, for example, you can't bear the worst-case scenario, or, alternatively, you can't bear missing out on the best-case scenario, MLATNA may misdirect you. Separately, MLATNA is usually framed as a single adviser's opaque estimate that leaves it unclear how the MLATNA was determined. In contrast, Notional BATNA is a decision method that spells out simple steps you can take to determine it yourself.

4 That's an example of something called an a priori method of risk assessment prized by statisticians. Just as a coin flip isn't dependent on past flips, so an a priori method doesn't assume past events determine future events, so you focus on what you can learn about the present and experts' expectations.

5 That's an example of an a posteriori method of risk assessment prized by insurance companies.

6 Russoff, Jane Wollman, "Charlie Munger: Buffett's 'Abominable No-Man,'" ThinkAdvisor, September 24, 2015, https://www.thinkadvisor.com/2015/09/24/charlie-munger-buffetts-abominable-no-man/.

7 In fact, Buffett and Munger downplay predictions and forecasts and ask if things will be OK even if the worst-case scenario happens.

8 E.g. Maximax, a decision rule that works like so: take the choice that produces the maximum value of the best predicted outcomes. (For example, if Choice 1 could produce values of $70K to $30K and Choice 2 $65K to $40K, pick Choice 1.)

9 E.g. Maximin, a decision rule that works like so: take the choice that produces the maximum value of the worst predicted outcomes. (For example, if Choice 1 could produce values of $70K to $30K and Choice 2 $65K to $40K, pick Choice 2.)

10 E.g. Laplace, a decision rule that works like an equally weighted average or Hurwicz, another decision rule (adjusted weighted average). For example, if Choice 1 could produce values of $70K to $30K and Choice 2 $65K to $40K, the average outcomes are $50K and $52.5K. Laplace would pick Choice 2. Hurwicz is more complicated.

11 E.g. Savage Regret, a decision rule that works like so: take the choice that produces the least regret; compare "what I could have made if I hadn't taken the sure thing" with "what I could have saved if I had taken the sure thing instead." For example, if with Choice 1 could produce values of $70K to $30K and Choice 2 $65K to $40K, then I could have saved up to $30K [$70K to $40K] if I'd gotten the best of Choice 1 instead of suffering the worst of Choice 2, and I could have made $35K more [$65K to $30K] if I'd gotten the best out of Choice 2 instead of suffering the worst of Choice 1. Savage Regret would pick Choice 2.

12 Cnet.com/news/what-would-happen-if-moores-law-did-fizzle/: "The hardest hit [by the end of Moore's law] would be companies dependent on consumers replacing their electronics every few years and tech companies such as Google whose long-term plans hinge on faster computers, cheaper storage, and better bandwidth."

13 "Study Finds Settling Is Better Than Going to Trial," *New York Times,* August 7, 2008, http://www.nytimes.com/2008/08/08/business/08law.html.

Chapter 13: Use a Yes/No Instrument Panel

1 "Part 2: Why Your Favorite Musicians Are Broke," 0:00–3:53, https://www.youtube.com/watch?v=o7OZLFGEDiI.

2 See, "Jewel Turned Down $1 Million Record Deal When She Was Homeless," The Joe Rogan Experience, https://www.youtube.com/watch?v=DTGtC7FC4oI; "Why Jewel says she turned down a million-dollar signing bonus when she was homeless," Dunn, August 5, 2017, ABC News, https://abcnews.go.com/Business/jewel-talks-human-growing-career-slowly/story?id=46598431#:~:text=%22Do%20I%20want%20to%20be,bonus%20as%20a%20homeless%20kid.%2.

3 Nalebuff, Barry, "Why You Shouldn't Be An Entrepreneur," Yale Enterprise Institute. Podcast audio. July 23, 2009. https://archive.org/details/podcast_yale-entrepreneurial-institute_why-you-shouldnt-be-an-entrep_1000085214450.

4 Bailey, Dave "Why You Shouldn't Raise Money Too Early (Even If Opportunity Comes Up)," Inc.com. April 11, 2017. https://www.inc.com/dave-bailey/why-raising-money-early-is-a-terrible-idea-and-what-to-do-instead.html.

"Fundraising: Going too quickly can negatively affect startup growth," Varun, Toucantoco.com, https://www.toucantoco.com/en/blog/fundraising-too-quickly-can-negatively-affect-the-growth-of-your-startup; "Why Raising Too Much Capital or Raising It Too Early Can Lead to the Failure of Your Startup," Fuld, Inc.com, https://www.inc.com/hillel-fuld/why-raising-too-much-capital-or-raising-too-early-can-lead-to-failure-of-your-startup.html.

https://www.startupgrind.com/blog/why-your-startup-doesnt-need-significant-if-any-early-stage-funding-to-succeed/.

5 Christiansen, Clayton, Alton, Richard, Rising, Curtis, and Waldeck, Andrew, "The Big Idea: The New M&A Playbook," *Harvard Business Review,* March 2011, https://hbr.org/2011/03/the -big-idea-the-new-ma-playbook; Kenny, Graham, "Don't Make This Common M&A Mistake," March 16, 2020, https://hbr.org/2020/03/dont-make-this-common-ma-mistake#:~:text =According%20to%20most%20studies%2C%20between,integrating%20the%20two%20 parties%20involved.

6 U.S. Federal Trade Commission, "Going out of business sales: What to know," 2019, https:// consumer.ftc.gov/consumer-alerts/2019/12/going-out-business-sales-what-know; "15 Locals Reveal Tourist Traps and Scams from Their Hometown (and How to Avoid Them)," Ranker, 2021, https://www.ranker.com/list/local-tourist-traps/blue-velvet.

7 455: "Continental Breakup / Act Three: Ooh, I Shouldn't Have Done That!," https://www .thisamericanlife.org/455/transcript.

8 https://en.wikipedia.org/wiki/Buchwald_v._Paramount. The [Buchwald v. Paramount] decision was important mainly for the court's determination in the damages phase of the trial that Paramount used "unconscionable" means of determining how much to pay authors, which is widely called "Hollywood Accounting." Paramount claimed, and provided accounting evidence to support the claim, that despite the movie's $288 million in revenues, it had earned no net profit, according to the definition of "net profit" in Buchwald's contract, and hence Buchwald was owed nothing.

9 Vitasek, Kate, Manrodt, Karl, Kling, Jeanne, and DiBenedetto, William, "Vested for Success Case Study: How Dell and FedEx Supply Chain Reinvented Their Relationship to Achieve Record-setting Results," Haslam College of Business, The University of Tennessee. No data provided.

10 Hopkins, Michael S., "How to Negotiate Practically Anything: Interview with an Attorney Who Has an Unconventional Negotiating Manner: kind, honest, fair," *Inc. Magazine,* February 1, 1989.

11 See Mnookin, Robert, *Bargaining with the Devil: When to Negotiate, When to Fight,* New York: Simon & Schuster (2011).

Chapter 14: Putting It Together to Roar Out of Recession

1 See "Supply Chain Financing," pgsupplier.com, https://pgsupplier.com/supplychainfinancing.

"Supply Chain Finance at Procter & Gamble," Harvard Business School Publishing case (2016) #216039-PDF-ENG; "Supply chain finance yields $5 billion for P&G," Dunbar, September 9, 2018, EuroFinance.com, https://www.eurofinance.com/news/supply-chain-finance-yields-5 -billion-for-pg/; "How treasury used a massive supplier chain finance programme to deliver huge free cash flow and productivity improvements," citibank.com case studies, https://www.citibank .com/tts/insights/case-studies/procter-gamble.html.

2 See "Supply Chain Finance at Procter & Gamble." The case warns there have been questions about the ethics of asking small and midsize enterprises to give longer payment terms. "[B]oth the US and the EU have promulgated directives encouraging large firms to pay their smaller suppliers promptly." The case leaves ambiguous whether SCF is ethical, suggesting it depends on the specific terms, rates, and risks suppliers end up bearing. Which means a sound use of Hard Data + Soft Skills should definitely take those needs into account. An article in EuroFinance acknowledges the question and offers a somewhat positive view of SCF. It reported in 2018, "Such extension of payment terms has attracted critics, concerned about the impact on small

to medium size enterprises (SMEs). Some argue that high days payable outstanding should be considered a black mark under corporate and social responsibility (CSR) guidelines. *SCF is one way of mitigating these criticisms*" (emphasis added). https://www.eurofinance.com/news/supply -chain-finance-yields-5-billion-for-pg/. In a 2018 Seidman Business Review article, "Supply Chain Finance—Should the Practice Be Adopted?" Roy McCammon noted SCF can be attractive for customer and supplier if handled well, though SCF can require real effort from the customer. "Adopting SCF practices is not a small project and does require time to analyze and process the potential benefits for the buying firm and depends on cooperation between functional areas of a company that would be responsible for the planning, development, and execution." Kerle (Kerle, P. (2009), "Supply Chain Finance—A Growing Need," *Corporate Finance Review*, 14(2)) draws from a survey of more than 1,000 finance directors who represent many of the largest corporations in the world, when he summarized that two-thirds of global companies are hesitant to adopt SCF due to the unclarity of how much buyers and suppliers would benefit. *While the research and academic support is abundant for SCF* (emphasis added), the lack of information available to practitioners seems to be the biggest barrier inhibiting the adoption of SCF practices (Gelsomino et al., 2016). That paper cites, among others: Luo and Zhang (2012), which studied the benefits of coordinating the supply chain through trade credit (i.e., operating on the accounts receivable collection period). Their results show that managing trade credit periods *might be a source of substantial benefits for the supply chain* (emphasis added). For example, a low-risk buyer can use trade credit to financially sustain a start-up supplier, to mutual benefit. However, the authors also demonstrated that such benefits depend on the information available throughout the chain: asymmetric information among the parties involved may lead to suboptimal solutions. Along the same line of reasoning, Hofmann and Kotzab (2010) showed how a collaborative approach (or, as it is called, a supply chain–oriented approach) to cash-to-cash management leads to "optimal solutions, whereas aggressive behaviour (i.e., pressure to shorten receivable collection and extend payable settlement times through the supply chain) might negatively affect the value of the organisations involved." Which supports the collaborative approach this chapter argues for. U.S. government efforts to accelerate payments to suppliers using a program called SupplierPay actually may have done less to help suppliers than policy makers had hoped. As ReceivableSavvy put it, "Without some type of affordable, easily accessible financing for smaller suppliers, SupplierPay is ineffective. Smart supply chain financing (SCF) solutions can assist businesses in extending their payment terms in a manner that is agreeable for both companies involved; yet SupplierPay does little to promote this."

3 Agustin Gutierrez et al., "Taking supplier collaboration to the next level," McKinsey & Company, July 2020, p. 2.

4 Intel-DHL-Teaching Case study.pdf, by Vitasek et al, https://www.vestedway.com/wp-content /uploads/2018/05/Intel-DHL-EMEA-TEACHING-case-study.pdf; "How DHL implemented a vested outsourcing model for reverse logistics," November 12, 2017, https://www.youtube.com /watch?v=OwjbH4ATui8; "Delivering Accurate and Automated Inventory Tracking," Intel white paper.

5 "High inflation: uncharted waters for supply management," A. T. Kearney, November 6, 2018, https://www.kearney.com/procurement/article/?/a/high-inflation-uncharted-waters-for-supply -management.

6 "Inflation: Negotiate with suppliers and don't panic," Weissman, August 26, 2021, Supplychaindrive.com, https://www.supplychaindive.com/news/supplier-negotiations -procurement-inflation/605380/.

Brown, A.B. "Starbucks says advance coffee purchasing helps it stay competitive," July 29, 2021, Supplychaindrive.com, https://www.supplychaindive.com/news/starbucks-says-advance-coffee-purchasing-helps-it-stay-competitive/604127/.

Ibáñez, Patricio et al, "How to deal with price increases in this inflationary market," January 13, 2022, McKinsey & Company, https://www.mckinsey.com/business-functions/operations/our-insights/how-to-deal-with-price-increases-in-this-inflationary-market.

"Responding to inflation and volatility: Time for procurement to lead," July 19, 2021, McKinsey & Company, https://www.mckinsey.com/business-functions/operations/our-insights/responding-to-inflation-and-volatility-time-for-procurement-to-lead.

Scaffidi, Pablo,"Supply chain negotiations during inflationary contexts," Multibriefs: Exclusive, January 19, 2018, https://exclusive.multibriefs.com/content/negotiations-during-inflationary-contexts/distribution-warehousing.

Stepanek, Paul, "Hit with a Price Increase? Seven Tips for Negotiating with Suppliers," IndustryWeek, April 5, 2021, https://www.industryweek.com/supply-chain/supplier-relationships/article/21160288/hit-with-a-price-increase-seven-tips-for-negotiating-with-suppliers.

Tevelson, Bob, Belz, Dan, Hemmige, Harish, and Rapp, Tom, "How Procurement Organizations Can Protect Against Inflation,"ISMworld.org, https://www.ismworld.org/supply-management-news-and-reports/news-publications/inside-supply-management-magazine/blog/2021/2021-04/how-procurement-organizations-can-protect-against-inflation.

Chapter 15: True Confession—I'm Powerless. You?

1   https://www.goodreads.com/quotes/134364-power-without-love-is-reckless-and-abusive-and-love-without.

2   See "NUMMI," (2015), This American Life #405 July 17, 2015.

Index

A page reference followed by n refers to a footnote or endnote on that page, with nn referring to multiple notes.